Writing = Learning

AATE Interface Series

Commissioning Editor: Sieta van der Hoeven

The AATE/Interface series comprises a range of books for teachers who are committed to researching their own teaching – teachers who work at the interface between theory and practice. Interface titles all have a practical edge, in that they include ideas developed in the classrooms, for use in the classrooms. Yet they are far more than a set of resources. The primary purpose of the AATE/Interface series is to address significant issues in English curriculum and pegagogy, and as such it represents a substantial contribution to our knowledge as English teachers and literacy educators. To date, the series consists of:

Gender and Texts: A Professional Development Package for English Teachers
Edited by Wayne Martino and Chris Cook 1998

Responding to Students' Writing: Continuing Conversations
Edited by Brenton Doecke with an introduction by Margaret Gill 1999

Exploring Narrative: A Guide to Teaching 'The Girl who married a fly'
and other stories
Val Kent with a contribution by Ray Misson 2000

Relocating the Personal: a critical writing pedagogy
Barbara Kamler with a foreword by Michelle Fine 2001

P(ict)ures of English: Teachers, Learners and Technology
Edited by Cal Durrant and Catherine Beavis 2001

For All Time? Critical Issues in Teaching Shakespeare
Edited by Paul Skrebels and Sieta van der Hoeven,
with a foreword by John Bell 2002

Empowering Readers: Ten Approaches to Narrative
Garry Gillard, with a foreword by Alec McHoul 2002

English Teachers at Work: Narratives, Counter Narratives and Arguments
Edited by Brenton Doecke, David Homer, Helen Nixon 2003

Writing = Learning

Edited by

Brenton Doecke and Graham Parr

Wakefield Press

THE AUSTRALIAN ASSOCIATION FOR THE TEACHING OF ENGLISH

KH

Wakefield Press
1 The Parade West
Kent Town
South Australia 5067
www.wakefieldpress.com.au

in association with

The Australian Association for the Teaching of English
416 Magill Road
Kensington Gardens
South Australia 5068
www.aate.org.au

First published 2005

AATE Interface Series Commissioning Editor, Sieta van der Hoeven

Designed and typeset by Clinton Ellicott, Wakefield Press
Cover designed by Stacey Zass, Colorperception Pty Ltd
Printed and bound by Hyde Park Press

ISBN 1 86254 677 0

Government
of South Australia   A R T S A

Wakefield Press thanks Fox Creek Wines
and Arts South Australia for their support.

10/19/06

Contents

1   Writing: A Common Project   1
    Brenton Doecke and Graham Parr

Professional Learning

2   Autobiographical Inquiry in Pre-Service and Early-Career
    Teacher Learning: The Dialogic Possibilities   19
    Graham Parr and Natalie Bellis

3   Conversation + Collaboration + Writing = Professional Learning   40
    Scott Bulfin

4   Talking Our Way to Understanding Writing   59
    Judie Mitchell

Counterpoint

5   Writing Positions and Rhetorical Spaces   75
    Terry Locke

6   Responding to Students' Writing: A Do-It-Yourself
    Inservice Kit   96
    Kevin Murray

7   (Trans)cultural Spaces of Writing   104
    Alex Kostogriz

8   Writing, Testing and Culture   120
    Michael Clyne

9   Becoming a *New* New Critic: Assessing Student Writing   129
    Wayne Sawyer

School Writing

10 Talking to Write: On Line Conversations in the
    Literature Classroom   149
    Prue Gill

11 Temporary Validation: The Challenges of Remedial
    'Literacy' Programs   166
    Bella Illesca

12 'I want you to write me a poem . . . and I don't want it
    to rhyme.'   182
    Val Kent

13 Hybridity, Creativity and Learning: Writing in the
    Science Classroom   205
    Gaell Hildebrand

14 Writing, English and Digital Culture   229
    Catherine Beavis and Claire Charles

15 Engaging in Valued Activities: Popular Culture in the
    English Classroom   247
    Brenton Doecke and Douglas McClenaghan

STELLA Language Modes

16 The Accomplished Teacher in the English/Literacy Classroom   263

Contributors

                                                                  269

Chapter 1

Writing: A Common Project

Brenton Doecke and Graham Parr

Stepping into the Future?

Recently much debate about curriculum has centered on the knowledge and skills required for participating in the 'knowledge economy'. Governments around Australia, as well as major international organizations like the Organization for Economic Cooperation and Development, have invested considerable resources into researching the requisite skills and knowledge for economic growth, questioning the relevance of traditional academic disciplines and exploring the viability of alternative understandings of human ability, including cross disciplinary knowledge and generic skills (see, e.g., McCurry 2004, OECD 2001). The 'reform challenge', according to a consultation paper distributed by the Victorian Curriculum and Assessment Authority last year, is 'to equip students with a range of knowledge, skills and attributes for them to prosper in this new social and economic environment and to foster the ability to manage constant change'. Schools are faced with the task of producing individuals who are capable of forming social relationships and contributing 'at a local, national and global level'. This means developing curriculum that focuses on generic skills and enables students 'to take their learning and apply it in new contexts', rather than remaining confined within traditional disciplinary boundaries (VCAA 2004, p. 2).

There is no doubt that the demands of the 'knowledge economy' have usefully prompted a renewed focus on learning and teaching, giving rise to alternative models of knowledge and curriculum. Any challenge to the stranglehold that the competitive, academic curriculum has had on schools is long overdue. A focus on generic skills, for example, can provide a useful lever for reconceptualising curriculum and questioning traditional divisions between 'academic' knowledge and the situated knowledge of the workplace (see McCurry 2004, Withers 1997, King & McRae 1997). Research on the learning that occurs in workplaces has produced useful concepts, such as 'situated learning' and 'communities of practice', that offer a critical perspective on school learning (e.g. Lave & Wenger 1991, Wenger 1998).

The alternative models of learning available to us might conveniently be set out in the following way:

Traditional understandings of learning	Alternative understandings of learning
Learning is conceived as purely a matter of individual cognitive development.	Learning is deeply social, something that occurs through interactions with others.
This understanding is evident in traditional school assessment practices, such as standardized testing and examinations for tertiary entrance, which treat students as individuals who are competing with one another.	The product of learning is conceived as a social product, what Neil Mercer calls 'the joint construction of knowledge' (Mercer 1996) or Gordon Wells defines as 'dialogic inquiry' (Wells 2001).
Accountability is conceived primarily in the form of showing improved performance by individuals against certain standards (e.g. 'typical progression' as mapped out by the National Profile – see AEC 1994).	The product of collaborative learning and inquiry is rich and complex, and more likely to match the kinds of learning that occur in workplace and community settings, requiring more complex forms of accountability than simply relying on standardised testing.
The notion of learning as 'individual cognitive development' spawns popular conceptions of learning, such as those kids who have 'ability' or 'brains' and those who don't.	A wider variety of knowledge and skills is valued in the process of learning, breaking down distinctions between pure and applied knowledge, theory and practice.
Such conceptions, and the practices associated with them, are meant to enable individuals to access another level of education and ultimately gain entry to high status professions.	Such conceptions of learning imply community involvement and socially productive work, promoting a sense of community obligation and membership of a larger social network.
Such practices are presented as having their own justification, as things that you 'do' to succeed in school; their meaning or value is rarely questioned.	Such learning is engaging and meaningful, not routine or simulated; learners can make connections with their daily lives and inquire into matters that are of significance to them.

Whether the rhetoric of the 'knowledge economy' ultimately brings about lasting educational reform remains to be seen, as does the precise nature that this reform might take (see Kenway, Bullen & Robb 2004). Several worthwhile initiatives have been taken at a systems wide level around Australia, most notably the Queensland New Basics and Productive Pedagogies, which firmly place the need for reconceptualising pedagogy, curriculum and assessment on the agenda. (See also Tasmanian Essential Learnings [Department of Education, Tasmania 2004] and Victorian Essential Learning Standards

[VCAA & DE&T 2005].) The challenge, according to Allan Luke, is not simply to give kids stuff that 'they feel is motivating and relevant', but 'to deliver high stakes knowledges, complex discipline and field-specific discourses, higher order thinking, critical meta-languages and intellectual engagement' (Luke 2000, p. 137). Luke tackles 'the silo mentality' of secondary schools, where curriculum is boxed into KLAs, and disciplines are treated as 'static corpuses of fact', and not 'dynamic sets of discourses and practices, literacies and knowledges' (Luke 2000, p. 139). The key is to enable students to establish 'some degree of connectedness' to the world, and the new economies and cultures that are forming around them (p. 137, p. 139).

Yet for all the excitement generated by such reforms, other factors remain at work that threaten the possibility of worthwhile change. You need only contrast New Basics with the opinions of neo-conservatives to recognize how deeply polarized debate about education in Australia has become. We shall use the name 'Donnelly' as a convenient shorthand for a cluster of neo-conservative views about education and schooling that are currently being propagated by mainstream media in Australia. According to Donnelly, the most successful educational systems 'adopt a strong, discipline-based approach to school subjects', enforce 'accountability', 'define clear educational standards', 'have greater time on task in the classroom and an emphasis on formal, whole-class teaching', and 'have regular testing and high risk examinations' (Donnelly 2004, p. 14, passim). Rather than a vision of the future, this reads like a scene out of *The Simpsons*. (We keep waiting for Bart to show how he feels about these types of regulation and control).

The populist character of Donnelly's rhetoric is largely due to the way he taps into some parents' fears and their desire for success for their children at school. The continuing drift towards private schools in Australia, for which Donnelly is an unashamed apologist, has likewise traded on these fears. Much of the publicity for private schools typically promotes an ideology of individual competitiveness and a traditional view of human ability as simply a personal attribute. This ideology flies in the face of theories about the distributed and socially grounded nature of learning to which we have just referred. Unfortunately, however, this same ideology is used by governments of both political persuasions around Australia to judge the performance of state schools, with the result that all students are subjected to the continuing hegemony of traditional notions of teaching and learning, involving normative practices that reflect the values and interests of a limited cross-section of the Australian population at the expense of any acknowledgement of cultural diversity and difference or alternative forms of knowledge (cf. Teese 2000).

A desirable scenario for educational reform in Australia would involve creatively mediating between the alternatives set out on the foregoing table, rather than treating them as hard and fast binaries. Common sense assumptions about measuring human ability cannot simply be wished away. Indeed, educators who are committed to enabling their students to experience more collaborative forms of learning often find themselves negotiating with students and parents who imagine that an activity only has validity if it can be tested and given a mark. Many writers in the following chapters show how they have managed to satisfy conventional expectations of schooling, meeting the 'outcomes' set out on literacy continua like *The National Profile* (AEC 1994), while opening up other dimensions of language and learning through collaborative work and dialogue that are grounded in the social relationships of the classroom. All English teachers are committed to the welfare of the individual students in their classrooms, and this means treating the values and expectations of students and parents with sensitivity, even when you do not agree with them. In this respect, working within a student-centred curriculum means negotiating with the range of values and beliefs that students bring with them into class. However, English teachers are also committed to enabling their students to learn from one another, when individual accomplishment – the writing of a poem or a play, the production of a video clip or pop song or website – is also at some deep level the product of the community in which those students are working, of their interactions with one another, of the talk and laughter they have enjoyed together. Despite the threat posed by neo-conservative political correctness, the following chapters provide abundant evidence of teachers who are working with their students to explore the complexities of language and meaning, and to share their worlds of experience and imagination.

The Role of English?

English has always been the centre piece of the competitive academic curriculum, and it seems fair to say that English teachers have been to some extent complicit in maintaining the hegemony of traditional models of learning. As Mark Howie observes, 'to teach is to live with guilt', and this applies not only to a daily sense of failure to accomplish everything they might have done (see Howie 2002), but to the way English teachers feel obliged to equip their students with the skills to compete successfully in statewide exams and other forms of standardized testing. In Victoria, for example, many teachers have become adept at teaching the conventions of essay writing (Teese 2000, p. 17, p. 50), spending hours coaching their students to produce essays within the time limit imposed by examinations. And the fluency shown by students who write the 'best' papers is indeed remarkable. But there is no walking away from the culturally loaded nature of this practice (Teese 2000, Clyne 1999, Kostogriz, this volume), even as teachers continue to meet their professional obligations to drill and skill students in handling the conventions of essay text literacy. Why should essay writing be prized over other literacy practices? To what extent should a capacity to write essays be equated with 'ability' in language and literacy? How does essay writing compare with the literacy practices in which students engage outside school? Why should schools focus on essay text literacy at the expense of enabling students to produce other kinds of text, most notably the multimodal texts they use in their everyday lives? These questions must be asked if teachers are to maintain a critical perspective on their professional practice, even though the answer might well be to reaffirm the value of school literacy practices as peculiarly suited to the intellectual and emotional growth of students (cf. Doecke & McClenaghan, Beavis & Charles, this volume).

Yet English teachers also rightfully feel obliged to explore the promise held out by alternatives to traditional models of language and learning. The research traditions behind alternative understandings of language and learning are extraordinarily rich, and it is a tell tale sign that conservative critics like Donnelly have baulked at engaging with arguments about the relationship between thought and language (Vygotsky 1986) or the way that language mediates the social relationships in which it is used (Bahktin 1981). Focusing on the complexities of language and meaning, language and social relationships, does not mean that school literacy practices as they have been traditionally enacted should be completely displaced by some kind of new age pedagogy that is completely unlike anything that has gone before. The challenge for English teachers is to remain sensitive to the ways that language mediates experience, as human beings think, learn, imagine, and negotiate their relationships with one another within the local and global networks available to them at any one moment in time (see Doecke, Locke & Petrosky 2004).

We are both teacher educators who have the privilege of observing pre-service teachers in action, as they attempt to negotiate the complexities of the social relationships they encounter in secondary English classrooms. The idealism of pre-service teachers is a key factor in keeping our own idealism afloat – they clearly believe, with William Blake, that classrooms should be sites for opening up 'immense world[s] of delight' (1790/1994), and that the imagination and language of young people should not simply be contained and controlled. Here are some anecdotes about their teaching, which show them exploring the complexities of language and meaning in precisely the way we are describing.

- *A pre-service teacher is teaching a Year 9 class in a state secondary school in an outer region of the Melbourne metropolitan area. You need to imagine an indifferent backdrop of the walls of a classroom in an under-resourced state school, the desks and chairs grouped haphazardly together. The kids are having a go at creating their own Garfield cartoon strips, attempting in three frames through a combination of imagery and text to tell jokes. The pre-service teacher laughs as he encourages them to present their jokes to their peers. The social relationships in this classroom form an inescapable context for learning and teaching – not delimitation, but a condition for learning – and the pre-service teacher has got it right by giving the kids an opportunity to work with a genre they know and to construct meaning by using those conventions. They are distilling their worlds of experience and imagination into cartoons that are actually very funny, and they laugh appreciatively when they show each other their work.*

- *Another pre-service teacher is teaching a class of Year 7 students, many of whom are learning English as a second language. But everyone knows* The Simpsons, *and the students laugh as Homer saves the day by preventing a disaster from occurring on the monorail. The pre-service teacher then invites the class to imagine how such an incident would be reported in the press, showing them an example of a front page which she has created, and the students then spend the rest of the lesson designing front page spreads depicting the incident.*

- *In a Grade 2 classroom, a pre-service teacher monitors his class of Year 9 students as they read stories to small groups of children. The stories have been specially written by the Year 9 students for their primary school audience; it is an audience they have come to know well through previous visits over the five-week teaching round. The pride of these Year 9 (often reluctant) writers in their own writing is palpable. Of particular interest to the pre-service teacher is Pedro, in one corner, who is reading his own horror story, 'Max the Vampire and the Monster from the Lake'. Young faces peer up at Pedro as he reads. Back at secondary school, Pedro had described his attitude to writing: 'I write when I am ordered to . . . I also prefer drawing over writing . . .' In Pedro's story, the eponymous Max seems to draw on Pedro's own experiences of having to produce school literacy texts. At Scaryville Primary School, Max can write 'when ordered to,' but growing fear at the onset of writer's block seems to provoke an especially frightening experience at the lake on the way home from school. And, yet, here is Pedro (like his other Year 9 peers) engaged and engaging as he discusses his story with his younger audience.*

- *A Year 8 class includes students from a wide range of cultural and educational backgrounds; they have not responded well to conventional 'creative writing' exercises in the past. The curriculum dictates that it's 'time to teach issues' and 'to learn about newspapers'. The pre-service teacher has found out, in a previous lesson, that few if any students even see a newspaper in their homes. And yet twenty minutes into the lesson, the classroom is a buzz of excited chatter and laughter as students relish the task of selecting fragments of newspaper text to produce collaborative poems or mini-narratives. The end of the lesson is 'a hit': students applaud the efforts of their peers as they read them out aloud. There is entertaining use of parody and absurd non-sequiturs. Some poems draw unlikely coherence out of disparate text fragments; other poems satirise the advertising discourses these students know so well. One group of writers has mounted a surprising social critique by juxtaposing the characters of George Bush, the principal of their school, and an Olympic champion. Most surprising of all, perhaps, is that these students have engaged in focused and animated work in association with newspapers – a form of media that might otherwise be deemed alien to their worlds.*

What these incidents have in common is not that they each model a successful strategy for enabling students to write, as though writing (or any aspect of English) can ever be a matter of learning and applying mechanical skills. The key element in each anecdote relates to the way the pre-service teacher was able to tap into the students' interests and enthusiasms and situate the activity within the social relationships of the classroom. What do we know about cartoons? Why do they make us laugh? How do you tell a good joke? How do incidents get reported in the press? How do you write a news-paper article? You could say that students and teachers alike were engaged in a joint inquiry into the complexities of language and meaning (see, e.g., Nystrand 1997, Beach & Myers 2001, Gill, this volume). The classrooms we have just observed are sites for genuinely critical engagement, imaginative play and inquiry, in which students jointly construct knowledge about their lives.

Language, as theorists like Vygotsky and Bahktin have shown, cannot be under-stood simply as a matter of personal 'expression' or 'intelligence'. In many ways, schools are locked into practices which treat language as though it were an individual property – this is perhaps no more perversely revealed than by the ritual of exami-nations, when students are obliged to sit in long rows of single desks, each individual engaged in a solitary struggle to write words for an anonymous marker. It may be impossible to imagine a world where schools or high stakes assessment are organized differently, and yet it is worth contemplating how educational institutions might enhance students' awareness of language as affirming the social nature of their being and as a medium through which they can work together to achieve common purposes. For all the emphasis on the imaginative 'flair' or 'ability' shown by the 'best' exam essays, the ritual of examinations reduces language to a preexisting body of agreed conventions to which students are obliged to conform (something which is painfully obvious when you encounter the naïve handling of the conventions of essay text literacy in papers of an 'inferior' quality). Bahktin's understanding of language as a field of con-flicting voices and dialectics, professional discourses, slang, the slogans of the moment, as well as echoes from the past, is more than a celebration of heterogeneity. It involves a tension between pressures towards standardization and conformity (as in a 'standard' language or grammar) and a rich human capacity for invention and resistance to such regulation and control. Paradoxically, Bahktin's understanding of the way that people appropriate language, of the way they struggle to occupy the space of the words that pre-exist them, is a more powerful model of human agency than the ideology of neo-liberal individualism enacted in the ritual of examinations and other forms of standardized testing (see Bahktin 1981).

Classrooms are sites for what Gordon Wells calls 'dialogic inquiry', by which he means the kind of joint inquiry into language and meaning that we are envisaging here (Wells 2001). It would be difficult to overestimate the significance of such inquiry and the ways it equips students to meet the demands of the 'knowledge economy'. We are imagining classrooms in which teachers and students explore the meaning-making potential of the complex range of literacy practices in which they engage in their everyday lives. English teachers can confidently affirm the need for such an inquiry to be at the centre of any curriculum design that might be introduced in order to enable students to handle the challenges of the future, whether this is driven by neo-conservative attempts to reduce English to a reified set of skills or more forward looking (but still problematic) initiatives, such as an emphasis on generic skills or multiple intelligences. As the authors in this book show, language cannot be boxed as simply one skill (e.g. 'communication' or 'intelligence'), as though it were one component of an array of skills or intelligences from which you might choose. Language is emphatically not one skill or intelligence amongst many. It is an indispensable medium for communication, for negotiating human relationships, for forming a social identity, for constructing knowledge, and for imagining worlds other than the one we currently inhabit. You might object that music or visual literacy coexists with language, and that they likewise cannot be explained in terms provided by any of the other 'intelligences'. Isadora Duncan shrugged off attempts to get her to explain her dancing by saying that if she could put it in words her dancing would be superfluous. And she was right. We can grant this without stepping back from the fact that language is always there, like life itself; that while one might wish to affirm the value of other forms of 'intelligence', our experiences are crucially mediated by words. This is what we understand by Derrida's famous statement that 'there is nothing outside the text' (1976), or Wittgenstein's aphorism that 'what cannot be said must be passed over in silence' (1994), or Vygotsky's explorations of the 'living' relationship between 'thought' and 'word' (1986), or Bahktin's meditations on the ways in which words 'sparkle' with ideology (1981) – all these theorists (who can roughly be bundled together as exemplifying the 'linguistic turn' in the human sciences) can be used to underline the inescapability of language, the centrality of language to our lives. They can also be used to argue that English is not one subject (or key learning area) amongst many, but that it should be the dynamic of any meaningful curriculum reform that enables students to step into the future.

To say this, however, is both to join the many voices demanding curriculum reform in order to create a 'knowledge economy' and to maintain a critical distance from such rhetoric. For to say that language is crucially bound up with thought is to acknowledge that any attempt to imagine the future (or a new 'knowledge economy') is likewise mediated by language. And just as we remain confined within our language, we remain confined within the present, as we continually grapple with words and meaning, language and experience, in order to make sense of our lives. A curriculum should therefore be not only about 'writing the future' (Kress 1995), but about writing the present. And yet we know that even as we try to find words to capture the present, it slips away from us. A curriculum cannot simply be shaped by future projections about the state of the economy or the kinds of citizens we feel we should be producing. Rather than viewing our students through the lens of such futuristic scenarios, we need to attend to their efforts to use language to understand the current moment, to articulate their needs and values, to achieve a sense of identity, and to find their place.

The classroom inquiry we are envisaging should crucially engage with the current moment, enabling students to grapple with their local and immediate concerns. Young people are confronted by a multiplicity of texts and images each day, many of which locate them in their immediate worlds, while others signal global settings and networks. Even as they actively participate in the social relationships of their immediate neighbourhoods or communities, they are participating within networks that stretch beyond them, challenging their capacity to think about and imagine their local world. To suppose, indeed, that the local and immediate do not open themselves up, with analysis, to being reconceptualised within the context of the global flows and networks of the information society, is to deny students the opportunity to make connections between their local contexts or spaces and larger international forces. A focus on the local and immediate can also become an inquiry into the connections between your local community and global forces, between what Castells calls the 'space of flows' and the 'space of places' (Castells 2000, pp. 408–409). It can take you beyond the immediacy of the present to an understanding of the way the present moment as you experience it is the product of complex mediations and relationships that challenge your sense that this is how things 'are'. Yet this is also to affirm the challenge and excitement of engaging in the present, of living this moment through.

Professional Learning = Student Learning?

While language is preeminently a social phenomenon, it is also an intensely personal experience – you need only think of how children puzzle about the mystery of words and things, or of those words that echo in your mind, conjuring up images of people and places you once knew: 'Down the passage which we did not take/Towards the door we never opened/Into the rose-garden' (Eliot 1999). As teacher educators, we invite our students to write about their earliest experiences of language and literacy and to reconstruct moments from their pasts that might explain their commitment to becoming English teachers. This is not simply because, as teachers of writing, they ought to practise what they preach, continually reminding themselves of (to borrow once again from *Four Quartets*) that writing is always 'a new beginning, a raid on the inarticulate' (Eliot 1999). We are equally concerned to promote the value of writing as a vehicle for grappling with issues emerging in their professional lives. A number of the chapters in this volume explore the nature of professional writing, showing how it enables teachers to refine their understanding of the complexities of teaching and learning. This is obviously of benefit to the students in their classes, although those benefits do not necessarily translate into tangible outcomes that can easily be measured.

It is possible to construct a table showing models of professional learning that matches the previous table.

Traditional understandings of professional learning	Alternative understandings of professional learning
Teachers are positioned as 'individual professionals' (Caldwell & Hayward 1998).	Teaching is considered to be collaborative in nature, a function of the network of relationships in which individual teachers and groups of teachers operate.
Professional learning is presumed to be generic in nature, and can be applied to all educational settings regardless of their particular character. It can be unproblematically transferred or exported from context to context.	Professional learning is anchored in the specific contexts in which teachers operate.
Knowledge of teachers and teaching is imported from outside and delivered through professional development programs.	Knowledge of teachers and teaching develops from, and involves, sustained inquiry into teaching and learning, including focused observation of learners.
Knowledge of teachers and teaching is unproblematically avowed, and is typically delivered as a remedy for deficiencies in teachers' existing practices.	The findings of research into the knowledge of teachers and teaching are considered provisional and contestable, especially with regard to how those findings might be applied to other settings.
Evidence of the knowledge of teachers and teaching is often *demonstrated* in large-scale surveys that systematically bracket out the specific nature of school communities.	Evidence of the knowledge of teachers and teaching is often *explored* in non-canonical forms of inquiry, such as action research, narrative inquiry, and other types of qualitative research that include some focus on the nature of school communities.
Teachers' professional practice is judged against pre-existing or traditional outcomes – outcomes which are unproblematically measurable, such as their students' standardised test results.	Teachers draw on academic and practitioner research and theory in order to review and critique their existing practices.
Teachers are rendered accountable through performance appraisals which require them to specify targets (for themselves and for their students) and to demonstrate that these targets are achieved.	Teachers work together to create a culture of critical inquiry at their school in which everyone – teachers, students, parents – can participate. They are mindful, nevertheless, of the managerial systems within which they continue to be accountable.

This table is perhaps misleading to the extent that what we are calling 'traditional understandings of professional learning' actually reflect a managerial culture that has only recently begun to affect the way teachers' work is understood (cf. Locke 2001,

Mahony & Hextall 2000). The threat and promise of the current moment described by this table broadly map on to the previous table, reflecting a conflict between an ideology of neo-liberal individualism and an alternative vision of human sociability and collaboration to achieve common goals.

As with the alternatives set out on the previous table, these contrasting under-standings of professional learning present themselves less as choices than as positions between which teachers must mediate in the course of their professional lives. They cannot close their eyes to the managerial forms of control and accountability that have been reshaping their professional practice, although they might still steadfastly adhere to an alternative model of professionalism and critique those forms (Parr 2004). But rather than supposing that they must choose between alternatives, as though their professional world splits right down the middle, they might more productively conceive of themselves as engaging in a dialogical struggle over the language used to describe their professional practice, in which they seek to appropriate the vocabulary of policy makers and use it for their own purposes. This has been the case with the word 'standards' (cf. Doecke & Gill 2000) – English teachers involved in the STELLA (see Section 4 of this volume) project have appropriated that word to name the values and aspirations that drive them as a profession, rather than allowing it to signify merely crude benchmarks against which their practice can be judged – and a similar struggle might be played out with respect to other managerial rhetoric.

Those chapters in the present volume which focus on professional learning might be read as engaging in this kind of struggle (see Bulfin, Parr & Bellis, Mitchell, this volume). A key theme in all these chapters is the way teachers talk and write their way into a shared understanding of the complexities of their professional practice. This presupposes the central role that teachers play in providing quality learning experiences to students. However, all the writers are careful to distinguish between the way they position teachers and recent claims that '"what matters most" is quality teachers and teaching, supported by strategic teacher professional development' (Rowe 2003, p. 1). These words are taken from a paper by Ken Rowe, in which he dismisses 'the tradi-tional and prevailing dogmas surrounding "factors" affecting students' experiences'. Rowe is especially dismissive of 'socio-cultural and socio-economic factors', which are merely 'the products of methodological and statistical artefact'. Those who emphasise the importance of such 'factors' are apparently guilty of '"religious" adherence to the moribund ideologies of biological and social determinism' (Rowe 2003, p. 1). Rowe's own brand of 'evidence-based' research presumably transcends the status of an 'artefact' and provides direct access to 'what matters most' – a curious position for anyone who is presenting research that by definition should be open to refutation. (How else could it have the status of 'knowledge'?)

The accounts of professional learning in this volume make far more tentative claims than so-called 'evidence based research', and in this respect they might paradoxically be said to be more 'scientific', reflecting a genuine spirit of inquiry that invites scrutiny of the assumptions that inform it (Freebody 2003, p. 37). Socio-cultural and socio-economic dimensions cannot be reduced to isolable 'factors' that can somehow be measured against 'teacher effects' (Delandshere & Petrosky 2004), but they form the inescapable conditions under which teachers try to establish relationships with their students. It follows that a crucial aspect of any teacher's professional engagement is a capacity to reflect on the values they bring to any school community and to monitor how those values might shape their dialogue with students (see Cochran-Smith & Lytle 2001, Goodson 2003, Etherington 2004). The writers on professional learning in the present volume all display this kind of reflexivity, and thereby subject themselves to a more rigorous form of accountability than managerialism's attempt to measure what it chooses to measure.

The professional learning of the practitioner researchers who have contributed to this book is closely linked to student learning. This is not to say that their learning is directly connected with improved learning outcomes as narrowly defined by Rowe and other advocates of school 'effectiveness'. (See other school effectiveness advocates: Reynolds 2002, Hargreaves 2001.) One of the most compelling chapters in the present volume recounts the efforts by a group of teachers at a state secondary school to implement a literacy intervention program. It concludes by questioning how students are classified as needing remediation, while still affirming the 'temporary validation' that the students experienced through participating in this program (see Illesca, this volume). Such insights into the complexities of implementing a literacy intervention program should not be dismissed, but might guide other teachers in their efforts to grapple with the contradictory nature of similar programs. However, the link between professional learning and student learning embraces more than just a capacity on the part of teachers to evaluate the success or otherwise of any initiative, important though such a capacity might be. Rather, the qualities that teachers value most in their students' learning – intellectual curiosity, a willingness to engage in exploratory talk, imagination, a preparedness to collaborate while also accepting a degree of autonomy, a capacity to engage in metacognition and reflexivity – are the very same qualities that characterize their own professional learning. Teachers who engage in practitioner inquiry are much more likely to be able to generate a 'culture of inquiry' in their own classrooms (Reid 2004, p. 12).

Conclusion

This collection of essays replaces *Responding to Students' Writing: Continuing Conversations* in AATE's Interface series (see Doecke 1999). The previous volume was organised around a dialogue between past and present, including the reprinting of seminal essays from the 1980s, such as Brian Johnston's 'How Can I Usefully Respond to Students' First Drafts?' and Frances Christie's 'Learning to Write: A Process of Learning How to

Mean', alongside essays in which writers reflected on the continuing significance of these texts for their professional practice. The collection signalled an attempt to move beyond the debates which had divided the English teaching profession during the 1980s, most notably the process/genre debate, and tried to facilitate a conversation between people who had hitherto belonged to opposing camps.

From the standpoint of the present, debates between advocates of 'process writing' and the 'genre' school seem to be a luxury we can no longer afford. This introduction has presented an account of a very different professional landscape, one in which the rich intellectual and professional tradition represented by the Australian Association for the Teaching of English and the wider English teaching profession is being challenged. Several of the chapters in this volume review this tradition, showing how the English teaching community has engaged in continuing inquiry and a refinement of its understanding of the complexities of student writing (see Locke, Sawyer, this volume). We have republished two influential essays by Kevin Murray and Michael Clyne (from *Responding to Students' Writing*) to show how, through their critiques of these writers, Locke and Kostogriz respectively are enacting a continuing process of reflection and inquiry. Other chapters show how writing continues to be a focus of research for English teachers, as well as for teachers of other subject areas (see Kent, Hildebrand, this volume). To conclude the volume, we have republished statements about the language modes which were developed in consultation with teachers of English around Australia as part of the STELLA project.

One aspect of the ongoing conversation that has not changed is the focus on writing and learning. Taken together, the authors in this book propose a three-fold (and interconnected) conceptualization of writing:

- *writing as artefact* – generated by students and/or educators in the process of teaching and learning, and constituting the object/s of critical and imaginative inquiry;
- *writing as process* – not constrained by expectations of particular artefacts but supporting and inspiring ongoing critical and imaginative inquiry and evaluation; and
- *writing as medium* – in which and through which this critical and imaginary inquiry can be enacted and enabled, stimulating richer learning for students, teachers, and teacher educators.

At the present time, the English teaching profession in Australia is indeed under serious attack from several quarters. English teachers in schools, their professional associations in supportive and advocacy roles, and teacher educators in collaborative inquiry with pre-service, early career and more experienced English teachers – all are threatened. Certainly, the profession cannot afford to rest complacently on its laurels, as if what they have done in the past were good enough for the present and the future. Nor is it time to adopt a bunker mentality: dig in and wait until the attack passes.

Rather, we believe it is time to work proactively, to take the initiative in public debates about English teaching and learning. If the English teaching profession is to maintain its integrity, if we as English educators are to continue to work in ways that allow us to inquire critically, imaginatively and collaboratively into our students' learning and our own practices, we must all accept the professional and political challenge of the moment. We need to generate and disseminate critical accounts of our practices, of the theory and conceptual framework underpinning these practices, of the beliefs and values driving the combination of theory and practices.

Traditionally, a focus on writing in research into English teaching has tended to concentrate mainly on writing-as-artefact. Yet such a focus, de-emphasising as it does writing-as-process and writing-as-medium, tends to limit the richness of any accounts of English educators' practices. By inquiring into the broadest possibilities and contexts of writing, as we have here, it can indeed be the case that writing = learning. In this book, by inquiring into all three aspects, we hope we have given an account of the rigour, the challenges and the possibilities of English teaching and learning.

References

Australian Education Council (AEC) (1994) *English – A Curriculum Profile for Australian Schools*, A joint project of the States, Territories and the Commonwealth of Australia initiated by the Australian Education Council, Carlton: Curriculum Corporation.

Bakhtin, M. M. (1981) *The Dialogic Imagination: Four Essays*, M. Holquist (trans.), C. Emerson and M. Holquist (eds), Austin: University of Texas.

Barnes, D. (1976) *From Communication to Curriculum*, Harmondsworth: Penguin.

Beach, R. and Myers, J. (2001) *Inquiry-based English instruction*, New York: Teachers' College Press.

Blake, W. (1790/1994) *The marriage of Heaven and Hell: In full color*, New York: Dover Publications.

Caldwell, B. J. and Hayward, D. H. (1998) *The Future of Schools: Lessons from the Reform of Public Education*, London: Falmer Press.

Castells, M. (2000) *The Information Age: Economy, Society and Culture, Volume 1, The Rise of the Network Society*, 2nd ed., Oxford: Blackwell Publishers.

Clark, C.M. (2001) *Talking Shop: Authentic Conversation and Teacher Learning*, New York and London: Teachers College Press.

Clyne, M. (1999) Writing, Testing and Culture, in B. Doecke (ed.), *Responding to Students' Writing: Continuing Conversations*, Norwood: AATE, pp. 165–176.

Cochran-Smith, M. and Lytle, S. (2001) Beyond Certainty: Taking an Inquiry Stance on Practice, in A. Liebermann and L. Miller (eds) *Teachers Caught in the Action: Professional Development that Matters*, New York: Teachers College Press, pp. 3–15.

Delandshere, G. and Petrosky, A. (2004) Political Rationales and Ideological Stances of the Standards-Based Reform in teacher Education in the US, in *Teaching and Teacher Education*, 20, pp. 1–15.

Department of Education, Tasmania (2004) Essential Connections: A Guide to Young Children's Learning, in Tasmanian Essential Learnings. Accessed in March 2005 at: http://www.education.tas.gov.au/ocll/currcons/Essential_learning.pdf

Derrida, J. (1976) *Of Grammatology*, G.C. Spivak (ed.), Baltimore: Johns Hopkins University.

Doecke, B. (ed.) (1999) *Responding to Students' Writing; Continuing Conversations*, Norwood: AATE.

Doecke, B. and Gill, M. (2000) Setting Standards: Confronting Paradox, *STELLA: English in Australia* 129–130 and *Literacy Learning: The Middle Years* 9(1), Dec. 2000–Jan. 2001, pp. 5–16.

Doecke, B., Locke, T. and Petrosky, A. (2004) Explaining Ourselves (To Ourselves): English Teachers, Professional Identity and Change, in *Literacy Learning: The Middle Years*, 12(1), and *English In Australia* 139, Feb. 2004, pp. 103–102.

Donnelly, K. (2004) *Why Our Schools are Failing: What Parents Need to Know about Australian Education*, Potts Point, NSW: Duffy & Snellgrove.

Eliot, T. S. (1999) *Four Quartets*, London: Faber & Faber.

Etherington, K. (2004) *Becoming a Reflexive Researcher: Using Our Selves in Research*, London and Philadelphia, PA: Jessica Kingsley Publishers.

Freebody, P. (2003) *Qualitative Research in Education: Interaction and Practice*, London: Sage.

Goodson, I. (2003) *Professional Knowledge, Professional Lives: Studies in Education and Change*, Maidenhead: Open University Press.

Hargreaves, D. (2001) *A Capital Theory of School Effectiveness and Improvement*, Jolimont, VIC: Incorporated Association of Registered Teachers of Victoria (IARTV).

Howie, M. (2002) Slow Learner, *English in Australia* 133, April 2002, pp. 25–29.

Kenway, J., Bullen, E. and Robb, S. (eds) (2004) *Innovation and Tradition: The Arts, Humanities and the Knowledge Economy*, New York: Peter Lang.

King, R. and McCrane, M. (1997) 'Teach Them to Fish': A Key Competencies Approach to the VCE English Classroom, *Idiom*, 32(1), pp. 24–32.

Kress, G. (1995) *Writing the Future: English and the Making of a Culture of Innovation*, Sheffield: NATE.

Lave, J. and Wenger, E. (1991) *Situated Learning: Legitimate Peripheral Participation*, Cambridge: Cambridge University Press.

Locke, T. (2001) English Teaching in New Zealand: In the Frame and Outside the Square, *L1 – Educational Studies in Language and Literature*, 1(2), pp. 135–148.

Luke, A. (2000) The Queensland 'New basics': An Interview with Allan Luke, in *STELLA: English in Australia*, 129–130, and *Literacy Learning: The Middle Years*, 9(1), Dec. 2000–Feb. 2001, pp. 132–141.

Mahony, P. and Hextall, I. (2000) *Reconstructing Teaching: Standards, Performance and Accountability*, London: RoutledgeFalmer.

Mercer, N. (1996) *The Guided Construction of Knowledge*, Adelaide: Multilingual Matters.

McCurry, D. (2004) Generic Skills in a Framework of Essential Learning, *Idiom*, 40(2), pp. 11–20.

Nystrand, M., with Gamoran, A., Kachur, R. and Prendergast, C. (1997) *Opening Dialogue: Understanding the Dynamics of Language and Learning in the English Classroom*, New York and London: Teachers' College Press.

Organization for Economic Cooperation and Development (OECD) (2001) Introduction to DeSeCo, Paris, Organisation for Economic Cooperation and Development. Accessed in March 2005 at: http://www.statistik.admin.cg/stat_ch/ber15/deseco/deseco_backgrpaper_dec01.pdf.

Parr, G. (2004) Professional Knowledge, Professional Learning, Professional Identity: A Bleak View, But Oh the Possibilities, in *English Teaching: Practice and Critique*, 3(2), Sept. 2004, pp. 21–47. Accessed in March 2005 at: http://www.tmc.waikato.ac.nz/english/ETPC/article/pdf/2004v3n2art2.pdf

Reid, A. (2004) Towards a Culture of Inquiry in DECS, Occasional Paper Series, No. 1, South Australia: Department of Education and Children's Service. Accessed in March 2005 at: http://www.decs.sa.gov.au/corporate/files/links/OP_01.pdf

Reynolds, D. (ed.) (2002) *World Class Schools: International Perspectives on School Effectiveness*, London and New York: RoutledgeFalmer.

Rowe, K. (2003) The Importance of Teacher Quality as a Key Determinant of Students' Experiences and Outcomes of Schooling, ACER Research Conference 2003, Building Teacher Quality: What Does the Research Tell Us?, pp. 15–23.

Teese, R. (2000) *Academic Success and Social Power*, Oakleigh: Cambridge University Press.

Victorian Curriculum and Assessment Authority (VCAA) (2004) Victorian Curriculum Reform 2004: Consultation Paper, East Melbourne: VCAA.

Victorian Curriculum and Assessment Authority (VCAA) and Department of Education and Training, Victoria (DE&T) (2005) Victorian Essential Learning Standards (VELS). Accessed March 2005 at: http://vels.vcaa.vic.edu.au.

Vygotsky, L. (1986) *Thought and Language*, E. Hanfmann and G. Vakar (eds and transls), Cambridge, MA: MIT Press.

Wells, G. (2001) The Case for Dialogic Inquiry, in G. Wells (ed.) *Action, Talk and Text: Learning and Teaching through Inquiry*, New York and London: Teachers College Press, pp. 171–194.

Wenger, E. (1998) *Communities of Practice: Learning, Meaning and Identity*, Cambridge: Cambridge University Press.

Withers, G. (1997) Competency-Based Education Revisited: the Mayer Report Five Years On, *Idiom*, 32(1), pp. 15–23.

Wittgenstein, L. (1994) *Tractatus Logico-Philosophicus*, D.F. Pears and B.F. McGuinness (transls), London and New York: Routledge.

Professional Learning

Chapter 2

Autobiographical Inquiry in Pre-Service and Early-Career Teacher Learning

The Dialogic Possibilities

Graham Parr and Natalie Bellis

Introductory note

This chapter is an attempt to represent and explore an ongoing inquiry-based dialogue about teaching and learning between two professional educators: Natalie, an early career teacher, and Graham, a teacher educator. Their dialogue began in 2003 in Melbourne, Australia, when Natalie was completing a one-year, postgraduate Diploma of Education (DipEd) for pre-service teachers, having completed a Bachelor of Arts (Honours) degree the previous year. Graham was one of Natalie's lecturers in English teacher education studies, a subject in her DipEd that involved inquiry into a wide range of pedagogical, curricular and professional perspectives on English teaching. Crucial to the professional inquiry that characterized this subject were two five-week long practicums – where pre-service teachers were 'placed' in two different schools – and two inquiry-based autobiographical pieces of writing (part of the assessment for this subject). The two written narratives were designed to encourage intellectual, affective and social engagement with the whole teacher education experience. In particular, they were intended to enable pre-service teachers to construct critical frameworks for making sense of learning experiences in their lives up till then, in their teaching practicums and in their professional learning beyond these particular settings.

As Natalie explains in her narrative below, the process of writing autobiographical narratives afforded rich possibilities for her professional learning as a pre-service teacher. In fact she continued to write autobiographical narratives throughout her first year of teaching. Sometimes these were addressed to colleagues in her own school setting, sometimes they were written for other professional forums – see Bellis (2004), where she constructed a hypertextual reflective narrative that was subsequently published in the journal, *English Teaching: Practice and Critique* – and sometimes they were part of an ongoing email conversation with Graham. For Natalie, this email dialogue became an important element in her attempt to maintain a learning continuum throughout her DipEd and first year of teaching, as well as an opportunity to develop a broader perspective of her immediate teaching contexts.

_____

Taking up the conversation . . .

Email to: Natalie
From: Graham
Subject: Writing = Learning
Hi Natalie,
How are things? I've finally finished my marking for the year. The last pieces I marked were those written by next year's graduate English teachers – they were writing narratives in which they were evaluating their teaching of writing on teaching rounds. The nature of the task is a little different from what you did last year, but I'm aware you haven't forgotten the autobiographical narratives you were writing then (and still are). I'm sure we both have projects and deadlines to meet in the near future, but I thought now would be a good time to take up our conversation about the chapter for the W=L book . . .
. . .
Email to: Graham
From: Natalie
Subject: Contrapuntal writing
Hi Graham,
I had a crack at some contrapuntal writing over part of the TS Eliot narrative I wrote at uni last year. Not sure how I did it in the midst of everything that is going on here today [at school]. Not a bad effort! I wouldn't expect that it would be able to fit into a chapter in this form . . . but I had a go in order to see if I could open up some new lines of inquiry . . .
. . . For me personally, the act of writing about teaching begins with uncertainty and confusion:
Can someone give me a map, please?
Where do I even begin? How do I begin?
Is looking back on an episode in the past really going to make me a better teacher?
Is it even relevant?
Perhaps, if . . .
But on the other hand . . .
Aaah! I'm not even sure what I'm being asked to do.
At the beginning of the process, I am not writing to find an answer. There is no set outcome that I am shaping the words to meet, no sense of anticipation that, when I put down the pen or lift my fingers from the keyboard, a moment of epiphany will suddenly occur. On the contrary, the writing process begins without the comforting presence of a map altogether.
In this way, the beginning of the writing process resembles the beginning of a teaching career. . . .

Fig. 1: Excerpts from email correspondence (Nov. 2004)

Narrative writing and autobiography: Some background

Many writers have commented upon the current proliferation of narrative forms in literature about teacher professional learning (e.g. Kamler 2003, Doyle & Carter 2003, Ritchie & Wilson 2000). A significant part of this proliferation comes from recent cohorts of pre-service and early-career teachers writing autobiographical narratives. They may be writing to 'capture their underlying conceptions of teaching' and or they may be just keeping journals 'to "story" their progress toward becoming a teacher' (Doyle et al. 2003, p. 131). In some contexts (such as in pre-service assignments or as in requirements for full professional registration) the mandating of some sort of auto-biographical writing constitutes a form of regulation. It is generally hoped that this mandating will somehow ensure pre-service and early career teachers are reflecting on their experiences in the classroom. Occasionally, the writing of narratives appears to be part of an inquiry-based professional culture (either within teacher education insti-tutions or in school settings), where it is considered intrinsically valuable for teachers (no matter how experienced) to inquire into their practice and professional identity by and through the process of writing autobiographical narratives.

Considering the time it takes to construct these narratives, one may well ask whether the narrative writing is worth all the trouble especially for time-poor early-career teachers, or whether this is an example of groupthink in education (Fullan & Hargreaves 1991), where large numbers of teachers are uncritically implicated in a narrative of follow-the-leader. Almost 15 years ago Maxine Green (1991) declared that story telling was 'everywhere' in educational research, and Barbara Kamler (2003) considers that interest in the writing of narratives has 'burgeoned' since that time (p. 38). It is as if some Duke of educational research has spoken and all have followed his call: 'Narratives be the food of teacher professional learning, so write on! Give us excess of it!'

Those educators engaged in narrative writing tend to fit into loose groupings like the following:

- an early manifestation of teachers as researchers (from the 1970s – eg. Stenhouse 1975): Perhaps for the first time, university researchers sought to position teachers as significant contributors to research into education by providing opportunities and spaces for them to write and publish stories about their work as teachers;
- the 'teacher lore project' (eg. Ayers & Schubert 1994): In this ongoing 'project', partnerships between school teachers and university researchers work together to construct and publish teacher narratives. They often claim that these narratives capture more of the authentic lived experience (and therefore the knowledge) of teachers in schools than writing generated by university researchers;
- the 'self-study movement' (eg. Loughran & Russell 2002): This is a loose com-munity of university-researcher and teacher-researcher partnerships, claiming to

follow in the footsteps of Donald Schön (1983/1991). They frequently refer to themselves as 'reflective practitioners,' and tend to base their writing on teaching and learning 'cases' in schools;

- critically reflective narrative writers (Richardson 2000, Goodson 1992): These writers tend to conceptualise their narratives within more rigorously theorized accounts of teaching practice, stressing the need to situate or locate any narrative within the socio-political contexts and environments of schooling. This grouping might also include those who call themselves 'narrative inquirers' (eg. Clandinin & Connelly 2000), although the degree of critical engagement in these narratives varies significantly from one narrative inquirer to another;
- critically reflexive narrative writers: These university-researchers and practitioner-researchers construct narratives that explicitly draw attention to the context of writing and the mediating nature of language in any writing project. They tend to frame their (autobiographical) narratives in opposition to humanistic or romantic narrative traditions of discovering 'truth' or 'the self' through narrative (Kamler 2001, Florio-Ruane 2001, Wells 1994, 2001).

Sounding a cautionary note in the midst of the 'burgeoning' of narrative, Goodson (2003) wryly apostrophizes about the 'Nirvana of the narrative, the Valhalla of the voice [in teacher research]'. He calls for careful critical scrutiny of narratives in educational research and in teacher professional learning: 'Stories and narratives are not an unquestioned good ... Individual and practical stories [can] reduce, seduce and reproduce particular teaching mentalities, and lead us away from broader patterns of understanding ... [They can] be as easily employed for closure as exposure' (Goodson 2003, pp. 26, 30, 48). In particular, Goodson points out the dangers of narratives that naively romanticize or sentimentalise teaching and teachers' work. They are the stuff of myths, he argues. In serving to mythologise and therefore mystify the work of teachers, such narratives discourage, if they don't actually shut down, any meaningful discussion of some critical issues affecting teachers and teaching.

Goodson's is not a lone voice. Several critics caution against the uncritical embracing of naïve or romantic notions of teacher narrative (e.g. Doecke, Loughran, & Brown 2000, Ritchie et al. 2000). Deborah Britzman (2003) takes this note of caution further. She is deeply critical of the 'glorification of firsthand experience' in teacher narratives. She identifies the danger of a narrative that 'nonproblematically scripts teacher identity as synonymous with the teacher's role and function' (p. 54). This is a concern for many writers, especially when these roles and functions are increasingly constructed by policy makers and employers in ways that impoverish teachers' professional autonomy and intellectual potential (see Cochran-Smith 2004, Doecke, Petrosky & Locke 2004, Parr 2004, Goodson 2003, Cochran-Smith & Fries 2001, Cochran-Smyth & Lytle 2001).

The problem of (not) questioning assumptions

All the narrative groupings summarized above would claim to be connecting with the concerns of practitioners in classroom settings, and yet there are marked differences in the nature of the narratives and in the professional knowledge and professional identity evoked in and through the writing. One explanation for this variation relates to the willingness, or otherwise, of narrative writers to critically reflect on the epistemological assumptions behind their narrative accounts. That is, they differ according to the extent to which they question and analyse the assumptions of how knowledge (and meaning) is constructed in and through their narratives.

Clearly, any narrative writing involves decisions about selection and omission, emphasis and de-emphasis. And all narrative writers in the groupings listed above would have made very different choices with respect to what is worth including and what is worth emphasizing. In this respect, they vary in the ways they *frame* their professional knowledge and their professional identity (MacLachlan & Reid 1994). It might be argued that this variation is a healthy indicator of plurality in educational research literature, evidence of a diversity of research perspectives. To some extent this is true. Certainly, as early career teacher and teacher educator we welcome notions of genuine plurality and diversity. But plurality (in the sense of several) does not necessarily mean diversity (in the sense of different critical positions). A collection of narratives that appears to be pluralistic and speaking with many voices can, on closer scrutiny, end up sounding more like one voice and lacking a certain authenticity.

Difficulties emerge when some narrative accounts, which would seem to be diverse and authentic, actually ignore crucial epistemological questions. For example let us consider a narrative whose description of teaching is sentimental in its simplicity. We could be thinking of many popular film representations of teaching from *Goodbye Mr Chips*, to *Dead Poets' Society*, to *Mona Lisa Smile*. Writers describing their teaching in such narratives are unlikely to 'waste their time' questioning epistemological assumptions; as such, they are always more likely to appeal to a wider audience (especially viewers or readers with little understanding of the complexity of teaching). Even for practising teachers, a simpler narrative that unproblematically claims to represent teacher knowledge and teaching practice can become seductive. What a relief to hear that it really is just that simple after all! It is seductive, in similar ways, when a written narrative claims to 'tell it like it really is' or when a particular perspective claims to be closer to the 'real life of teaching'. However, in all these cases there is a strong correlation between the seductive and the dangerously spurious. Any project that claims to reveal the simple truth (or the real story?) of teaching surely needs to be scrutinized to determine whether it is more engaged in mystification than clarification. As Goodson (2003, 1997) says, narratives are capable of concealing more than they reveal, and if they are concealing then they are failing in the very respect they hope most to succeed in (ie. to 'tell it like it really is').

At the most benign level this concealing is just unhelpful to teachers, especially pre-service and beginning teachers, who are (one hopes) exploring written resources that will help them develop their critical knowledge and understanding of teaching and seeking out people who will talk openly about teaching. It is more worrying when these pre-service and beginning teachers read unproblematic accounts of teaching and find that their own sense of teaching does not translate into such unproblematic frames. Britzman (2003) explains how beginning teachers 'feel an inordinate responsibility to single-handedly make students learn … [and] hope there is a direct relation between teaching and learning' (p. 3). Unfortunately, this sense of inordinate responsibility is reinforced by some researchers, such as effective schooling researchers, who constitute a politically powerful voice in education debates. This 'voice', often appropriated by politicians seeking quick and simple solutions to complex educational problems, characteristically valorises the notion of the individual 'quality teacher' and brackets out as insignificant a multitude of complicating socio-cultural factors in any teaching and learning dynamic (cf. Rowe 2003, Kleinhenz & Invarson 2004, Hattie 2004, Hargreaves 2001, Teddlie & Reynolds 2000).

Autobiography as dialogue

Given the proliferation of autobiographical narratives in education research literature, and given the wide range of quality of these narratives, one might be tempted to call, 'Enough. No more!' Indeed, in the last ten years, much research into teacher professional learning has been calling for the development of more dynamic *collaborative* inquiry-based cultures to resist the 'intellectual isolationism' characteristic of utilitarian constructions of teaching (Ball 1995, p. 256; see also Cochran-Smith 2001). Much research has also bemoaned the fact that cultures of *collaborative* inquiry operate so rarely at the level of particular school settings and at the systemic level (Reid 2004, Stokes 2001). And yet, here we are, an early career teacher and a teacher educator, advocating (with some caveats) a seemingly individualistic form of narrative writing for pre-service and early career teachers.

One might well ask, 'Why?' Part of the answer to this question comes from Florio-Ruane's reflection on her 2001 research project, where a group of 'writing teachers' met together over several months to talk about and to write autobiographical narratives. The approach of the group, as she explains, was to take the genre of autobiography that is 'typically thought of as personal and individual and [paradoxically] read it as a dialogic one' (Florio-Ruane 2001, p. xii). This paradox is at the heart of our approach and our argument.

Let us say from the outset, we are concerned to prevent our narrative becoming a 'victory' narrative (Lather 1994, in Stronach et al. 1997, p. 128) or a 'valorizing' narrative (Doecke et al. 2000, p. 347), and we wish to avoid positioning ourselves as the heroes of our own tale (Swidler 2001). In one respect, we share an enthusiasm for the possibilities of autobiographical narratives that seek to inquire into teacher identity, classroom practices and teaching spaces (in the richest sense of this term); we're interested in critical and imaginative autobiographical narratives that explore cultures and discourses within a range of contexts. But our enthusiasm doesn't speak with one voice. We are mindful of the criticism of Andy Hargreaves (1996) that much teacher education literature, particularly that involving teacher educators co-writing with early career teachers, tends to de-emphasise any potential difference in the voices between the two, which usually means silencing the early career teacher perspectives (see also Doecke 2003; Schultz, Schroeder & Brody 1997). Indeed, it is fair to say that this was an ongoing and generative tension in our collaboration in writing this chapter.

Rather than presenting a monologue about the joys and professional benefits of writing autobiographical narratives, our intention is to be dialogic. We want to open up, and inquire into, the critical and imaginative possibilities for teachers' professional learning through and in autobiographical writing. We want to draw on and speak with a range of voices as we inquire into these possibilities. We see any notion of an uncomplicated monologic communication to be misleading, anyway, and contrary to the fundamentally dialogic dynamic of all language (see below). On the one hand, this is to signal a connection with the traditions of an 'expressive and exploratory language' (Britton 1970; see also Nystrand 1997, McEwan 1994, Wells 1999, 2001), where open-ended talk, either literally or through writing, constitutes a suitable medium for critical and imaginative grappling with problems and ideas in education settings. On the other hand, as we discuss in the following section, we believe that teachers' autobiographical writing is not, and cannot ever be, 'a vehicle for the one-way transmission of knowledge.' It is almost inevitably dialogic.

The dialogic possibilities of counterpoint

Partly in order to illustrate the nature of this dialogic dynamic, and partly as a means of opening up further possibilities for our own professional learning, we intend to engage with Edward Said's (1983) notion of counterpoint. Rather than quoting Said directly, we want to draw on the musical notion of counterpoint to help explain our thinking:

> The term counterpoint . . . is used to describe music in which the chief interest lies in the various strands that make up the texture, and particularly in the combination of these strands and their relationship to each other and the texture as a whole. (*Grove's Dictionary of Music and Musicians, vol. 2*)

We see this metaphor of counterpoint[1], with its 'various strands' or voices, being generative for us because of its value in (i) exposing multiple voices where one narrative voice traditionally dominates over (ie. colonises) others and (ii) representing the dialogic possibilities of language, knowledge and identity in autobiographical narratives. And we see the notion of dialogic possibilities, expressed through and in this metaphor of counterpoint, operating in all the different ways we generate and construct meaning. Importantly, the notion of dialogic possibilities in counterpoint applies as much to our collaborative conversations – literally our dialogue – as to our own learning as individuals. That is, the learning of each us as individuals is also dialogic.

To illustrate the dialogic possibilities of counterpoint, we might inquire into an excerpt of a well known text indirectly alluded to earlier in this chapter. It is a monologue, and a narrative of sorts, spoken by Duke Orsino at the opening of Shakespeare's *Twelfth Night*.

> If music be the food of love, play on.
> Give me excess of it, that, surfeiting
> The appetite may sicken and so die.
> That strain again! It had a dying fall;
> O, it came o'er my ear like the sweet sound
> That breathes upon a bank of violets
> Stealing and giving odour. Enough, no more!
>
> *Twelfth Night*, I.i. 1–7

One familiar (dominant?) reading of this speech is of a paean to the joys of love – blissful, perhaps dignified love. Such a reading might be possible, might indeed be valid: (i) if the dynamic of the language were to be reduced to the narrowest monological terms; (ii) if the images were to be shorn from their original context; and (iii) if the ideas were to be translated into a simple, uncomplicated greeting card message. And, indeed, the first line of the text does appear in greeting cards all over the world, perhaps evincing the dominant status of this reading.

It is helpful to see this 'dominant' and monological reading as a response to one dominant 'voice' only. In such a reading, the singular voice must effectively silence other voices that are trying to explain how *Twelfth Night* ridicules the contrivances and baroque excesses of Elizabethan courtly love. This voice would also need to ignore the voices that might tell how the speech is delivered by a Duke, who is soon to be revealed in the play as ridiculously narcissistic and prone to flights of absurdly romantic self-indulgence. And in deferring to a monologic reading of the speech, the metaphoric voices of the text need to be narrowed, collapsed – perhaps 'blanched' is a better word – into only the blandest possibility. This dominant reading needs to be deaf to the playful but distasteful possibility, for instance, that 'surfeiting' – 'Give me excess of it, that, surfeiting / The appetite may sicken and so die' – might suggest literally 'throwing up', and that the duke might be construed as indulging in a kind of bizarre bulimic ritual where 'surfeiting' is a romantic response to an excess of love! Further, this dominant reading would need to pass over any critical voice that inquired into the effect of the incongruous mixing of metaphors in lines 5–7. Finally, a monological reading needs to ignore any critically reflexive voice that, depending on the particular context and biography of the reader/s, might want to sigh at the beauty of the imagery or 'throw up' with disgust at what seems to be a litany of saccharine platitudes.

Of course, when one engages with these other voices one begins to appreciate the rich dynamic of dialogic possibilities such a text affords. A monologic reading of this brief excerpt must defer to a simple and singular strand of meaning. Yes, shorn of all dialogic possibilities, the speech can be an ode to the beauty of love, for what it's worth. However, in stark contrast, a contrapuntal reading is receptive to the rich, multifarious strands or voices in terms of ideas, contexts, metaphors ... In a contrapuntal reading, different, interconnecting voices speak through and in the text, contributing to a rich, imaginative and problematic reading of the speech. Bakhtin's notion of dialogism goes further than this. He argues that all language, like all knowing, is dialogic in nature. In fact, even '*a word is a two-sided act*. It is determined equally by *whose* word it is and for *whom* it is meant' (Bakhtin 1994, p. 58). The corollary of this is that any state-ment (or 'utterance,' as Bakhtin terms it) 'makes response to something [spoken previously] and is calculated to be responded to in turn' (1994, p. 35). This applies as much to previous and succeeding words in any one sentence, as to previous and suc-ceeding lines in the poetry, and as to (previous and) succeeding speakers in a dialogue (including links with texts previously written or read).

So a space for contrapuntal reading is a site of ceaseless epistemological activity: there is a constant movement to and fro, built into the dynamic of dialogic language itself, and embedded in this is the constant interaction between and among voices or strands that constitute the counterpoint. Counterpoint in autobiographical narrative would seem to offer itself as a compelling metaphor and intellectual space for inquiring into and enacting teacher professional learning.

Co-Writing as counterpoint – a representational challenge

In our conversations leading up to the writing of this chapter, we considered many options for enacting and representing, on the page, our sense of the dialogic and contrapuntal dynamics of our ongoing professional conversation. (cf. Bulfin & Mathews 2003, Etherington 2004.) We spent considerable time, and several emails, exploring various geographical metaphors, to help elucidate our notion of dynamic dialogic spaces. In so many ways, we feel the visual metaphor of dynamically interconnected voices that we ended up with (drawn from the musical metaphor of counterpoint), does have possibilities in tentatively representing our dialogue on a two dimensional space. We like to think that, in some ways, this is making concrete something of the counterpoint that constitutes the critical inquiry of this chapter too. In our co-written text, which contains some narrative elements, we hope to show that collaborative inquiry-based dialogue does not always come together neatly with one voice.

Sometimes the voices 'sound' together, sometimes they sound in turn; sometimes one voice responds to another, sometimes two voices are 'in harmony with' each other; occasionally the voices are dissonant. (And occasionally we leave the dissonance unresolved.) In the discourse of the musical dictionary (see page 25), we hope to represent multiple 'interrelated strands' in the counterpoint of our ongoing conversation.

In passing, it is worth noting that we affirm the metaphor of voice/s in dialogic writing. But we don't just mean to suggest that writing can replicate the dynamic of several human voices responding to each other (sometimes referred to as polyphony) in autobiographical narratives. We recognize something of Kamler's (2003) concerns about the temptation to see the metaphor of voice in writing as closely linked to the body, and the danger when this suggests writing is a natural process of merely 'giving voice' to an idea or a process. (See also Sawyer, this volume.) Kamler quotes Pam Gilbert (1990) in stating her resistance to any notion of voice that 'naturalise[s] personal writing as authentic, "individual, spontaneous, natural, truthful, involved, emotional, real"' (Kamler 2003, p. 37).

This connects with Kamler's concern not to lose touch with 'the personal engagement' that can come from writing using the conventional metaphor of 'voice' (Kamler 2003, p. 39). Indeed, there is a danger when a discourse, or an autobiographical narrative, is preoccupied only with critique, in that the personal may be de-personalised, and a bleak critical perspective may prove unable to imagine an alternative brighter future. Such a narrative may lack what Giroux (1988) calls a 'language of possibility' (see also Leonardo 2004). Kamler (2003) calls for 'other discursive and pedagogic means' to achieve this personal engagement and to explore the possibilities (p. 39). To that end–and since, incidentally, we are both musicians 'in another life'[2]–we look again to musical discourse, and the discursive possibilities afforded by the German notion of *Stimme*. The term *Stimme* is usually translated as 'voice' in musical terminology, but it can mean *either* a human voice (singing a particular line or strand in a counterpoint texture, for instance) *or* a musical line or part (not necessarily a human voice) in the texture of a contrapuntal piece of music. In musical discourse and in narrative writing, the human involvement of the 'voice' in counterpoint may be emphasized, but the very ambiguity of the notion of *Stimme* serves to problematise any glib assumptions about the naturalness or otherwise of its production. We believe this ambiguity provides an appropriately open space to enact a 'language of possibilities,' and we hope to present this in and through a contrapuntal/dialogic autobiographical narrative in the following section.

The dialogue in this next section emerges from, and in response to, a narrative that Natalie had written in the early part of her DipEd year. (A fragment of this narrative, part of a poem titled, 'The student teacher's wasteland,' is included on the left hand side.) By calling it 'Natalie's (?) narrative,' we wish to signal some important tensions. On the hand, it *is* Natalie's narrative; for the first time the first person pronoun 'I' is used throughout this section to indicate Natalie's ownership. And yet the question mark in the sub-heading serves to signal the many levels on which it might be possible to read the section as a whole, and even Natalie's poetic autobiographical fragment, as dialogic (ie. a dialogue).

Natalie's (?) narrative . . . a counterpoint of 'voices'

Email to: Natalie
From: Graham
Subject: How's it going?
Thanks for your previous email. I got a rich sense of Natalie in the classroom. You've been in the job now for a few weeks. Does it feel that long? How are you coping with the workload?
. . .
To: Graham
From: Natalie
Subject: The Micro and the Macro
. . .I still don't quite understand why this whole narrative thing seems to be having such an impact on me. I thought when school began [a month ago now] that I wouldn't have much time or energy to write more narratives, but here I am still writing. I have never felt a greater need to write than I do presently. I feel almost as if I am in the process of inventing a new 'personal genre' for myself, if that makes any sense. I get the feeling that I'll have quite a collection of reflective narratives after my first year of teaching . . .

Fig. 2: Email from Natalie to Graham (Feb. 2004)

Obstruction, obscurity, emptiness, disorientation, twilight, blackout, often com-bined with a struggle or path or journey – an inability to see one's way forward, but a feeling that there was a way forward, and that the act of going forward would eventually bring about the conditions for vision . . . Possibly, then, writing has to do with darkness, and a desire or compulsion to enter it, and, with luck, to illuminate it, and to bring something back to the light (Atwood 2003).

In Margaret Atwood's book about writing, *Negotiating with the Dead*, she highlights the mysterious nature of writing. In describing the writing process as a journey into darkness, she invokes Marlow's description of his journey into the Congo in Joseph Conrad's (1995) *Heart of Darkness*. Marlow departs into the darkness driven by a glimmer of hope that he may find a vessel of light, or truth, that will illuminate not only his own iden-tity, but the views and values of his society, hidden somewhere deep within the jungle: 'It was the farthest point of navigation and the culminating point of my experience. It seemed somehow to throw a kind of light on everything about me – and into my thoughts' (p. 21). Considering the writing process in this way does have some value in that it draws attention to its serendipitous quality – that some value and benefit may arise 'with luck', as it were. And there is the sense, as many writers would attest to, that if you hack through the vines and tramp through the undergrowth for long enough eventually some sort of truth will be uncovered and that will be that. Destination reached. Journey over. Problem solved. It is a view of the writing process that appeals in many ways.

Indeed, there have been times, particularly during my pre-service year, when this metaphor of a journey did seem fitting. Perhaps it was because of the dominant voices in society, those 'cultural myths' (Britzman 2003) that confidently describe what are supposedly the primary functions of teachers – marking essays, imparting knowledge, enforcing discipline. Or perhaps it was because of the reductive discourses that position beginning teachers as individuals whose sole responsibility is to survive the tumult of their first year. For a variety of reasons, the process of constructing my professional identity, particularly through writing, did seem to me to be a highly individual and solitary process. As I have articulated in the above email extract, grappling with and making sense of the disparate elements of my professional identity was often confusing. And as seen in the email to Graham quoted at the start of the chapter, there was a disconcerting sense in which I was 'not even sure what I was being asked to do'. Not surprisingly, I wasn't entirely sure where it was going to end up. I was, however, attracted to the notion of constructing a professional identity, in some sense trying to define it. This seemed to me to be the only way to make sense of the cacophony of voices that seemed to be competing for my attention at any given time in my preservice year.

And yet, describing the process of writing my autobiographical narrative as a journey into the 'heart of darkness' now seems to me to be a suitable metaphor for only *some* aspects of the writing process. For a start, the image of myself as a hapless wanderer journeying without a map ignores the value of the beliefs and knowledge that I as an early career teacher already bring to the beginning of my career. The first autobiographical narrative that I wrote highlights in a number of ways how inappropriate it was to suggest that the process of my learning to teach would one day reach a conclusion, or even that this journey had a tangible beginning.

The narrative was written in response to the following task outline:

Task 1: A reflective autobiographical narrative, inquiring into your beliefs and values about English and English teaching

Brief description of the task

You will inquire into, and reflect on, your experiences as a learner of English, in order to clarify for yourself and to articulate for your reader the views and values you hold (and are developing) about English teaching.

Fig. 3: Instructions for autobiographical assignment in the early part of Natalie's pre-service teacher education year.

I found the task to be particularly appealing because of the emphasis my lecturers placed on experimenting with unconventional structures and modes of narrative/ autobiography, and particularly genre. Just as the process of 'learning to teach' occurs at a site of contestation, subversion, and possibilities, so too does the process of writing and grappling with meaning: 'genres become borders to cross over and over again, simulacra of a past to be resurrected and erased, palimpsests that are constantly rewritten' (Curti 1998, p. 53). This idea of experimentation and testing the boundaries of genre and structure is not only a powerful metaphor for the professional learning continuum of teachers. Its inclusion in the writing process also allows the viewpoint of both the writer and the reader to be widened, explored and reconsidered, resulting in diversions and changes in direction that were not previously possible.

In the spirit of 'testing the boundaries', the narrative excerpt that I will share here is a parody of T.S. Eliot's 'The Wasteland' that I wrote to explore the crossroads that I found myself standing on in the midst of my pre-service year. As I saw it, the pathways of myself as student and myself as teacher were crossing in a way which was confronting. In an email to Graham after the completion of writing this narrative, I explained my reasons for approaching the task in this way: 'To me, Eliot's *The Wasteland* is partly about creating a new text (or, on a broader scale, a new literature) out of the old ... And I think that for me, this task has been about creating, or at least defining, a new direction out of past experiences' (July 2003). This part of the narrative followed on from inquiry into some of my learning experiences as a student in a secondary English classroom. It emerged as a somewhat tentative 'sounding-out or trying-out' of my emerging professional identity (Dickerson 1989) as I set about forging a place to begin as a teacher.

I include an excerpt (see over), partly to illustrate some of my early experiments in autobiography, and partly in order to show how dialogue between Graham and me emerged from the writing of the artefact. In many ways, the dialogic dynamic that we are enacting in this whole chapter is represented by the counterpoint of voices on the following two pages. Initially, it is helpful to consider the voices in three categories: (i) the textual artefact (the excerpt from Natalie's pre-service autobiography), (ii) the text boxes (Natalie's reflection on her earlier text) and (iii) the callout bubbles (Graham's reflection and prompts).

Some further reflection

To us, the sense of dialogic counterpoint between and among the voices on these pages is evident in many ways. First, in the excerpt from the original autobiographical artefact, Natalie the preservice teacher was constructing meaning from, and reshaping, past events. This process necessarily involved, and was mediated by, the various *Stimmen* from her teaching and learning experiences before and during her DipEd year. Second, the ways in which Natalie the early career teacher engages now with her original text

The Student Teacher's Waste Land

I. The Burial of the Dead

I see the silhouette of a young woman with
Questioning eyes, searching for a way clear
Through alternate swirls of red and blue
Chalk dust.
She brandishes a light sabre, or is it a pen,
And writes to seek her path.

She yearns to teach, though all she knows is
A heap of broken images that are only now
Slowly, sneakily, silently shifting to form anew.
(A curse? Or a gift?)
She wants to be like Persephone,
To shift between her numerous dreams as
The sky changes.

In Egami Rorrim Land,
A crowd of influences flows through her soul,
Reflecting and refracting,
Dispersing then diffusing
Light through a web of
Multiple selves.

Natalie: My sense of self is strongly embedded in the words that I was writing here. I still use writing to understand, celebrate, extrapolate and critique my teaching and learning experiences. Although Kamler (2003) argues for a separation between the text/artefact and the self (p. 35) that often feels difficult to achieve, especially when my 'voice' seems so clear to me in my writing, and I feel like I am investing so much of myself in the act of giving voice to my ideas and experiences and then sharing them with others.

Graham: Yes, I know what you mean. Stronach et al. (1997) (and many others) suggest that we are 'all predisposed to build stories in this way' (p. 127). But they go on to argue that this says as much about the power of modernist (social) conventions of autobiography as it says about the psychology of individual writers. I guess, it's not a matter of 'either … or'.

Natalie: On the other hand, I understand and appreciate the more poststructuralist notion of a polyphonic identity ('a web of/Multiple selves') – that my professional identity is grounded in my interactions with others, both past and present, and it will continue to shift and change through future interactions with students, colleagues, texts and experiences. Sharing this and other autobiographical narratives with others and listening to and reading other voices respond to them – voices that can shift, embellish, affirm or question my thinking – ideally results in both my critical engagement in my own practices and the engagement of others in theirs.

Graham: Mmm. This is an interesting tension. I take it that you're saying you intellectualise your position in this dialogic particular way and yet there is an emotional sense of writing as discovery that is still powerful!

Natalie: I think that it is difficult to escape the seduction of writing to seek understanding. And the emotional connection that the writer feels with 'their' text seems to me to be completely unavoidable. Besides, surely it's an important part of the writing process? But I am realizing that this doesn't mean I can't step away from the original text (to a certain extent) and consider it from difficult angles. In fact, the notion of it helps me to do that – to be able to view the text as something that was constructed dialogically and therefore I (we!) can analyse the language and consider various readings of it.

Graham: What have been some of the most powerful influences on your students' attention (and yours) in your first year of teaching? I know it's a big question, but can you just mention a few?

Natalie: Gosh, where do I start? The looming threat of exams would be one – their presence sometimes seemed to narrow the ways that my students wanted to explore the texts. And for me, there was the constant battle of trying to remain up to date in the curriculum in order to prove to my school that I was not only coping, but capable. There never seemed to be enough time to achieve everything that I felt that I should be achieving in the classroom. And then, when you add athletics carnivals, public holidays, co-curricular activities, music lessons, and powering up laptops to the mix, well …

Natalie: In this section of the 'poem' I am in the process of developing and articulating some of the beliefs and values that I want to inform my teaching. There is a sense of uncertainty conveyed through the words 'Maybe / Hopefully' as I ponder how the reality of the profession that I had not yet entered would connect with my vision of what it should be like. The desire to ask open-ended questions and encourage my students to do the same hasn't changed this year, although this voice has occasionally gotten lost amidst the competing influences on both my and my students' attentions.

Graham: I sense a hint of irony here. What do you now think about this metaphor of a 'key that will open any door'? Do you remember what you were referring to here?

Natalie: Well, I certainly wasn't meaning to be ironic at the time! Perhaps the idea of education as a 'key that can open any door' is a romantic notion, but I still think there is room for idealism in teaching, and my experiences this year haven't changed that. Although, looking back on those lines now, I can see that a possible reading of them is a highly individualised view of teaching in the words 'this is what I will give'. I would like to think that my classroom is a place of partnership between me and my students, rather than me as the teacher holding all the 'keys' as it were. Oh, look, I've just used the term 'my classroom' - not a particularly inclusive term! It seems that it's not as easy to avoid these discourses as one might think!

Natalie: The narrative ends with a sense of incompletion. When I revisit it now, it still feels unfinished. I don't feel that, now that I've been teaching for a year, the questions that I was contemplating while I was writing this narrative have necessarily been answered. My viewpoint has been expanded in many ways by my experiences this year however. I guess that explains why we consider the act of 'learning to teach' to be a process, rather than something more definitive. What we 'know' can never really be considered concrete.

II. What the Teacher Said

"What if?"

    "But if?"

        "And if?"

That is what I ask ("What if?")
And that is what I will teach my students
To ask, to dream, to create, to engineer,
Maybe.
Hopefully.

Yes, always.

This is what I will give:
A key that can open any door
Smash any window
Vanquish any monster
Reach any shelf.

On this rising hill *among the mountains*
The trees are stretching, *the grass is singing*
And the rivers are flowing.
I rise from the ashes like a
Phoenix. And dream.

Shantih shantih shantih?

We'll see.

(and responds to Graham's questions and comments) illustrates the ongoing nature of her autobiographical inquiry, and it points to the enriched range of *Stimmen* that now interact with each other in her professional learning. As an early career teacher, she continues to 'try-out or sound-out' her professional identities. Third, Graham's text in the callout balloons serves as a gesture, only, with respect to the multiplicity of other voices/*Stimmen* that continue to open up dialogic possibilities for Natalie's learning. In that respect, there is a sense that Graham's callout balloons do not really build a new level into the dialogue at all, but rather make more explicit the different strands that are already embedded within Natalie's dialogic professional learning in the first place.

It is worth spending a moment reflecting on the collaborative nature of the dialogue between Natalie and Graham and the ways that the metaphor of a musical counterpoint might be helpful in elucidating this. As with the notes on the manuscript for a piece of musical counterpoint, there is something incomplete and inadequate in the words on a page representing a dialogic writing process. Certainly, they do not tell the whole 'story.' And any aspects of the story that are notionally present are mediated by the conventions of language, by the dialogic nature of all communication and by the mediums in which they are embedded. For instance, there is a suggestion of some linear logic to the page – top to bottom, and left to right – although this does not determine the way readers will read it, just as musical notes on a piece of manuscript do not completely determine how a piece of music will be heard. There are different voices speaking on the page (the poem, the text boxes and callout balloons): they speak to each other, sometimes together, sometimes in turn ... But still there is a sense in which any representation of the dialogic dynamic can only ever be a tentative and incomplete reproduction. Even the sense of the individual voices (Natalie's text or Graham's text) as discrete entities should be considered problematic. In our representation of collaborative inquiry into autobiography the overall effect tends to blur any ostensible line of demarcation between the individual voices. What is more powerful than the sense of any particular and individual voice is the 'texture' overall, the holistic sense of a rich counterpoint of ideas, voices, *Stimmen*: ie. a dynamic of dialogic possibilities. In practical terms, these possibilities may come in the form of colleagues, practical experiences, critical readings, and professional learning resources and professional learning spaces generally. Just as they have in the past, all of these *Stimmen* continue to stimulate and mediate Natalie's and Graham's professional learning.

Coda

We have been arguing throughout this chapter that a dialogic understanding of autobiographical narrative offers rich possibilities, particularly, but not exclusively, for pre-service and early career teachers. Indeed, we see these possibilities as generative for so many aspects of education today:

- in classrooms (both school classrooms and classrooms in teacher education institutions), in the ways teachers interact with their students as they write, and in the ways students interact with each other in the same situation;
- in staffrooms, in the ways teachers interact with their colleagues in some form of collaborative writing process; and
- in other professional learning spaces, where teachers look beyond their immediate teaching context and dialogically interact with the wider world.

It may well be that the dialogic *process* of sharing and discussing such written artefacts is more valuable than the actual construction of the written texts per se. In acknowledging this, we hope we are making clear that we do not wish to fetishise autobiographical writing, as if it were a solution to all educational problems.

In advocating for autobiographical inquiry we have been arguing, in effect, for a broader notion of professional inquiry that involves teachers, administrators and policy makers opening up spaces for the richest dialogic possibilities to unfold (cf. Reid 2004). We see this professional inquiry potentially operating on three levels: systemic, interpersonal (and personal), and linguistic. Underpinning all of these levels is the sense that just as the richest professional identity is dialogic (or contrapuntal, with different strands or *Stimmen* interacting with each other), so too the richest professional learning and knowledge is dialogic. While this would suggest that educators could benefit from more collaborative models of working and writing together, this can also apply to apparently individual work (like autobiographical writing).

For both of us, exploring the dialogic potential of autobiographical writing has crystallized some fundamental questions about dominant discourses of individual professional identity and individual professional knowledge. There are important questions that need to be asked of policy makers who invoke individualistic notions of 'the quality teacher,' and in doing so, seek to regulate and control teacher learning, especially that of pre-service and early career teachers. Etienne Wenger writes about all manner of professional learning, not just teachers', but his insights are valuable for the teaching profession and for pre-service and early-career teachers in particular. He has an interesting take on the notion of professional learning and the knowledge that emerges from this learning:

> Our knowing – even of the most unexceptional kind – is always too big, too rich, too ancient, and too connected for us to be the source of it individually. At the same time, our knowing – even of the most elevated kind – is too engaged, too precise, too tailored, too active, and too experiential for it to be just of a generic size. The experience of knowing is no less unique, no less creative, and no less extraordinary for being one of participation. (Wenger 1998, pp. 141–2)

Natalie's narrative attests to the widely held perception that this 'experience of knowing' for pre-service and early career teachers is a place of constant change and contestation. Beginning a teaching career is an uncertain time when the myth of a definitive knowledge can seem particularly beguiling. However, a *participatory* conceptualization of professional knowledge and identity evokes an idea of knowing that can be interacted with – a sense of 'knowing' that can be expanded, amended, shaped, questioned and enhanced by a diverse range of voices over time. Like a musical counterpoint, it is an experience of knowing that is rendered meaningful by the combination of voices that make up its texture, rather than the particular voice that contains the dominant melody.

We, ourselves, have found that critically and imaginatively inquiring into our own autobiographies, and capitalizing on the dialogic possibilities inherent in this process, brings meaningful rewards in terms of our own professional learning and engagement. Needless to say, in co-writing this chapter we have found the process of collaborative inquiry into autobiography, and capitalizing on the dialogic possibilities, brings meaningful benefits too. But in the face of the proliferation of autobiographical teacher narratives, we are clearly not arguing for a surfeit of autobiographical inquiry – as if more is always better.

We are recommending a particular approach to autobiographical inquiry writing: one that is critical, imaginative, reflexive and perhaps collaborative; an approach that builds in some consideration of the epistemological questions raised by such writing. We're not recommending it as an easy process with guaranteed benefits. However, we believe that this sort of approach can enable pre-service and early-career teachers to better understand their new profession; and it may well help to develop a 'language of possibilities' that will encourage beginning teachers to contest those dominant discourses that serve to limit their professional identities and constrain their professional growth. Finally, we recommend this approach to autobiographical writing (and collaborative inquiry into autobiography) to all teachers and teacher educators interested in exploring the rich dialogic possibilities that teaching as a profession holds.

References

Atwood, M. (2003) *Negotiating With the Dead: A Writer on Writing*, Cambridge: Cambridge University Press.

Ayers, W. and Shubert, W. (1994) Teacher Lore, Learning about Teaching from Teachers, in T. Shanahan (ed.) *Teachers Thinking, Teachers Knowing: Reflections on Literacy and Language Education*, Urbana, IL: NCTE, pp. 105–121.

Bakhtin, M. (1986) The Problem with Speech Genres, in C. Emerson and M. Holquist (eds) *Speech Genres and Other Late Essays: M. M. Bakhtin*, V. McGee (transl), Austin: University of Texas Press, pp. 60–102.

Bakhtin, M. (1994) *The Bakhtin Reader: Selected Writings of Bakhtin, Medvedev and Voloshinov*, P. Morris (ed.), London: Edward Arnold.

Ball, S. (1995) Intellectuals or Technicians? The Urgent Role of Theory in Educational Studies, *British Journal of Educational Studies* 43(3), Sept. 1995, pp. 255–271.

Bellis, N. (2004) A Beginning: Using Writing and STELLA to Construct a Professional Identity, *English Teaching: Practice and Critique* 3(2), Sept. 2004. Accessed in Dec. 2004 at: http://www.tmc.waikato.ac.nz/english/ETPC/narrative/html/BellisPP_files/frame.htm

Britton, J. (1970) *Language and Learning*, Ringwood: Penguin.

Britzman, D. (2003) *Practice Makes Practice: A Critical Study of Learning to Teach*, Revised Edition, Albany: State University of New York.

Bulfin, S. and Mathews, K. (2003) Reframing Beginning English Teachers as Knowledge Producers: Learning to Teach and Transgress, in *English Teaching: Practice and Critique* 2(3), Dec. 2003, pp. 47–58. Accessed in Dec. 2004 at: http://www.tmc.waikato.ac.nz/english/ETPC/article/pdf/2003v2n3art4.pdf)

Clandinin, J. and Connelly, M. (2000) *Narrative Inquiry: Experience and Story in Qualitative Research*, San-Francisco: Jossey-Bass.

Cochran-Smith, M. and Fries, M. (2001) Sticks, Stones and Ideology: The Discourse of Reform in Teacher Education, *Educational Researcher* 30(8), pp. 3–15.

Cochran-Smith, M. (2004) The Report of the Teaching Commission: What's Really at Risk? (Editorial), *Journal of Teacher Education* 55(3), May-June 2004, pp. 195–200.

Cochran-Smith, M. and Lytle, S. (2001) Beyond Certainty: Taking an Inquiry Stance on Practice, in A. Liebermann and L. Miller (eds) *Teachers Caught in the Action: Professional Development that Matters*, New York: Teachers' College Press, 3–15.

Conrad, J. (1995) *Heart of Darkness*, London: Penguin Books.

Curti, L. (1998) 'D' for Difference: Gender, Genre and Writing, in *Female Stories, Female Bodies: Narrative, Identity and Representation*, London: Macmillan.

Dickerson, M. (1989) 'Shades of Deeper Meaning': On Writing Autobiography, in *Journal of Advanced Composition* 9, http://jac.gsu.edu/jac/9/articles2/11.htm

Doecke, B. (2003) Ethical Issues in Practitioner Research, *Professional Educator* 2(4), October 2003, pp. 8–9.

Doecke, B., Brown, J. and Loughran, J. (2000) Teacher Talk: The Role of Story and Anecdote in Constructing Professional Knowledge for Beginning Teachers, in *Teaching and Teacher Education* 16, pp. 335–348.

Doecke, B., Locke, T. and Petrosky, A. (2004) Explaining Ourselves (to Ourselves): English Teachers, Professional Identity and Change, in *Literacy Learning: The Middle Years* 12(1), and *English in Australia* 139, Feb. 2004, pp. 103–102.

Doyle, W. and Carter, K. (2003) Narrative and Learning to Teach: Implications for Teacher Education Curriculum, *Journal of Curriculum Studies* 35(2), pp. 129–137.

Etherington, K. (2004) *Becoming a Reflexive Researcher: Using our Selves in Research*, London and Philadelphia, PA: Jessica Kingsley Publishers.

Florio-Ruane, S. (2001) *Teacher Education and the Cultural Imagination: Autobiography, Conversation and Narrative*, Mahwah, NJ: Lawrence Erlbaum Associates.

Fullan, M. and Hargreaves, A. (1991) *What's Worth Fighting For?: Working Together for your School: Strategies for Developing Interactive Professionalism in your School*, Hawthorn, VIC: ACEA.

Giroux, H. (1988) *Teachers as Intellectuals: Toward a Critical Pedagogy of Learning*, Granby, MASS: Bergin & Garvey.

Goodson, I. (1992) Studying Teachers' Lives: An Emergent Field of Inquiry, in *Studying Teachers' Lives*, I. Goodson (ed.), London: Routledge, pp. 1–17.

Goodson, I. (1997) Representing Teachers, *Teaching and Teacher Education* 13(1), pp. 111–117.

Goodson, I. (2003) *Professional Knowledge, Professional Lives: Studies in Education and Change*, Maidenhead: Open University Press.

Green, M. (1991) Foreword, in C. Witherel and N. Noddings (eds) *Stories Lives Tell: Narrative and Dialogue in Education*, New York: Teachers College Press, pp. i–xii.

Grove, G. (1961) *Grove's Dictionary of Music and Musicians*, 5th ed., E. Bloom (ed), London: Macmillan.

Hargreaves, A. (1996) Revisiting Voice, *Educational Researcher* 25(1), Jan.–Feb. 1996, pp. 12–19.

Hargreaves, D. (2001) *A Capital Theory of School Effectiveness and Improvement*, Jolimont, VIC: IARTV.

Hattie, J. (2004) It's Official: Teachers Make a Difference, *Educare News*, Feb. 2004, pp. 24–31.

Kamler, B. (2001) *Relocating the Personal: A Critical Writing Pedagogy*, Norwood, SA: AATE.

Kamler, B. (2003) Relocating the Writer's Voice – From Voice to Story and Beyond, in *English in Australia* 138, Spring 2003, pp. 34–40.

Kincheloe, J. (2003) *Teachers as Researchers: Qualitative Inquiry as a Path to Empowerment*, London and New York: RoutledgeFalmer.

Kleinhenz, E. and Ingvarson, L. (2004) Teacher Accountability in Australia: Current Policies and Practices and their Relation to the Improvement of Teaching and Learning, *Research Papers in Education* 19(1), March 2004, pp. 31–49.

Leonardo, Z. (2004) Critical Social Theory and Transformative Knowledge: The Functions of Criticism in Quality Education, *Educational Researcher* 33(6), Aug./Sept. 2004, pp. 11–18.

Loughran, J. and Russell, T. (eds) (2002) *Improving Teacher Education Practices Through Self-Study*, London: RoutledgeFalmer.

MacLachlan, G. and Reid, I. (1994) *Framing and Interpretation*, Carlton, VIC: Melbourne University Press.

McEwan, H. (1997) The Functions of Narrative and Research on Teaching, *Teaching and Teacher Education* 13(1), pp. 85–92.

Nystrand, M. (1997) Preface, in M. Nystrand, with A. Gamoran, R. Kachur, and C. Prendergast, *Opening Dialogue: Understanding the Dynamics of Language and Learning in the English Classroom*, New York and London: Teachers College Press, pp. xiii–xiv.

Reid, A (2004) Towards a Culture of Inquiry in DECS, Occasional Paper No. 1, Sept. 2004, Department of Education and Children's Services, Government of South Australia. Accessed in Dec. 2004 at: http://www.decs.sa.gov.au/corporate/files/links/OP_01.pdf

Richardson, L. (2000) Writing: A Method of Inquiry, in N. Denzin and Y. Lincoln (eds) *Handbook of Qualitative Research, 2nd ed.*, Thousand Oaks/London: SAGE.

Ritchie, J. and Wilson, D. (2000) *Teacher Narrative as Critical Inquiry: Rewriting the Script*, NY and London: Teachers' College Press.

Rowe, K. (2003) *The Importance of Teacher Quality as a Key Determinant of Students' Experiences and Outcomes of Schooling*, Discussion Paper Prepared on Behalf of the Interim Committee for a NSW Institute of Teaching, Feb. 2003, ACER. Accessed in Dec. 2004 at: http://www.acer.edu.au/research/programs/documents/Rowe_ACER_Research Conf2003_Paper.pdf

Shakespeare, W. (1985) *Twelfth Night, or What You Will*, E. Story (ed.) Cambridge and New York: Cambridge University Press.

Said, E. (1983) *The World, the Text, and the Critic*, Cambridge, MA: Harvard University Press

Schön, D. (1983/1991) *The Reflective Practitioner: How Professionals Think in Action*, London: Avebury.

Schultz, R., Schroeder, D. and Brody, C. (1997) Collaborative Narrative Inquiry: Fidelity and the Ethics of Caring in Teacher Research, *Qualitative Studies in Education* 10(4), pp. 473–485.

Stokes, L. (2001) Lessons from an Inquiring School: Forms of Inquiry and Conditions for Teacher Learning, in A. Liebermann and L. Miller (eds) *Teachers Caught in the Action: Professional Development That Matters*, New York: Teachers College Press, pp. 141–158.

Stenhouse, L. (1975) *An Introduction to Curriculum Research and Development*, London: Heinemann.

Stronach, I. and MacLure, M. (1997) *Educational Research Undone: The Postmodern Embrace*, Buckingham: Open University Press.

Swidler, S. (2001) Heroes of Our Own Tales: Presentation of Self in Conversation and Story, in C. Clark (ed.) *Talking Shop: Authentic Conversation and Teacher Learning*, New York: Teachers College Press, pp. 118–136.

Teddlie, C. and Reynolds, D. (eds) (2000) *The International Handbook of School Effectiveness Research*, London and New York: Falmer Press.

Vygotsky, L. (1962) Thought and Word, in *Thought and Language*, E. Hanfmann and G. Vakar (eds and transls), Cambridge, MA: MIT Press, pp. 119–153.

Vygotsky, L. (1981) The Genesis of Higher Mental Functions, in J. Wertsch (ed. and transl.) *The Concept of Activity in Soviet Psychology*, Armonk, NY: Sharpe.

Wells, G. (2001) The Development of a Community of Inquirers, in G. Wells et al, *Action, Talk, and Text: Learning and Teaching Through Inquiry*, New York and London: Teachers College Press, pp. 1–22.

Wells, G. (1999) *Dialogic Inquiry: Towards a Sociocultural Practice and Theory of Education*, Cambridge: Cambridge University Press.

Wells, G. (1994) Introduction: Teacher Research and Educational Change, in G. Wells (ed.), *Changing Schools from Within: Creating Communities of Inquiry*, Toronto: OISE Press, pp. 1–35.

Wenger, E. (1998) *Communities of Practice: Learning, Meaning and Identity*, Cambridge, MA: Cambridge University Press.

Notes

1 We should point out here that this metaphor of counterpoint is different from the linear notion of point and counterpoint, such as in a debate, where one voice sounds at a time, each time responding to an earlier voice. Rather, we want to emphasise the non-linear notion of counterpoint where several interweaving voices ('strands') are speaking to and with each other – perhaps at the same time – in the manner of a contrapuntal musical texture.

2 We both studied music before becoming English teachers.

Chapter 3

Conversation + Collaboration + Writing = Professional Learning

Scott Bulfin

(Blogpost@http://thisteachinglife.blogspot.com)

FRIDAY, JANUARY 07, 2005
>so it begins
I managed to continue with the chapter today, but not very far. I have written bits and pieces over the last couple of months and need to pull it all together and push it further again. Sometimes it's just cracking the beginning that is the difficult thing; framing things in an interesting way and not producing another boring piece of dry academic writing – sometimes I think I have some idea of how to do this and at others I sit in despair, agonising and wrestling with words that won't seem to do what I want them to do . . .

Email from: Meg
To: Mr Bulfin
Hey Mr. Bulfin,
I have attached my poem sorry it is so late in the day but i totally forgot hahaha. i have also been to the library after skool and tried to hire the book making laws for clouds and couldnt find it so instead of trying to find it at another library i have just found another book which is 48 shades of brown but it is very thick so i am going to do that as my next [book report] seeing as i dont have much time left to do it so i have gone on to read the book hot or what which is another margaret clark book.
Please tell me if you think i should read this or not as i am a bit lost.

Introduction

This chapter explores some of the learning opportunities I have experienced in my early teaching career. Over the past few years, I have enjoyed many conversations with colleagues, some of which have led to productive collaborations, and I shall argue the value of these activities as opening up spaces for critical reflection, where we have been able to work together to resist the pressures of the daily routines of classrooms and schools, and to imagine other possibilities for learning, knowing, and being. I also want to show how writing (email conversations, coauthoring an article with a colleague, blogging etc.) has been integral to my professional learning, providing in turn a context for my continuing dialogue with students. When my students' emails arrive, demanding a response, I know that together we are engaged in this complex business of wrestling with words and making meaning.

There is a growing number of early career teachers and practitioner-researchers who are talking and writing about their professional learning (see Bellis 2004, Bulfin 2003, Bulfin & Mathews 2003, Griffin 2002, 2003, Hopton 2003, Illesca 2003, 2004, Mallord 2003, Wild 2003). This 'work' is the product of a particular discursive community where texts – narratives, counter narratives, and arguments (cf. Doecke, Homer & Nixon 2003) – frame and reframe each other (cf. MacLachlan & Reid 1994). These texts 'speak' to each other in generative, though sometimes dissonant ways, creating a space where knowledge is co-constructed – a whole universe of discourse that now includes digital technologies and associated emergent cultural forms, such as blogs and wikis.[1]

As well as these conversations between early career teachers, there is the talk between experienced teacher-researchers and teacher educators who have been around for much longer. (For a good selection just flip back to the contents page of this book!) The writing by early career teachers is itself framed and positioned by writing 'about' early career teachers and their experiences: an intergenerational dialogue where texts, experiences, histories and biographies mix and mingle and sometimes clash (a noisy, Friday afternoon, period six conversation). Divergent certainly, but a dialogue in which there is more than a hint of potential for teacher renewal and change, and an argument in favour of a broader notion of professional identity and learning than is implied by the notion of 'professional development', involving a recognition of the value of other dialogic spaces (Bakhtin 1981, Bulfin & Mathews 2003) and the sociocultural nature of learning and identity (Lave & Wenger 1991, Renshaw 1998, Rogoff 1994, Witherell 1991).

When considering learning for early career teachers, a personal-private/public-political dialectic (cf. Doecke 2001) is a useful metaphor. Teachers' work is deeply personal and private, but also unavoidably public and political. In fact the daily workings of schools are so completely tied up in this tension that the dialectic, or movement between the private and public (or personal and political), is one of continual exchange. Those who occupy school spaces are obliged to operate simultaneously in both domains. My learning has been similarly non-linear, characterised by negotiation, provisionality, uncertainty and a certain sense of discomfort (and excitement!)

What follows is yet another attempt by me to join this noisy conversation.

Beginning Teaching

I began my teaching career in a government high school of about 650 students. A 'middle-to-lower status' school, 'Hilltop' competes with a number of higher status schools in the area for students and resources. Of course, such things as school 'status' and 'credibility' depend on who you talk to rather than reflecting any objective measurement. Demographically, middle class white-Australian students form an over-whelming majority of the school population, especially at the senior levels, although lately there has been a welcome increase in the number of Asian-Australian and overseas students, who have generally had a positive influence on the academic and social culture of the school. While most teachers at Hilltop have many years experience, there is a small number of younger or newly qualified teachers joining the staff. My 'official' induction was a fairly simple event, if it can be called an induction at all, and the real work was largely left to my English faculty colleagues, to whom I am deeply indebted for taking an interest in me, for listening patiently to my idealistic statements about the importance of English teaching and for recognising when I did occasionally have something important to say.

I am not being critical of the administration's 'hands-off' approach to induction – it was obvious that they were not used to welcoming new teachers to the school and they were doing what they thought would be helpful. They too were overworked and rightly concerned that the school year got off to a good start. Beginning work at a 'new' school, regardless of whether you are experienced or only at the start of your career, has its challenges: you need to suss out the unwritten and unspoken laws, traditions, and values, to fit in with different policies, processes, discourses and relation-ships. Despite some difficulties, the professionalism of my immediate colleagues, amid the hurly-burly of full teaching loads and additional responsibilities, was never more evident than in the way they accepted me as a colleague and friend, and not as a young person in need of development. I was quickly made to feel that I could contribute to the life of the faculty as much as anybody else, and that my ideas and input were valued.

My experience of induction was certainly different from my expectations before I began teaching. The collegial relationships that I have just mentioned did not spring up overnight, but took much longer than I have suggested and were much more compli-cated. Leaving the university after I had apparently 'finished' my education or teacher preparation and getting on with the 'real' job of teaching was both exciting and dis-concerting. On the one hand, I felt uncomfortable (and annoyed) with what seemed to me a pervasive discourse suggesting I should 'forget all that uni stuff and get on with the job of teaching' and that as a 'beginner' I 'just' needed to 'survive THE FIRST YEAR', as if it would make or break the rest of my career (and life). I am still suspicious of such assumptions and the implications they have for university teacher education and research in general.

On the other hand, I had intensely enjoyed much of my undergraduate education studies and knew I would miss the opportunity to explore interesting and powerful ideas through conversations and writing – especially when I considered the kinds of stories and discourses that surrounded 'beginning teaching' and the 'reality' of class-room life. There are many stories about the lack of opportunity and time for serious reflection (on ideology, belief, motivation, etc.), for wider reading, or just for chatting with colleagues about the work. From the perspective of teaching rounds, and a university tutorial room, these stories seemed to be the stuff of staffroom lore, and as it turned out, despite their often dramatic retelling, they were not without their truth. In such circumstances, I wondered if it were possible to continue the type of conversations my university colleagues and I had enjoyed before being silenced by school-based discourses. Rather than see my time at university as a waste of time, I was interested in finding my own links between the theory I had read and my professional practice.

I have argued elsewhere (Bulfin 2003, Bulfin & Mathews 2003) that established discourses and conditions in schools often work to make it more difficult for early career teachers (if not all teachers) to create space to engage in sustained dialogue and writing about their work and learning. Strictly behavioural or psychologistic notions of learning tend to privilege individual knowledge and action, making it difficult for schools and teachers to meet the challenges posed by outcomes-oriented curriculum, standards-based reforms, professional accreditation and regulation. These and other top-down 'reforms' largely ignore the learning that can occur through dialogue, col-laboration and writing, and can seriously undermine the efforts of teachers to work together. So while there is plenty of talk and conversation that goes on in schools (my Year 8 students will show you that), there are also many barriers to the type of 'authentic conversation' (Clark 2001) or sustained intellectual dialogue that is impor-tant for quality teacher learning. The situation is similar with respect to writing – while a lot of writing goes on, very little could be regarded as reflective or exploratory. Most is done in order to meet administrative demands.

When my colleagues and I began teaching, our excitement at finally getting our own classes was dampened by a quiet realisation that we would have to work much harder if we wanted to continue the kinds of authentic conversations we had engaged in at university and which had been such an important part of our learning as pre-service English teachers. Now that some time has passed since these early difficulties, I realise that this dilemma was not only a function of schools and work conditions, but also that we were still 'outsiders' in our school contexts. We had not yet had oppor-tunities to develop trusting relationships with colleagues and find like-minded teachers with whom we could talk and write. They were there, but it took some time for these relationships to strengthen.

Learning against the grain?

It was in an effort to resist the relentless pressures associated with beginning teaching that a colleague and I began meeting regularly. We talked about our teaching – the concerns, pressures, successes and failures that we experienced from day to day, and whatever else came up. We created a space for conversations that we could not have at our respective schools, at least not in the first few months of our first year of teaching. Importantly, we also wrote narratives of our teaching and other reflections on critical incidents, sharing these with each other. This gave us space to unpack and to theorise our experiences, to re-examine our basic assumptions, to 'try on' the talk and mind of professional teachers in a more personal-private setting.

Below is an email exchange that captures a sense of these conversations and gives some indication of how we positioned ourselves in relation to others and the events of the time: as radicals, as knowledgeable about educational issues, as passionate professionals. In email exchanges and other conversations such as these we were able to set up alternative 'spaces' for our professional learning, where we could pursue our own interests, in our own ways.

Email from: Katrina
To: Scott
Why is it that professionals don't strike? Seems to me that you are buying into some crap idea of economics here – whatever happened to collective action as espoused by your mate Mr. Marx? Why is it that if people strike they are seen to be, in the hierarchy of work, somehow lesser for having done so? What about exercising your right to have a voice and a show of solidarity with others in the PROFESSION? Isn't striking a (established, recognised, bonafide) part of the discourse of collective bargaining? Is striking not a kind of lobbying? Are you working for the media?
The state governments have decided to cap teacher salaries at no more than 3% increase – which when you account for inflation is the equivalent of a zero pay rise indefinitely. I think, (from what I can make out anyway) that this is the first time all state governments have worked together to create an agreement about teacher salaries. To give the full picture (and being honest) I think it has also undermined the power of state union action in some respects as they have (in the past) been able to play off the pay and working conditions in other states. Some people at school tend to think that you have to push the issue while you can – think Kennett, history of IR in VIC – and while the government isn't necessarily in a position of authority (low retention rates, teacher shortages, etc.) They said the last strike was 99, but I think it may have been 2000 – hmmm. Others think it is a waste of time and others are worried about missing out on a day's pay. So, its been an interesting response and I'm confused and don't really know what to do.

Email from: Scott
To: Katrina
Yeah all good points – but for your bravado you still don't know what to do! Oh, and 'collective action' doesn't have to be militant – i.e. Gandhi. It's a shame that these calls for

strikes are given from above – probably mostly by people who don't even teach anymore – where is the collective action you speak of in terms of the other problems and issues the profession faces? VIT, class sizes, quality prof. learning, private schooling–academic success–social power a la Teese? Is the AEU and the majority of teachers who will strike marching down the same road it is apparently 'fighting'? – an overriding concern for pay/remuneration/economics/market capitalism/greed! Nobody bloody well strikes when they tell beg. teachers to suck provisional eggs for a year and then undergo some lame ass 'professional' accreditation hurdle jumping exercise – no one bloody well strikes about contract teaching positions where young teachers have to take time off to reapply for jobs they already do well! I guess I'm wondering why the AEU is choosing this issue over all the others? It seems to me that in the end, for them, as with the government, it is also a politically motivated move – one designed to increase their own power and status as much as making a statement about teachers' pay (what about conditions!). The AEU serves its own agenda and powerful constituents – not the minority of members who have different concerns. Anyway … I'm going to whack on a Billy Brag CD. I'm waiting for the great leap forward.

It is refreshing to reread this text now from a distance and see a number of larger concerns emerge: the individual caught up in conflict with the larger structures of state, reminding us – to borrow C. Wright Mills' words – that 'the human meaning of public issues must be revealed by relating them to personal troubles and to the problems of the individual life' (Mills 1959, p. 248). There is also a sense that we have been left out of an 'official' conversation, but that we still attempt to understand the situation for ourselves by 'writing our way to meaning' (cf. Christie 1999). Many questions are raised: what does a professional do in these circumstances? What are the professional consequences for acting out of step with other colleagues? This example of 'authentic conversation' shows us pushing each other for clarification, challenging ideas and assumptions. At the time we felt uncertain about the value of these conversations (did they simply reveal our anxieties and uncertainties about moving from university to school?), but in time, and as we persisted, we became convinced of their value.

At times our conversations were opportunities to share varying perspectives and to open up new ways of seeing experience, as in the narrative below, which was written in response to a frustrated email from Katrina.

Email from: Katrina
To: Scott
Hi, I have a million things that I should be correcting at the minute as I seek out ways to procrastinate. It's like, I know there are a million things that I need to work on improving and I seem incapable of doing any of it. I've decided my focus is too much on the 'everything' and I need to settle in and concentrate on one area or problem at a time. Easier said than done though. Half way into doing something OK I think, shit, my year nine classes need 'fixing up' and then I'm off on a different path without having finished

the first one. So tell me . . . do you think there are things you aren't happy with in your practice? Are these big or little concerns and how do you or don't you address these? See, I want to put you in the light for a minute and don't cop out.

Email from: Scott
To: Katrina
Um . . . hello? Let me tell you a story from yesterday. First I'll set the scene . . . Generally I have not had many problems with my year 9 English class, even period 6 seems generally OK, they have a go – most – those that don't are usually good natured about it and we get along. I had planned to begin our debates about a week ago but b/c of one thing or another they have been delayed and put off and postponed and shifted and avoided etc. So this was it, I had decided that we were starting today, no matter what. Your question prompted this short narrative response in my journal;

'OK, guys, I'll put the debate order on the board and you get into your groups and get your thoughts together. I've made some executive decisions and no correspondence will be entered into concerning the order of debates . . . OK'

Assorted murmurs and some slow movement. I quickly look for the team groupings I have written down somewhere – this is the second version – I lost the first. Located, I jot the order on the board knowing that I'm sure to get some resistance.

It seems OK. So afterwards I turn to the class. There are a couple of hands up and so I brace myself.

'Mr Bulfin, Sophie is away! We CAN'T do our debate today, OK!?'

'Mr Bulfin, Perry is away too! We can't do out debate either.'

'Mr Bulfin, Hamilton is away as well. We're not doin' our debate.'

'Mr Bulfin, Cate and Nellie are away. How can we do our debate!? We're not doin' ours either!'

With this I remember that Cate and Nellie saw me on the way to class and asked 'permission' to attend a 'Tournament of the Minds' practice. I consented without thinking.

The unease slowly begins to register. I sigh. The beginning of class has not gone smoothly (even though I have skipped it). I have asked a couple of students to rearrange some tables at the front of the room for the debate and there is lots of noise and commotion, students wandering around, chatting and laughing. When I finally realise that I won't be kicking many goals this lesson, most students are doing their own thing and waiting for me to 'get into gear'. I'm not sure whether time froze and I just stood there and phased out or whether it all happened during an instant but felt like an age.

'OK, folks, can you open your exercise books to a new page and copy down what I write on the board.' I remember that I have some 'word puzzles' with me – for early finishers in my year 8, period 5 class. I found these puzzles in the *Age* and I'm already regretting my decision to use them with this class – but when you choose a path, you choose where it leads . . .

So things are going OK. There is some productive talk about the task but also a sense of barely restrained anarchy. As I'm writing the next puzzle on the board I'm hit in the back with a screwed up piece of paper – not a malicious throw just a lob. There is laughter as I turn around. How do I react here? What do I say – how should I hold myself?

I choose not to say anything but just look around the room with my eyebrows raised and tilted. I wait a few seconds . . . then Brad owns up. I calmly but firmly ask him to wait outside the room. I need to be careful here as in the past when I have asked students to wait outside the room I have forgotten about them. I finish writing on the board then go outside to talk to Brad.

'Are you going to yell at me? I didn't mean it. Someone else threw it at me and I just threw it away and it accidentally went in your direction.'

Umm . . . what do I do now? Usually when faced with one-on-ones I get soft and lose my frustration and/or anger, but I don't want to lose it now. I also realise that getting angry with this young man won't have the effect I want it to. Instead I look at him and say,

'Brad, I don't throw paper at you, do I?

'No,' (resigned tone).

'I treat you like I expect to be treated. I don't throw things at you and I expect that you won't throw things at me. Is that fair enough?'

'Aren't you going to yell at me? You can yell at me if you want!'

This narrative describes just one example of the 'millions' of things I am unhappy with in my practice. I seem to wander from mess to mess all day long and just try to shrug it off (it's not really that bad). In a way it gives me strange comfort to know that it's me that should be doing better, or planning more, or thinking more creatively or something. I can't blame the kids for being off the wall, although I can expect them to be sensible and have a go. But the problem is not theirs or mine alone. We need to work together. Your comments about changing focus on the 'everything' and the many parts reminds me of a problem that sociologists often have (apparently) which I think connects to some ideas in the actor-network literature (ANT). The changing focus between the micro and the macro comes about because of eventual dissatisfaction with on the one hand a focus on the individual's power to effect change (the micro, for example) and on the other hand with the confining and positioning forces of institutions, culture, technology (!) etc. (the macro). It seems that we often change focus between these two, and in reality probably work with both at the same time, or at least an overlap. The tension between these two concepts is really interesting and I think borne out in teaching practice every day.

I wrote this narrative as a way of reflecting on the 'millions of things that I should be correcting' about my own practice and the ways in which I had begun learning about teaching from my students. I do not want to glorify teacher narrative, or to suggest that we arrived at some kind of truth by engaging in this kind of activity, only that it afforded us chances to talk about our practice and how we both had begun to construct ourselves as teachers – to engage in a form of reflexive practice. At the time, I had framed this narrative as an example of 'my' failure or of 'my' struggle to come up with 'answers' for this group of students; but Katrina read it differently and much more positively. Being presented with a different reading of one's own text can result in a type of fracturing of original intent, and that can be very generative.

You could also say that we were engaged in developing our teacherly identities or subjectivities. Learning to be a teacher is much more than mastering content knowledge and teaching procedures; it involves talking and speaking like a teacher, acting like a teacher, 'thinking, feeling, believing and valuing in ways that are recognised as characteristic of teachers' (Doecke & McKnight 2003, p. 297, cf. Gee 1991). This process of taking on and refashioning a particular discursive identity (cf. Bulfin & Mathews 2003, Gee 1996, Marsh 2002, Santoro 1997) was at once challenging and rewarding. Our professional learning was closely bound up with issues of professional identity and how teachers see and understand themselves as professionals.

As we shared ideas and readings and then held these ideas up alongside our experiences, our conversations became an opportunity to engage more meaningfully in a personal-public knowledge dialectic where theory became more meaningful because it helped us better understand our teaching and other concerns. An important part of this was finding a language to frame our experiences and give them shape. As a result, we were able to see further than we could see alone. This is not to say that we always agreed or that harmony was the order of the day; sometimes good conversation means listening as someone 'unloads' or gets stuff 'off their chest'. Furthermore, I came to understand that as much as we were learning about our teaching, we were also thinking deeply about our learning; a kind of inquiry into the 'scholarship of teaching', if you like, where the content (substance) of our learning (our conversations and writing) was the learning process itself.

I was writing my honours thesis at the time that I was engaging in these conversations, and this also became an important writing=learning event. Our conversations fed into my thinking and writing to the extent that it became more natural and representative of the collaborative and dialogic processes to think and write about 'our' learning, rather than to think that we were on completely separate journeys. Struggling with my own thinking and writing, while in 'conversation' with many other ideas, texts, colleagues and experiences made the process of writing my thesis a more collaborative experience than it is often thought to be. My thesis provided me with an opportunity to reflect on the value of collaborative learning experiences in which I was participating.

Adventures in the public-political domain

Our early experiences as interlocutors had been firmly in the personal domain, but this began to change. We were invited by a teacher educator colleague to join a small working party to plan the Professional Identity and Change (PIC) strand of the International Federation for the Teaching of English (IFTE) conference held in Melbourne during 2003. In an effort to continue the conversations that began in the planning stages in the months prior to the conference, those involved with the work of the PIC strand have since written about the experience from varying perspectives

(Bulfin & Mathews 2003, Doecke, Locke & Petrosky 2004, Parr 2004). As this writing points out, the PIC/IFTE experience was a significant one and offered occasion to engage in extended dialogue about issues such as professional identity, change, and learning for English teachers. As early career English teachers we found an opportunity to take our thinking and conversations into more public domains.

My involvement in the IFTE conference and in the PIC working party were major turning points in how I have come to think about my professional learning and identity. In the lead up to the conference, the PIC group, as we came to call ourselves (there were about eight of us, including experienced English teachers and teacher educators), met regularly to prepare our contribution to the conference. During our planning efforts, we were able to create an authentic discursive space where opportunities to reflect on and theorise our experiences in preparation for the conference offered a source of rich learning rarely found within the day-to-day experience of teaching. This professional dialogue brought together teachers of varying ages and experience, who were all committed professionals. The intergenerational dialogue that occurred strengthened my view of teachers as legitimate knowledge professionals, capable of intellectual and critically active work.

In an effort to further broaden the discussion a couple of us younger teachers selected snippets from our online conversations and sent these as an email to people in Australia and around the world who had registered to attend the PIC strand. Our comments were not designed to present 'the' voice of beginning teachers, as if there could be such a thing (in preparing for the conference, we often disagreed amongst ourselves), but to present several perspectives on a range of issues.

From: Scott, Katrina & Anna
To: IFTE–PIC registered delegates
Subject: The PIC Beginning Teachers have something to say!
Hi everyone (we are not sure exactly who you are but we hope you're out there). We are a bunch of beginning teachers helping out with the PIC strand and we wanted to let everyone know what we have been up to the last couple of weeks. To give beginning teachers some 'space amidst the crowd', we have been asked to prepare a panel of sorts and have assembled some committed beginning teachers who have been discussing issues relevant to us. Below are some snippets from our discussions that we offer in the hope of opening up the conversation.
Scott, Katrina, Anna
. . .

Katrina>
I have to do a series of things in my classes that I don't want to do, or talk about them in a really superficial way that doesn't actually tell me anything – like some crap task we did at uni (sorry, but if anyone did that subject you might appreciate what I am saying) And then that's it, it feels like it's not so much a practice in joint reflection as it is in setting up

---

a situation where you go through a script with someone who will assess you on your ability to read

Anna>
It's interesting what you mention about journal writing being cathartic as well as isolating – I agree! Your comment about other teachers saying that you won't have time to reflect is really scary and not true at all – sure teaching is a chaotic job at times but it's not as though you can't spend 1/2 an hour reflecting. I think it stems from the little importance some more experienced teachers place on this practice. It's all about classroom management and budgets!

Scott>
I also find it ironic that in finding language to talk about our experiences as beginning teachers we inevitably take on the discourse of experienced teachers – a discourse that is owned not by us, but by those who often construct versions of what beginning teaching is like. To talk about these experiences in ways that are meaningful to older teachers we adopt the 'cultural tools' and frameworks that they have developed as experienced teachers and researchers. But do these help us make meaning from our own experiences or do they mediate or filter our experiences so that we end up sounding like everyone else and not really hitting the mark – only the wall of concrete utterances?

In response to our conversation starter, we received several responses, one of which is presented below.

From: Barbara Comber[2]
To: IFTE-PIC registered delegates
Subject: Re: The PIC Beginning Teachers have something to say!
Hi Scott, Katrina and Anna
Thanks for your post. I'm one of the mid/late career folks trying to hear what early career teachers are saying about being an English teacher now, what it means, what we could do better in preservice, what kinds of induction and support would help when you begin, what kinds of knowledge about English and about teaching has proven useful to you, what kinds of ethics is essential etc. etc. so I really appreciate your contribution to the list. You all raised questions for me, which I raise in the interests of continuing this conversation:

Katrina: What were the things you didn't want to do? What made these "uni tasks" superficial/sham? How would you improve it for future new teachers? Tell us more about the scripts you felt you had to rehearse/regurgitate?

Anna: How have you made the time for reflection? Is journal writing a part of that? What else helps? Are there situations in which you do get to engage in proper educational/educative conversations beyond budgets and behaviour?

> Scott: Can you imagine places/sites/discourses where beginning teachers were not
> dominated by experienced teachers' discourses? Is there a way that "new teachers" can be
> inducted into the profession that doesn't impose and dominate, or is that an impossible
> fiction? When you "meet" without experienced teachers (if you do) do you do
> something different/more productive for you, where you don't sound like everyone else?
> Cheers
> Barbara

Joining a wider, more public conversation, which was international in scope, involving
teachers and academics from Australia, New Zealand, England, the USA, Canada and
South Africa, helped lay to rest the self-doubt and uncertainty that surrounded our
more personal discussions and sense of professional identity as valued members of a
knowledge community. In making the shift to a more public-political dialogue, we
found that we had more in common with other English teachers, at all stages of their
careers, than at first we had imagined. Our personal and private 'knowledge' was made
increasingly 'public' through our involvement in a wider community of English
teaching professionals. Perhaps this could be read as relief at having been recognised as
'legitimate peripheral participants' (Lave & Wenger 1991) by established 'old timers' in
the field. Regardless, in this larger conversation the knowledge creation process was
joint, dialogic and public. This in turn gave us confidence to write about our experiences of beginning English teaching (see Bulfin & Mathews 2003), a process that, for
me, embodied the personal/public tension that we had been talking about and that I
have been exploring throughout this chapter. This important learning opportunity gave
us ways of seeing ourselves as writers, learners and knowledge producers rather than
simply the subjects of others' writing and research.

Writing (in and on) my professional landscape

While my involvement in PIC and IFTE provided different ways of seeing myself and
others as teachers and professionals, and of 'doing' teachers' work, it also had the effect
of turning my thoughts back on (or forward to) my immediate concerns and context.
In this way my learning has increasingly 'come home' to my school setting – but not
simply in a personal or private way. Rather, it is again a case of a shifting between
personal-private and public-political domains while keeping a broader perspective on
the issues at hand. Whatever else you do, the demands of the day-to-day have a way of
remaining omnipresent.

During my first year teaching, I had become increasingly aware of how I was being
positioned as an early career teacher, or indeed how all teachers are positioned by
various discourses, values, histories and a variety of other factors (cf. Gee 1996).
Understanding how I was positioned helped turn my interests and attention more to
the conditions of my work and the practices of my workplace, colleagues and students.
I began to see these relationships not as natural or given, but as the products of both

'biography and history, and the range of their intricate relations' (Mills 1959, p. 248). This also suggested that the pressures and tensions I felt as a young teacher were not entirely due to my limitations and foibles. Furthermore, many of the problems at Hilltop (or wherever you are) were (or are) not simply a function of context 'but must be understood in terms of public issues – and in terms of the problems of history making' (p. 248).

I am fortunate to have a couple of colleagues who are interested by these same tensions, and who also understand the importance of good conversation, one of whom enjoys writing. Because teaching seems to take so much out of us, we find it refreshing to talk and write together. In fact we blog many of our experiences. Our conversations are also often of day-to-day kinds of stuff; sometimes we just talk about our students or colleagues who are just so tired and worn down. We also write narratives of events where we try to explore the effects of the issues we face. I wrote the following after lunch at a local café brought to a head some issues we faced as a faculty.

As an English faculty we occasionally go out for lunch together – quite ordinary you might think – but very important, in fact some of the best PD you'll ever get your hands on. But, of course, you have to eat fast otherwise you'll miss period five. So, last week while sitting around a table at a local café, I imagined our own beer hall putsch.

Why? Well, our head of faculty relayed to us an experience she had had that very morning. She had been 'called in to see' the principals. What did they talk about? Well, let's just say there wasn't any congratulations handed out, in fact they discussed (or the principals discussed) some 'alarming' figures showing our 'terrible' performance in VCE English last year compared to other 'like schools' in our region and across the state.

'Don't try to rationalise the figures! They mean what they mean ... I just want you to tell me what we need to do?! What is the problem and how do we fix it?'

This is the general refrain when anything is being 'discussed'. A few weeks before at a staff meeting we were supposed to be analysing student survey data; same story here, 'don't try and explain the figures, don't rationalise them, just give us some strategies to fix the problem'.

Sitting at the café that day we all understood what the problem was ...

THE PROBLEM IS THERE IS NO OPPORTUNITY TO TALK ABOUT OUR PROBLEMS.

Curriculum days are so chocked full that we have a token 30mins as an English faculty for vitally important matters such as the validity of our CSF judgments and how these map on to (or don't map on to) students' AIM results. Yep, the days are long and the nights are even longer.

The irony of our situation was not lost on us as we sat around the café table surrounded by the usual corporate and business lunch crowd, who began casting odd glances at us and looking a little worried as our talk becoming louder and louder as we became more and more worked up.

'They want us to lift our percentage of students scoring over 40 for English – the goal is 5.9%. They want us to identify who achieved an A or A+ in year 11 and work with these students especially to ensure they receive 40 or over; but they don't want too many, just a select few around the benchmark. They want an even spread.'

'They cannot understand why we are doing so badly in English at Y12 when there seem to be many more students succeeding at Y11. They want to know what is happening. I think that they think we are perhaps marking things too easy in Y11, or too hard in Y12, and that we are not preparing students well enough for the exam, as our kids coursework scores are often scaled down.'

And so the conversation continues. We talk about what we can do and some arguments we can use against this kind of managerial effacement of teacher professionalism, this kind of vacant obsession with that much loved mantra of the 'business community', 'continuous improvement'. We also talk about that great versatile line, lie, and mantra, 'It is the teacher that matters most . . . It is the teacher that matters most.'

But period 5 always comes too soon.

The school is in the throes of writing a new charter and English has been singled out as an area of concern. The whispering in the corridors is that if something is 'wrong' with our VCE results then there must be a problem with our 7–10 curriculum; fix this and you've solved the VCE problem. Simple.

I guess I have noticed some good from all of this though. We are talking more as a faculty. Some of us are always at it, every chance we get. Others are not so interested. But things are changing. Discussion is building and good reflective conversation is beginning to occur.

Writing such as this is important for many reasons, not in the least because it provides a sense of distance from which it is possible to critique practices, discourses and assumptions, especially one's own (cf. Kamler 2001). Despite the content, our writing and conversations are always fuelled by a desire to understand why things are the way they are and how we might go about changing some of them. We try not to whinge all the time, as this tends to strangle good productive dialogue; rather, we talk over ideas and experiences. Once again, as with the PIC group, in these collegiate relationships there is no sense that age is necessarily the deciding factor in all experience. We work to create a dialogic space (often online), where we can begin to imagine possibilities and to find support to teach (and think) in different ways.

Opening classroom doors

There is no denying the value of conversation, collaboration and writing for professional learning. As a corollary, I have thought it important to bring these understandings into the classroom and to model these ideas and actions for students. In addition to our class work, I try to encourage students to engage with these same issues outside of class time in greater depth and complexity than our time together usually allows. I invite students to continue our conversations online, through email and instant message programs (MSN Messenger, etc.).

One particular exchange was prompted in response to a visit to Hilltop by an experienced and well-respected English teacher, who came to share some end of year English exam 'tips and tricks' with senior students. The presenter was so self-assured and opinionated that it was as though his reading of the text was the only valid one. The message seemed to be that if students wanted to 'ace' the exam they should take on the presenter's point of view. The presenter further suggested that Hilltop students were fortunate because they now had the same information that this teacher shares each year with his own top performing students at an exclusive private school in Melbourne. A day after the event, Louisa, a student in my Senior English class wrote to me about an issue she had been pondering. The context concerns Scott Anderson's novel, *Triage*.

Email from: Louisa
To: Mr Bulfin
Subject: Triage
Hey Mr Bulfin,
I'm sorry to bother you, but I've been thinking about [the visitor's] talk yesterday and how he said that Mark feels guilty because he doesn't bring Colin home and wanted to say what I thought ... I don't know if this is right, or it might be obvious, but I think he does bring him home. Mark leaves Colin's body in Kurdistan because a body is just a body – a physical object – that doesn't mean anything. He made the choice to not take Colin home – Mark's guilt is not from failing to take the body back to America, but his failure to take Colin home to his family by not speaking of his death – he keeps the man from his loved ones for quite a long time. But he takes Colin home spiritually eventually, with the help of nature. When Mark visits the Alpujarra, he visits a river and sits upon a rock – he recalls the death of Colin. Whilst in the Alpujarra around surroundings that remind him of the day, Mark is slowly bringing Colin home – he says 'I'm taking you home.' In the end, by speaking of Colin's death, Mark returns himself and Colin back to his family – he must do this to say goodbye and give peace to Colin's family. Home is not a physical place or the returning of a body, but rather an explanation for Colin's family about Colin's death and a final goodbye for Mark to his friend.
Louisa.

Louisa's desire to continue the conversation, to create her own meanings, to speak her own mind and to engage in a productive struggle with words and ideas, is obvious. I was delighted by her confidence in questioning the authoritative position this experienced teacher had assumed during his address. Here she is offering an alternative point of view in an environment in which she felt more supported. She is able to support her own ideas and writes in an exploratory and open-ended way, inviting response. This kind of 'writing conversation' is nothing new, but further illustrates the importance of conversation, collaboration and writing, not only for teacher professional learning, but for student learning. My challenge as a teacher was to help Louisa move from this personal-private space of communicating with me to the public domain of performing well in the VCE exam, while also understanding the reductive way in which such exams frame student knowledge and constrain response.

Whether the kinds of conversations I have been arguing for in this chapter are enacted in classrooms, corridors, staffrooms, cafés, or in online spaces, they must be directed at engaging participants in an open dialogue about possibilities. The extent to which these different conversational spaces mediate the kinds of language practices, communications and relationships that develop is a question that is certainly worth further consideration. There are many issues associated with 'writing conversation' as opposed to physical conversation that have implications for participants in any exchange: power and authority, access and disadvantage, to name just a few.

My 'conversation' with Louisa also speaks productively to the challenges early career teachers face when negotiating their professional identities and a sense of personal and public authority about their experiences. In order to reflect on and write about their interests and concerns, many teachers require active support, encouragement and opportunities – in ways similar to those I was able to provide for Louisa – otherwise they might not ever speak or write 'out'. For my part, I am grateful to have received such support from colleagues

Conclusion

Opportunities to work in the ways I have described have been very rewarding. I know this has also been the case for colleagues and students I have had the privilege to work, talk and write with over the last couple of years. In the end, there are opportunities for professional learning in all experience, but I believe that this learning must also include efforts at pushing back against the pressures and dilemmas teachers live and work with everyday. I am thinking not only about the need to resist the prescriptiveness of narrow inservice professional development, but working out ways in which we can push back the 'normalising' practices of mainstream schooling (cf. Popkewitz 1998) which can squeeze the life and hope out of both students and teachers. These 'normalising' practices largely ignore that schools are shaped by complex social, political, historical, technological and economic forces – and that reading, writing, teaching and learning are similarly shaped.

I am reminded of H. L. Mencken's observation that 'for every complex problem, there is a simple solution that is always wrong'. The complex problems that teachers and schools face cannot be solved by greater government control of teachers, their education, work and conditions. Nor can teachers 'make a difference' on their own. What we need are productive partnerships and collaborations between teachers, schools, governments, professional associations and universities – the STELLA project[3] is one that comes to mind. This is a project conceived in a completely different way to others that attempt to create public knowledge about English teaching and teachers' professionalism, one that has involved the kinds of 'authentic' conversations and writing that I have been arguing for here. So interesting and useful work can be done, but it is not easy.

Teacher conversation, collaboration, and writing have the potential to generate learning opportunities that are more meaningful than professional development as typically conceived by governments and schools. The processes that I have been describing better recognise the complexity and professionalism of teachers' work and knowledge, and the contextual factors that play such an important part in any work-place. This said, the kinds of conversations and writing that I am arguing for really only become critically useful when participants are engaged in sustained theoretical reflec-tion about their work. Such learning is not just a matter of 'talking' or 'working together' or scribbling journal notes about how a lesson may have gone – important though these activities may be. It is about self-reflexive, practice-based inquiry that contributes to our knowledge as a profession.

The idea of learning that continually or simultaneously moves between the personal-private and the public-political domains provides an alternative and broader notion of professional learning for early career teachers than traditional ways of thinking about beginning teaching. This notion emphasises the importance of looking for 'conversations' beyond the immediate context of one's school. It also encourages recognition of how the problems particular to the practice setting are connected through people to those larger issues and problems. This must surely be the beginning of thoughtful conversation, collaboration and writing.

So in the end, as always, I am left wondering what to make of all this for me and those who share my practice setting and classroom space. Certainly, it is important to do more than just reflect, talk and write. So while professional learning for teachers is often about ourselves, we must go on to 'organise ourselves for future *action* in our classrooms and schools' (Clark 2001, p. 180), action that must be both practical and critical.

Acknowledgements
Thanks to Karen Bares, Brenton Doecke, Natalie Bellis and Graham Parr for responding to various drafts of this chapter.

References

Bakhtin, M. M. (1981) *The Dialogic Imagination: Four Essays*, C. Emerson and M. Holquist (trans.), Austin: University of Texas Press.

Bellis, N. (2004) A Beginning: Using Writing and STELLA to construct a professional identity, *English Teaching: Practice and Critique* 3(2), September, html document
http://www.tmc.waikato.ac.nz/english/ETPC/narrative/html/2004v3n2nar2.htm

Bulfin, S. (2003) Learning to Learn Against the Grain: Beginning English Teaching and the Processes of Professional Learning, Unpublished Honours Thesis, Monash University, Melbourne.

Bulfin, S. and Mathews, K. (2003) Reframing Beginning English Teachers as Knowledge Producers: Learning to Teach and Transgress, *English Teaching: Practice and Critique* 2(3), December, pp. 47–58.
http://www.tmc.waikato.ac.nz/english/ETPC/article/pdf/2003v2n3art4.pdf

Christie, F. (1999) Learning to Write: A Process of Learning How To Mean, in B. Doecke (ed), *Responding To Students' Writing: Continuing Conversations*, Norwood, SA: AATE, pp. 67–83.

Clark, C. M. (2001) *Talking Shop: Authentic Conversation and Teacher Learning*, New York: Teachers College Press.

Doecke, B. (2001) Public and Personal Domains: Professional Standards for Teachers of English in Australia, *L1 – Educational Studies in Language and Literature* 1(2), pp. 163–177.

Doecke, B. and Gill, M. (2001) Setting Standards: Confronting Paradox, *English in Australia* 129–130, December 2000–February 2001, pp. 5–15.

Doecke, B., Homer, D. and Nixon, H. (eds) (2003) *English Teachers at Work: Narratives, Counter Narratives and Arguments*, Norwood, South Australia: AATE/Wakefield Press.

Doecke, B., Locke, T. and Petrosky, A. (2004) Explaining Ourselves (To Ourselves): English Teachers, Professional Identity and Change, *English in Australia* 139, pp. 103–112.

Doecke, B. and McKnight, L. (2003) Handling Irony: Forming a Professional Identity as an English Teacher, in B. Doecke, D. Homer and H. Nixon (eds), *English Teachers at Work: Narratives, Counter Narratives and Arguments*, South Australia: AATE – Wakefield Press, pp. 291–311.

Gee, J. P. (1991) What is Literacy? in C. Mitchell and K. Weiler (eds) *Rewriting Literacy: Culture and the Discourse of the Other*, New York: Bergin and Garvey, pp. 77–102.

Gee, J. P. (1996) *Social Linguistics and Literacies: Ideology in Discourses* (2nd edn), London, New York: RoutledgeFalmer.

Griffin, A. (2002) 'Self' and 'Other' / 'Self' and 'Situation': The construction of professional knowledge for the beginning English teacher, Unpublished Honours Thesis, Monash University, Melbourne.

Griffin, A. (2003) 'I Am a Teacher – Oimigod!': The Construction of Knowledge for the Beginning English Teacher', in B. Doecke, D. Homer and H. Nixon (eds) *English Teachers at Work: Narratives, Counter Narratives and Arguments*, South Australia: AATE/Wakefield Press, pp. 312–325.

Hopton, N. (2003) English Teaching as a Profession: To Leave or Not to Leave, *English Teaching: Practice and Critique* 2(3), December, pp. 95–98.
http://www.tmc.waikato.ac.nz/english.ETPC/narrative/pdf/2003v2n3nar1.pdf

Illesca, B. (2003) Speaking as 'Other', in B. Doecke, D. Homer and H. Nixon (eds) *English Teachers at Work: Narratives, Counter Narratives and Arguments*, Norwood, South Australia: AATE/Wakefield Press.

Illesca, B. (2004) Teachers' work and professional identity: Living a contradiction on the margin, *English Teaching: Practice and Critique* 3(3), December, pp. 79–87.
http://www.tmc.waikato.ac.nz/english/ETPC/narrative/pdf/2004v3n3nar3.pdf

Kamler, B. (2001) *Relocating the Personal: A Critical Writing Pedagogy*, Norwood, South Australia: AATE/Wakefield Press.

Lave, J. and Wenger, E. (1991) *Situated Learning: Legitimate peripheral participation*, Cambridge: Cambridge University Press.

MacLachlan, G. and Reid, I. (1994) *Framing and Interpretation*, Melbourne: Melbourne University Press.

Mallord, C. (2003) Rollarcoasters and Rioja, in B. Doecke, D. Homer and H. Nixon (eds) *English Teachers at Work: Narratives, Counter Narratives and Arguments*, Norwood, South Australia: AATE/Wakefield.

Marsh, M. M. (2002) The Shaping of Ms. Nicholi: The Discursive Fashioning of Teacher Identities, *International Journal of Qualitative Studies in Education* 15(3), pp. 333–347.

Mills, C. W. (1959, rpt. 1978) *The Sociological Imagination*, Harmondsworth: Penguin.

Parr, G. (2004) Teachers' Professional Learning Environments: Impoverishment and Possibilities, *Idiom: Journal of the Victorian Association for the Teaching of English* 41(1).

Popkewitz, T. S. (1998) *Struggling For The Soul: The Politics of Schooling And The Construction Of The Teacher*, New York: Teachers College Press.

Renshaw, P. (1998) Sociocultural Pedagogy for New Times: Reframing Key Concepts, *Australian Educational Researcher* 25(3), December 1998, pp. 83–100.

Rogoff, B. (1994) Developing Understanding of the Idea of Communities of Learners, *Mind, Culture and Activity* 1(4), pp. 209–229.

Santoro, N. (1997) The Construction of Teacher Identity: An Analysis of School Practicum Discourse, *Asia-Pacific Journal of Teacher Education* 25(1), March, pp. 91–99.

Wild, A. (2003) What am I doing and where am I going? Conversations with beginning English teachers, *English Teaching: Practice and Critique* 2(1), May 2003, pp. 68–79. http://www.tmc.waikato.ac.nz/english/ETPC/narrative/pdf/2003v2n1nar1.pdf

Witherell, C. (1991) The Self in Narrative: A Journey into Paradox, in C. Witherell and N. Noddings (eds), *Stories Lives Tell: Narrative and Dialogue in Education*, New York: Teachers College Press, pp. 83–95.

Notes

1 There are many examples of education blogs used for such purposes. See for example:
Mike Arnzen, 'Pedablogue' http://blogs.setonhill.edu/MikeArnzen/;
John Lovas, 'A Writing Teacher's Blog' http://faculty.deanza.fhda.edu/jocalo/;
Lectrice, 'The Blackboard Jungle' http://blackboardjungle.blogspot.com/;
mshoff, 'It's probably me' http://www.unc.edu/~mshoff/blogger.html);
Hipteacher, http://hipteacher.typepad.com/.
For an explanation of wikis see: http://en.wikibooks.org/wiki/Main_Page

2 Barbara Comber is Professor of Education at the University of South Australia, and Director of the Centre for Studies in Literacy, Policy and Learning Cultures. She has researched and published widely in literacy education and social justice and has been active in the profession on an international level for many years.

3 Standards for Teachers of English Language and Literacy in Australia (STELLA). For information regarding the STELLA project, see http://www.stella.org.au or Doecke and Gill (2000).

Chapter 4

Talking Our Way to Understanding Writing

Judie Mitchell

What do teachers know about writing? And how do they (and anyone else) know they know? What exactly is teacher professional knowledge? How do teachers construct this knowledge? And what validity does it have in comparison with more traditional understandings of knowledge?

In this chapter I draw on the work of a professional learning community of teachers drawn from Erinswood[1] Secondary College's four campuses. The group comprised English and language teachers who were interested in grammar. By 'grammar' we did not mean just a traditional understanding of nouns, verbs, and so on – the kind of stuff that gets recycled in course books – but a metalanguage about language. This was largely in response to expressions of anxiety from our students about being able to handle the linguistic demands associated with Year 12 English. They knew they did not have the cultural baggage to succeed at Year 12, and they were asking us how they might get it.[2] As a group of teachers, we decided to meet regularly to share aspects of our practice, develop new teaching strategies, explore relevant literature, and engage in practitioner research that would address this issue. This lasted over a period of five years.

This chapter provides a snapshot of the ways in which the teachers talked their way into understanding their own knowledge of the teaching of writing. My position in the group was that of teaching colleague. However as the convenor of the group I was also engaged in studying the professional working of the group for my doctorate.

A view of knowledge

The conception of knowledge underpinning this chapter is that it is something constructed out of a situation of practice, when people engage in action and reflect on the matches and mismatches between their intentions or ideas and what they actually achieve. Knowledge, in this view, is constructed by teachers as they reflect on their practice; it is not something that is simply imported from the 'outside'. This is not to discount the knowledge of academic discourse or traditional research, which might likewise be conceived as the product of a certain set of cultural practices (Wells 1999). But, for too long, the voices of practitioner researchers have been marginalised in comparison with the voices of the academy and other authorities.

I present two narratives which document and describe some of the conversations and activities that the Erinswood Grammar Group (we called ourselves the EGG) teachers engaged in during the five years we met. These narratives reveal characteristics of the knowledge jointly constructed by the teachers through their participation in this professional learning community. This knowledge was always provisional, jointly constructed through their discourse, and arising out of a complex interaction between their experiences, beliefs, values, their reflection–in (and on) –action (Schon 1983), and their critical reflection on theory. The episodes convey a sense of the intellectual work accomplished by members of the EGG, as they went about devising new teaching procedures, constructing practical knowledge, making tacit understandings explicit, and establishing links between the research literature and their teaching practice. Over a period of five years we engaged in sustained inquiry into how to teach writing, with the result that we built up a substantial body of knowledge about the complexities of the writing process and the difficulties our students were experiencing.

By presenting this account of the intellectual work of the EGG, I am addressing concerns about the status of teachers' knowledge, most notably those expressed by Fenstermacher (1994). This is a concern about warrant, or the extent to which the teachers' knowledge claims can be justified as 'knowledge'. Fenstermacher (1994, p. 13) argues that three forms of inquiry closely associated with professional practice, namely reflective practice, personal practical knowledge, and narrative inquiry, fail to recognise 'the importance of truth by employing criteria that are not epistemically relevant'. He argues that truth claims must be accompanied by epistemic warrants in order to count as truth. Fenstermacher argues that knowledge can be 'inferred' from the narratives told by teachers, or from action arising in the course of a teacher's experiences (ibid.), but he rejects 'inference' as sufficient grounds for claiming that teachers 'know' in the sense of being about to make claims that have 'epistemic status'.

Fenstermacher's call for teachers to justify their knowledge claims is a reasonable one. But what criteria should be used when offering such justification? Fenstermacher eventually concedes that teachers' knowledge should not necessarily be subjected to the kind of epistemological scrutiny associated with traditional philosophy, observing that 'there are a number of ways of warranting a knowledge claim'. One of these is 'the good reasons approach' whereby 'practical reasoning makes action sensible to the actor and the observer' (p. 44).

Such reasoning may also show that an action is, for example, the reasonable thing to do, or the only thing one could do under the circumstance ... Practical reasoning may also address the moral aspects of action, indicating that it was fair, right, or the best of a number of poor alternatives. (Fenstermacher 1994, p. 45)

Practical reasoning also has the advantage of 'transforming the tacit quality of the teacher's knowing to a level of awareness that opens the possibility for reflective consideration' (p. 45).

The examples of professional conversations presented in this chapter show teachers engaging in the kind of practical reasoning which Fenstermacher describes. During the life of the EGG, I recorded all our conversations, thus maintaining an account of our research. The teachers were constantly reflecting on the extent to which their claims about their practice were justifiable (i.e. whether they actually 'knew' what they were claiming to know) and whether they were acting ethically. Teachers who engage in practitioner inquiry are not simply driven by a desire to know the 'truth' (if it is acceptable to use that word), but by a desire to meet the needs of their students. They are constantly striving to make their tacit (or 'inferred') knowledge explicit and thereby opening it up for reflection and critique.

Narrative One: Constructing new teaching procedures

This narrative draws on data collected from several meetings of the EGG. We would meet every month after school in order to share our concerns and our practice with regard to our students' language and learning. There were six regular participants: myself, Liz, Kerry, Denise, Bernie and Keith. We taught at three different campuses of the college, three of us at the senior campus and three at junior campuses. We were all volunteers who were sufficiently concerned about our students and their learning that we were prepared to devote some of our time to on-going professional conversations and the sharing of our practice.

This narrative shows how teachers in the EGG jointly constructed new teaching procedures for responding to students' writing in the course of their meetings. Liz begins with a story from her classroom.

Liz: My Year 7s had done a writing folio piece and it got to be a couple of weeks and I hadn't had a look at them and I thought to myself how can I use this to my advantage? I thought I'm going to leave it for another three weeks and not show them their writing folio pieces, their drafts. I didn't even look at them and the idea being that they would look at them with fresh eyes because they hadn't seen them for so long. I got them to read it and then they had to write four or five lines on the back and some of the things that kids wrote were really interesting. One kid wrote – this is really good I usually make a lot more mistakes, I'm really pleased. But other comments were things like – one kid said I don't even recognise this as me having written it, it sounds like somebody else. They didn't even own it – it was nothing – it was just a list of events – it was about their first week – a lot just said 'Oh the spelling's really bad', one said 'It sounds like a baby's written it – I can write much better sentences than that!' Someone said – 'Oh I needed to put a first paragraph in because it wasn't in the right order'.

Liz proceeded to elaborate how she 'pushed to them the idea that [she] wanted them to see it with fresh eyes and that they would see mistakes that they wouldn't normally see'. She asked them to look at their spelling and punctuation, 'and my instructions were: "What were you thinking about when you were reading it, what were the thoughts that came into your mind?" So it wasn't just mistakes – feelings – so it was also "Oh this is interesting or this is tedious"'. She then recounted what she said to them:

> I pushed the line to them that they don't deliberately make mistakes – if you think something's wrong you're not going to write it anyway are you? – and they all agreed, so when you go back to read your work you don't see your mistakes because you don't either know that they were there or you don't see them because you don't expect to see them. I said to them 'I'm going to show you something really quickly and I want you to read it quickly and tell me what it says'.

Liz showed us what she had shown her students – a piece of paper, on which she had written:

Once upon a
a time.

She asked us to read it out loud, and of course we all read 'Once upon a time', completely missing the fact that 'a' was repeated.

Liz told us a story about her teaching, beginning with a traditional orientation of her classroom situation, the complication she experienced, and the way in which she resolved it. This story resonated strongly with the rest of us; we had all been in a similar situation but none of us had resolved it in quite the same way. Stories are an ideal medium for sharing and communicating knowledge about teaching, as many researchers have noted (see Carter 1993, Florio-Ruane 1991). However Liz's narrative was more than simply a story about her teaching. She was engaging in theorizing about the way people write, indicating (Fenstermacher would say 'inferring') her understanding of cognitive aspects of writing, and explaining an experiment she conducted on the basis of this understanding.

Like many episodes in teaching, the idea for this procedure came about through reflection-on-action – a combination of a set of circumstances. Liz had not found the time to read their writing, she did not want to seem unprofessional or lazy, and she (found) discovered a way to turn the situation to her advantage. The rest of us agreed that this could be categorized as a new procedure for teaching writing – we called it 'Delay Return of Work'. In fact, the procedure has serious educational merit. As noted earlier, we had, as a group, been exploring literature relevant to our concerns. In my reading I discovered (and shared with the group) Zebroski, who talks about the need for a 'cooling off' period in the writing process:

> A dialogic view of writing explains why we so often need a 'cooling off' period after we have composed a piece, why it is necessary to go away from our texts for a while in order to revise them. The writer hears new voices from both the text and from the mind and needs to consider the relations between these voices. (Zebroski 1995, p. 235)

I also shared with the group a study by Emig of twelfth grade writing, in which she notes how, in school writing, the context in which students write is not conducive to revision, or rewriting:

> Lyn does not really reformulate any of the three pieces she writes. There are several features of the design and Lyn's attitudes toward the sessions that may explain, in at least two of the pieces, why she does not. ...the design does not explicitly provide for reformulation, an activity which requires quiet, if not solitude, leisure, and some separation in time from the act of writing. (Emig 1971, p. 67)

Emig regards school writing as artificial because it 'truncates the process of composing'. She goes on to contrast this process with that of 'self-sponsored' writing (meaning writing for oneself rather than for a teacher or other assessor): 'From the accounts of the twelfth grade writers in this sample one can see that in self-sponsored writing, students engage in pre-writing activities that last as long as two years' (p. 98).

Continuing with this process of constructing knowledge about the writing process, Keith took up Liz's idea and elaborated on it, suggesting that she might use the students' comments as a checklist. The checklist would include items which the students had identified as being errors or other 'mistakes' in their writing and which they could use to monitor their future writing. 'When you do the next piece of work, give them back the checklist at some stage and they can use the checklist . . .'. The conversation then continued with speculation about how both individual and whole class checklists could be generated and why these would be worthwhile:

> Liz: You mean individual checklists –

Keith: – generate a whole class checklist?

Liz: – they know that checklist of improvements has come from what they've written in those four or five lines – that might be meaningful ... for them and when you do the next lot you might think there are other things you might want to build in – well let's see if there are some others kids can pick up on some other areas that are not on the original checklist and just keep building up a bigger and better checklist.

Judie: Next step is to go through and see what changes they did make – I like Keith's idea of actually putting together a checklist from things they said – might be interesting to show all the kids comments that other kids made – not name them but ...

Liz: They are always interested in their own peers' questions and comments – fascinated – and they look for their own – oh, there's mine ...

Bernie: Even if they knew what they were looking for as an individual (it) would be a big step, wouldn't it? If at the end of the year you could sit down next to a kid, not taking their draft up, and say what are you going to do with this next? – what's the next step? If they knew enough to know that 'Oh I always forget capital letters, or I always do there, their and they're wrong – or I always use commas when I should be using full stops'.

Liz: So if each student made up their own list of things – and at the end of the year ...

Kerry: It could be automatic – if you were able to sit down next to them and they could say 'I know if I do these things' – this would be one way of measuring –

Liz: There's two parts to that – knowing that they do the wrong things, but then they also have to do be able to do something about it.

Bernie: But you can't do anything about it until you know it!

The teachers fed off one another's comments, drawing on their own experiences of working with students – 'They are always interested in each other's questions and comments' – and exploring ideas and building on them. They finish each other's sentences, continuing each other's thoughts with 'even if', 'so' and 'but'. These turns signal cohesion, a joint construction of knowledge (see Mercer 1995, p. 66) about better ways of attending to individual student needs. Liz's idea is developed into a procedure that will help students monitor their own errors. Kerry extends Liz's suggestion of student monitoring to teacher monitoring ('one way of measuring'). The idea is then taken further to include the possibility of building on the checklists so that teachers can provide ways of 'doing something about it'. In the end the teachers have teased out jointly not only the 'what' and the 'how' of the procedure, but also the 'why'—in fact the purpose of the new procedure is to encourage students to take responsibility for their own learning. The end product is a rich range of procedures which, taken together, provide a strategy for helping students to proof-read their work.

The teachers' discourse is marked by mutual respect for each other's ideas ('I like Keith's idea'), and a sense of a meeting of equals. They believe that the sum of the ideas of the group is greater than those of any one individual. The teachers make statements that are grounded in the authority of their own experience. However, these statements always attest to the provisional nature of any knowledge. Liz's comment that their own checklist 'might be meaningful' remains tentative—the idea needs to be tried out in a real classroom, tested and retested, before we can make any kind of categorical claims about it. This indicates a willingness to resist or question the kind of 'best practice' handed down from so-called expert sources.

I shared the research literature quoted above (Emig 1979 and Zebroski 1995) with the group after this meeting. As a result of reading this material, and hearing Liz's new procedure, Bernie described how she used it with her ESL students, who were horrified when she told them she would not be returning their work immediately. She needed to carefully explain her reasons to her students and she was able here to draw on the literature cited earlier. Bernie could not mechanically carry this idea over into her own classroom when working with her particular group of students, but was obliged to negotiate with them, and to devise new strategies in order to implement this idea.

Some time later, with these experiences in mind, I also drew on Emig's (1971, p. 98) findings about 'pre-writing activities that last as long as two years', and Zebroski's (1995, p. 325) notion of hearing 'new voices' from the text'. I proposed to my Year 11 students that they might like to use writing pieces they had produced in previous years as a basis for their writing folio pieces. In other words, they could bring along pieces of writing they had done in Years 9 or 10 which they felt were successful and, drawing on their more sophisticated understandings of writing (e.g. genre, aspects of language, character development), develop them into more complex texts. This came as a shock for most of them as it required rethinking the notion that this might be 'cheating'. However, I emphasized that they would find themselves extensively reworking the piece, drawing upon their enhanced writing skills, and that this work would produce differences between the original piece (seen now as a draft) and the new work. Several students took up this offer with great relief because they claimed they found thinking of new ideas difficult.

Several months later Kerry and Denise both described how they had continued with the idea of an editing sheet—which had now become a generic sheet designed by Denise and which they both found highly successful.

Judie: Tell us a bit more about those editing sheets –

Kerry: I've used them with two classes and both classes took well to the idea that rather than just having to proofread their own writing they'd be proofreading a partner's writing and the fact that they had focus questions that they had to tick and they were on a continuum – it just gave them more of a focus – I don't know if it's the way it was phrased but then that's a question that could be asked – what did you find helpful or unhelpful about these sheets? I said that I wanted it handed in with their draft and their good copy.

Denise: It does say that on the sheet –

Kerry: But I think why they had an impact was because they were seen as a whole process – not only their feedback to the writer but at the bottom of that is my final evaluation so it's all linked together, the proofreading and then the final editing that I do and the final assessment that I do.

Judie: I think that's very important . . . I'm in there in the classroom in this sea of bloody paper – oh you've got to have this sheet, you've got to attach that sheet and have you had feedback from so and so – and there's paper everywhere and the kids are going aarrgh!

(laughter of recognition)

Denise: What goes with what!

Judie: – and I'm saying stapler, stapler – and I'm thinking 'My God is this really worth it?', but I think it is, I reckon that all that – their work is only a small part of the whole thing – they're getting feedback from someone else, assessing their own work, all of those things are just as important as the piece of work. (Transcript, August 1999)

Again this discussion moves from simply describing a successful strategy to the wider purpose of the strategy and its place within the bigger picture of the teaching and learning of writing. Kerry's narrative refers to the 'whole process' and how it is all 'linked together'. My comments raise the practical difficulties of having this 'big picture' where multiple levels of reflection and feedback result in a 'sea of paper'. My remark about whether it is all worth it reveals the hard work and commitment that accompanies any genuinely effective teaching practice – it is much easier on everybody for the teacher to simply grade the writing and hand it back.

The discussion had moved from Liz's story, and the value of standing back from one's writing, to the use and value of checklists. We had developed a new procedure and shared our knowledge of the use of checklists. But the discussion did not end there:

Kerry: Can I just say also that they were so keen to be reading each other's writing – they wanted to keep on reading other people's writing – that I said they could have a reading lesson – when they had handed in their written piece they could actually take any other one that they wanted and we just had a reading lesson. I actually left them for a couple of minutes and went down to the staffroom and said to a couple of people 'Just come and have a listen to 8G', and I think they thought I meant they were off the planet – but you could have heard a pin drop. This wasn't with me saying I want silent reading – they were just so involved and the instruction that went with that was I want you to give a comment just in the plastic pocket on how you enjoyed the story. It's another audience for their writing. (Transcript, August 1999)

Kerry's final comment reveals an unexpected spin-off of the procedure. Not only were the students reflecting on their own and each other's writing, but they were gaining real pleasure from reading each other's work. Kerry here is flush with both the success of her procedure and the spin-off.

The reflection in which the EGG teachers engaged in these episodes is grounded in their own classroom situations. In their classrooms, they test the claims made by researchers about writing, comparing it with their knowledge of the ways in which students learn. They have developed this knowledge over years of experience, and they obviously see themselves as continuing with this learning. Every classroom situation is different and so they are continually revisiting, refining and redefining this knowledge in the light of new experiences.

Liz's original idea had focused on revision for grammatical errors and improving expression. Her actions were based on her knowledge that people do not deliberately make mistakes, and that when writers see their work with fresh eyes, they see mistakes that they would not initially see. Her knowledge came from personal experience – her justification is based on a kind of trick or game which proves that even seasoned writers can be deceived by seeing what they think is there rather than what is there. (This isn't the strongest justification she gives or implies, merely a teaching strategy she used to enable the kids to gain insight into the complexities of the process.) The success of the 'experiment', combined with prior experiential knowledge, enabled her to construct a case for acting the way she did. In sharing her experience with the group there were multiple outcomes. Other members trialed the same procedure and shared their experiences. We engaged in reading and discussing theory which supported our actions. We developed an extension procedure – the checklist. We explored our intentions, reasons, and justifications for using checklists which incorporated peer and self evaluation. I extended the procedure when I suggested my students rework pieces they had previously written. This required them to focus on the more complex aspects of the writing process – such as experimenting with different genres, more sophisticated language use, and character development.

Was this knowledge which the Erinswood Grammar Group constructed about the teaching of writing valid? I have already observed that it involved a complex interplay between Liz's suggested strategy for teaching writing, the prior experiences we each had of teaching writing (which framed our reactions to her account), and our critical reflections after implementing and extending this strategy. Perhaps rather than invoking the notion of 'validity', it would be more appropriate to employ Mishler's notion of 'trustworthiness' to describe the way we developed our understanding of writing by exploring the implications of this strategy. Mishler (1990, p. 419) notes that 'If our overall assessment of a study's trustworthiness is high enough for us to act on it, we are granting the findings a sufficient degree of validity to invest our own time and energy, and to put at risk our reputations as competent investigators'. Both Bernie and I acted upon Liz's idea because we trusted that it would lead to improvements in our students' learning. We were prepared to risk our reputations as competent teachers, believing that we could justify our actions to both students and parents who queried them. That we did so further attests to the trust we put in the initial idea. However, it was not simply that we accepted Liz's idea uncritically. We all took steps to implement this idea and to test it against our own experience, as well as seeking support in the existing research literature.

Narrative Two: More than propositional knowledge?

In the following discussion Kerry tells a narrative in which she makes a knowledge claim that could be distilled into a proposition. The proposition could be phrased thus:

> One reason why students write run-on sentences is due to the increased cognitive demand when writing analytical responses to a text.

Compared with the discussion below, the proposition seems dry, highly specific and technical. The following discussion is rich because it not only gives a justification for the above statement about run-on sentences, but draws out its implications for future teaching, raising fundamental questions about the nature of literacy and learning.

> Kerry: You know how we began the EGG with concerns about students at Year 11 and 12 still making basic errors? I was just observing my English classes – my Year 8 home group that I had in Year 7. There comes a point in Year 8 where I start consciously changing what I expect from them in a piece of work and that change comes about now – half way through Year 8, because I consider that now it is my role for preparing them for what's going to be expected of them in Year 9. I start introducing a different approach – say a text response. In Year 7 and 8 I might have given a decent mark to structural features given in response to a text but about half way through Year 8 I'm expecting them to develop skills of becoming more

analytical about the texts and the questions. Previously one or two sentences would have fulfilled the criteria and got a high mark – what I'm finding now is because I'm expecting more of them in terms of analysis of the text, discussion in their groups and length of answers – what am I coming across now? That I haven't encountered as much previously? Run-on sentences!

All: OOH!

Judie: You're saying writes more –

Bernie: You can just see them thinking – I've got to say more about this so it's got to go into that sentence –

Kerry: Yes – so then I'm having to reteach or prompt their recollection of what is a sentence – a sentence contains one idea, must have a noun and a verb. Of course you can have an extended sentence which has phrases and clauses in it but then when you go on to a new idea you must change sentence. I thought that was an interesting insight that I've gained over the last weeks – whereas I hadn't encountered so much now. I thought that was a pertinent point to share.

Judie: Excellent point!

Kerry: Now I'm teaching them the benefit to be gained from varying the length of their sentences – it's not as if they haven't been taught or haven't learned but because now they're having to combine it now with a different level of thought process they're now having to be retaught. How to incorporate this different level of thought process into the structural aspect of it.

Keith: Why aren't they able to retain the original sentence structure?

Kerry: I'll take copies to show you.

Judie: Good – cos some of it might be – there's a couple of reasons that Shaughnessy gives – they've had so much trouble starting – and the other one is because it's all on the same topic –

Kerry: That's where I find it pertinent that everyone has their own way of teaching the sentence.

Keith: Are they reverting back into oral language do you think?

Kerry: No, no.

Keith: Or just recording their thinking –

Judie: What happens with the ESL kids?

Bernie: We were discussing the new CSF [Curriculum and Standards Framework, a curriculum framework mandatory for Victorian schools] – one guy [another

ESL teacher] was arguing really strongly that with the secondary support documents that there should be no need to put in things about grammar cos they should all have learnt it – once they've learned surely there is no need to keep repeating it. We talked about how they do go through the stages of abandoning the structures that they've mastered when they have to – when it's necessary for them to use a more complex structure –

Judie: I'm vaguely remembering a theory I read years ago – that if the cognitive demands are too great then the human brain or mind will ditch something to accommodate the higher level of cognitive demands. They ditch the grammar stuff because they have to concentrate on getting ideas down.

Kerry's insight is achieved through reflecting on her own teaching and her students' work, combined with her reading of theory (especially Shaughnessy 1977, from whom she has the construct of a run-on sentence, an American term not used widely in Australia). She has been able to analyse her students' problems through a lens she might previously not have had. The extent to which Kerry's insight makes sense to the other teachers in a very personal way is evident in Bernie's comment: 'You can just see them thinking – I've got to say more about this so it's got to go into that sentence …'

Kerry here is very pleased with herself for having this insight. She shares it with the group and gets a unanimous round of applause – the collective 'OOH!' which on tape has the sound of pure admiration. The fact that they could get feedback and support for their ideas was an important part of the functioning of the group and one of the reasons why the teachers kept coming.

Positive feedback is rare in teaching, as evidenced in current trends in staffrooms to have 'thankyou days' and weeks where teachers give each other 'random acts of kindness'. However, feedback in these situations is often for personal or administrative achievements, hardly ever for good teaching. Like many of the students they teach, teachers themselves are rarely accorded intellectual respect in their daily lives.

Kerry's insight is theoretically sound. She and the other teachers 'know' that literacy is not a skill which can be mastered once and for all – knowledge which conflicts with the understanding of literacy that is currently being promoted by governments and the media. Bernie notes how a colleague (the ESL teacher) makes this competing claim and how she is able to argue that this claim is not supported by her experience or by Kerry's example.

In his search for a definition of knowledge Fenstermacher (1995, p. 24) states that 'it is sufficient for our purposes (and in accord with a fair body of epistemological thought) to state that a proposition is known by its holder if the holder believes the proposition and has evidence to establish its reasonableness in relation to other, competing claims'. He also labels this 'objectively reasonable belief'. Kerry's insight into the complexity of learning literacy skills, and the evidence she gives, as well as the way her observations resonate with the rest of the group, gives her knowledge the status of 'objectively reasonable belief'. She has 'proved' that she is now justified in reteaching basic sentence structure.

Conclusion

Teachers do need to be accountable for their professional knowledge and practice. They should be able to justify what they know, and to put this knowledge into practice in their teaching. Fenstermacher (1994, p. 36) makes the point that 'Performance knowledge, particularly when it falls within the domain of expert, specialist or professional practice, must meet evidentiary standards if it is to have epistemic merit'. As teachers, we acknowledge his notion of 'practical reasoning' as being 'a contribution to the epistemic merit of a practical knowledge claim' (p. 45). The teachers in the EGG demonstrated their capacity to make knowledge claims which were backed up by practical reasoning.

So, to return to the questions with which I commenced this discussion, how did the teachers of the Erinswood Grammar Group know what they knew? And how did they know they knew what they knew? The answers lie in the discourse in which they participated by joining the EGG, their continuing conversations when they each drew from their individual experiences and their reading to construct a professional knowledge about the complexities of language and learning. The teachers used practical reasoning to establish what they knew, and the fact that they were willing to share what they knew, and to test out theories, indicates that they knew they knew. They also knew, however, that their knowledge was always provisional. In other words, it is always subject to revision, a set of frames for interpreting experience which can always be refined or replaced. Teachers know there is always more to see than we actually see, and more to understand than we actually understand.

In listening to these teachers' voices, it is difficult to accept the view that the only worthwhile knowledge in teaching must be 'scientifically' researched, at a remove from the complexities that teachers experience in their professional lives. This is not to argue that academic research and the knowledge it produces is always irrelevant to teaching. In fact, as this chapter indicates, the teachers in the EGG found important insights in some of the literature and these insights informed their work. However, as these narratives indicate, teachers also develop and construct knowledge as they engage in their work, and it seems important to assert the need to establish more dialogue across these discourse communities.

References

Carter, K. (1993) The Place of Story in the Study of Teaching and Teacher Education, *Educational Researcher* 22(1), pp. 5–12

Doyle, W. (1997) Heard any good stories lately? A critique of the critics of narrative in educational research, *Teaching and Teacher Education* 15(1), pp. 93–99

Emig, J. (1971) *The Composing Processes of Twelfth Graders*, Urbana Illinois: NCTE.

Fenstermacher, G. (1986) Philosophy of Research on Teaching: Three Aspects, in M.C. Wittrock (ed.), *Handbook of Research on Teaching* (3rd ed), New York: Macmillan.

Fenstermacher, G. (1994) The knower and the known: The nature of knowledge in research on teaching, L. Darling-Hammond (ed.), *Review of Research in Education* 20, Washington, DC: American Educational Research Association.

Georgakopoulou, A. and Goutsos, D. (1997) *Discourse Analysis: an Introduction*, Edinburgh: Edinburgh University Press.

Mercer, N. (1995) *The Guided Construction of Knowledge*, Clevedon: Multilingual Matters.

Mishler, E.G (1990) Validation in Inquiry-Guided Research; The Role of Exemplars in Narrative Studies, *Harvard Education Review* 60(4), pp. 415–443

Schon, D. (1987) *The Reflective Practitioner*, California, USA: Jossey-Bass Inc.

Shaughnessy, M.P. (1977) *Errors and Expectations – A Guide for the Teacher of Basic Writing*, New York: Oxford University Press

Wells, G. (1999) *Dialogic Inquiry: Towards a Sociocultural Practice and Theory of Education*, Cambridge: Cambridge University Press.

Zebroski, J. (1995) *Thinking Through Theory: Vygotskian Perspectives on the Teaching of Writing*, Portsmouth, NH: Boynton Cook, Heinemann.

Notes

1 Erinswood, like the names of the teachers in the study below, is a pseudonym.

2 For more information about the original impetus of the study, see Mitchell, J.A. (1999) Responding to Student Writing: A PEEL Perspective, in B. Doecke (ed.), *Responding to Students' Writing*, Norwood: AATE.

Counterpoint

The term 'counterpoint' . . . is used to describe music in which the
chief interest lies in the various strands that make up the texture,
and particularly in the combination of these strands and their
relationship to each other and the texture as a whole.

(*Grove's Dictionary of Music and Musicians*, 5th edn, vol. 2)

Chapter 5

Writing Positions and Rhetorical Spaces

Terry Locke

Introduction

My starting point for this chapter is a short article by Kevin Murray entitled 'Responding to students' writing: A do-it-yourself in-service kit' first published in 1984 and republished in 1996 and 1999, and again here (see chapter 6 – the page references below are to pages in this volume). You might say that I am engaging in a conversation across two decades with a man whom I have never met but whom I have come to admire. This act of writing of mine is, of course, historically situated. I describe myself as occupying a rhetorical space, because I am deferring to the position Murray himself occupied, as an initiator of this conversation and as a special member of my imagined audience. I am also keenly aware that this audience includes pre-service and beginning teachers, that group my editors, Brenton and Graham, have described to me as my intended audience. However, as I will be indicating later in this chapter, the rhetorical space I am occupying as a writer also includes other participants; and they too have a part to play in response to my gesture of addressing them.

Murray's concern in his article is with those factors beyond surface (i.e. spelling, punctuation, syntax) errors that make a piece of writing good or bad. His basic question of a piece of writing is: 'Does it work?' As a focus, he provides two 'stories' written by two boys from the same Year 8 class, who had been asked to write on the topic 'An Exciting Day'. At the start, Murray draws a distinction between 'intuitive' and 'objective' marking, noting the reputation English teachers have for reliability in the former. However, he points out, such marking does not help address questions from students which ask teachers to identify what they did wrong and what they need to do to improve. To answer such questions, marking needs to be put on some kind of 'objective' footing (96).

He offers two approaches:

- A theory of narrative which views story-telling as a vital human function which generates significance out of the 'daily flood of events'. In this view, 'the test of a quality narrative lies not so much in the bare events alone but in the evaluation or significance imposed on the events by the writer'.
- A discourse analytical approach 'which examines the ways we use language to string sentences together to make a coherent and understandable whole'. Such an approach goes beyond a narrow concern with syntax, to examine '...meaning and how a writer sustains his thought across extended pieces of spoken or written text (semantics)' (98).

Both approaches are applied to the stories of Gavin and Harry. In respect of the theory of narrative, Gavin's story fails miserably on the grounds that it records events without bestowing significance. Using the second, linguistically based approach, Murray chooses to examine Gavin's story for an identifiable structure and for two aspects of cohesion[1] ('reference' and 'conjunction'). In relation to linguistic theories of 'schematic structure', Murray asserts that 'autobiographical narrative' (as with such forms as the essay, sonnet or Western movie) has a characteristic pattern or structure:

- 'The scene is set in time and place.
- 'A chronological sequence of events is presented.
- 'The critical event emerges and is focused.
- 'The critical event and its aftermath is evaluated or commented on' (99).

It is worth noting, I think, that the theory is prompting Murray to apply a more specific description ('autobiographical narrative') to the boys' writing – signalling a break with the practices of his time which would have labeled the stories as simply 'school' writing.

Anyway, in terms of these criteria, Gavin's story is also unsuccessful, since it does not display the characteristic features of a successful 'autobiographical narrative'. It fails to focus on and evaluate a 'critical event'. In terms of 'reference', Gavin's story *does* get a pass. In terms of 'conjunction', the implication from Murray is that Gavin's story is lacking in its sophisticated use, and such a lack can be connected with a lack in rich complexity.

How might a teacher usefully give feedback to Gavin? Murray's two approaches lead to differing strategies. The first would suggest that Gavin needs to be told 'gently but firmly that this is a flawed story'. Murray goes on to affirm that part of the problem is that information which might trigger the act of sense-making (that is, the imposition of significance on events) is still in Gavin's head; there is a gap between his 'intentions' and 'their realization' in text. This is not, I think, suggesting that the problem lies with Gavin alone, though it is being diagnosed in cognitive terms. Rather, a crucial kind of dialogue with a 'genuine respondent' has not occurred.

'Until he verbalizes this [presumably, the experience as mental event] explicitly the experience will not be truly available to him at all.' The second strategy, a kind of linguistically based, direct remediation via workshopping, might use (as an example) cloze tests to address Gavin's problems with cohesion (100).

In contrast, Harry's story is deemed to be successful. In Murray's judgement, he has passed the test of signification; he has 'selected a single incident from a crowded world' and rendered it meaningful in terms of a tone of 'bravado, excitement and jaunty defeat'. From a linguistic standpoint, Harry is seen as in command of narrative structure and as having few problems with cohesion.

Murray concludes his article by asking a question about the informality of Harry's style and its appropriateness. Citing Hallidayan linguistics, he suggests that such a question needs to be related to three variables: a) subject matter; b) audience; and c) genre (the first mention of this term in the article). In terms of these variables, as manifested in Harry's story (which Murray now describes as an example of a 'simple anecdote'), he has passed the test of appropriateness.

Let's recall that Murray wrote this article in 1984. I like what he wrote for a number of reasons. Firstly, his article takes seriously the need to develop 'objective' criteria for assessing writing. In this respect, Murray is part of the move towards criterion-referenced assessment which took place in a number of educational settings in the 1980s and which enabled teachers to be more sharply focused in response to such questions as: 'What do I need to do to get an "A", Miss?'

Secondly, it moves beyond a concern with surface features to broader questions about writing such as: What is the relationship between writing and meaning-making? We see this concern at work in the sentence previously quoted: 'Until he verbalizes this explicitly the experience will not be truly available to him at all' (100). The suggestion here is that 'languaging' experience is, in itself, the means of constructing meaning and communicating it.

Thirdly, there is a focus on writing at text level, with an emphasis on features such as structure and cohesion that go beyond the level of word and sentence. Moreover, there is a preparedness to be explicit in the use of a grammatical metalanguage, which differs from that traditionally used in the formal teaching of 'grammar'. Though the term is used only once, there is a gesture in the direction of a concept of 'genre' in ref-erences to the predictable patterning of particular text-types.

As a means of establishing the basis for a respectful critique of Murray's article and to identify some gaps in his text, I would like to move to the broad question:

What happens in the act of writing?

Let me start by stating that literacy is a cognitive, social and technologically mediated practice, utilizing agreed systems of signification, to communicate messages about experience. As a definition, this one is broad enough to paper over a fair number of fishhooks. In contrast with the time Murray wrote his article, our period in history favours a view of literacy as multiple. The prevailing view would say that what it means to be 'literate' is socially (or *discursively*) constructed (see, for example, Cope & Kalantzis 2000, Gee 1996, Lemke 1998, Roberts 1997).

Referring to literacy as 'discursively constructed', let me define a discourse as a coherent way of making sense of the world (or some aspect of it) as reflected in human sign systems (including verbal language) (Locke 2004a). One approach to a view of literacy as discursively constructed is to identify the elements that have a (potential) role to play in constructing it. While recognising the non-exclusive nature of the following elements, I posit them as a list offering a handy kind of heuristic for this approach to literacy and specifically the teaching of writing:

- writer
- reader (or audience)
- text
- meaning-making mind
- meaning
- language (and other sign systems)
- technological mediation
- and social context.

I suggest that *how* we view these elements and the relationships between them has a central role in the discursive construction of literacy, and therefore the act of writing – the focus of this book. As I have argued elsewhere (Locke 2003a), the ways in which these elements are constructed and configured result in different ways of conceptualising practices around texts (reading, writing and disseminating) and can be related to differing 'versions' or 'models' of subject English itself. These versions can be distinguished according to varying emphases such as:

- *Cultural heritage:* There is a traditional body of knowledge (including a canon of precious texts and grammatical knowledge) which is to be valued and inculcated as a means of 'rounding out' learners so that they become fully participating and discriminating members of a society or culture that is often promoted at the expense of groups, communities or discourses that would threaten its homogeneity or sense of superiority.
- *Personal growth:* This is sometimes called the New English (Green 1997) or 'progressive' English (Cope & Kalantzis 1993). It is valuable to engage in literary and language-centred enterprises because this facilitates the personal, individual growth of learners, for whom the acquisition of certain linguistic competencies will play a central role in their ongoing capacity to make sense of their world.

- *Textual and sub-textual skills:* At its worst, this promotes a decontextualised knowledge about language and the acquisition of grammatical skills based on narrow and formulaic definitions of correctness. On the other hand, such an emphasis can also mean valuing the mastery of the forms and conventions of a range of genres deemed to be socially significant – an approach which is related to but significantly different from the linguistic table manners promoted by traditional grammar.
- *Critical practice:* Often called 'critical literacy', this emphasis puts a value on encouraging language-users to see themselves as engaged in textual acts which are part of a wider set of discursive practices that actively produce and sustain patterns of dominance and subordination in the wider society and offer members of society prescribed subject positions (or ways of self-identifying) (Locke 2000).

Each of these emphases, I would argue, offers teachers of writing a particular position or stance in respect of what writing is about. These positions (schematised, perhaps simplistically, in Table 1), as they are taken up by teachers, can be expected to impact upon both understandings of what writing is or should be, and pedagogical practice (including formative and summative assessment).

Cultural heritage	Personal growth
Writer orientation: • Appreciation and emulation • Deference • Acculturation	Writer orientation: • Self-realisation through meaning-making • Creative exploration • Personal integration
Skills acquisition	Critical literacy
Writer orientation: • Formal mastery of textual practices • Pragmatic competence • Social adeptness	Writer orientation: • Critical linguistic analysis • Detachment • Social transformation

Table 1: Versions of English and writer orientation

In what follows, I elaborate, in respect of each of these orientations, a view of what happens in the act of writing.

In their classic 'New Critical' text, *Understanding Poetry*, Brooks and Warren (1976) assert that 'literature is the most sophisticated example of the process by which we come to grasp our own environment, especially our human environment, with its complex and ambiguous values …' Such a statement, in harmony as it is with a cultural heritage view of English, explains why for years writing was the poor cousin of reading (especially literary reading) in the English classroom. In a cultural heritage model, literature was the product of the best human minds (usually male) putting the best words in the best order. How could merely mortal school pupils ever hope to emulate the feats of the great writers! (Murray distances himself from cultural heritage discourse, by treating his students seriously as writers of a literary genre – 'story' or 'autobiographical narrative' – and positioning himself as a 'genuine reader' of their work (100).

The Brooks and Warren statement also explains why certain kinds of non-fiction, 'real world' texts such as editorials, newspaper columns, feature articles, reports, submissions, and media texts, have had to wait patiently for admission to the English classroom. Somehow these genres were non-canonical, second-rate and therefore unworthy of emulation. Meaning-making, in the grandest sense, was performed by the individual, creative genius on a literary stage. Language was the raw material for this act of meaning-making, and something to be wrestled with and shaped. Meaning, with a capital 'M', was something to be enshrined in the text to be elicited by the humble reader trained in the art of explication. Technology did not come into it. A text was a text was a text, whether produced by quill, ball-point or typewriter. If poetry was best words in the best order, as Coleridge claimed, then grammar was the key to the Order itself, and parsing was a rite signalling admittance to the inner sanctum of syntax.

The discourses that underpin the progressive English classroom are not a radical departure from those underpinning the cultural heritage model of English. In a telling phrase in *Growth through English*, John Dixon (1975) refers to 'the acceptance of pupils' work as embryonic literature' (p. 55). Literature has not been knocked off its pedestal. Rather the category has been enlarged to encompass the propensity of all human beings to create meaning through language in their engagement with experience. The meaning-making mind is still an individual one; creative genius has simply become democratized.

Murray's article is in large part underpinned by progressive or 'personal growth' discourse. His pupil Gavin's problem is not a lack of creativity. He has 'real messages' to send and part of the teacher's job is to 'trigger' his awareness of this. The problem with Gavin is that much of his story is still in his head, beyond his awareness, and requires a particular kind of dialogic engagement if it is to be externalized and made meaningful. 'Until he verbalizes this explicitly the experience will not be truly avail-able to him at all.' Nor will his 'intentions' be realised (100). What is this 'experience'? Well, it's clearly not the original experience. Rather, it is the experience as recreated in Gavin's mind and imbued with sense. It is *this* experience that progressive English teachers aim to have students put on paper. It is through such acts of sense-making that self-realisation or personal growth occurs.

One can see why such a construction of writing might be described as a process, as in the expression 'process writing', and why Donald Graves' approach, with its emphasis on 'conferencing' dovetailed with the discourses of personal growth. Teachers of writing, in terms of this discourse, are constructed as sympathetic listeners and facilitators. As with the cultural heritage model, language is a means whereby inner meanings are communicated – a medium providing a clear window to the world and the possibility of shared meanings between human beings.

The 1966 Anglo-American Dartmouth Seminar was perhaps the first and last time English teachers reached a consensus on the nature of their subject – and, with a few problems glossed over, it was a progressive consensus. Reporting on the conference, the American, Herbert Muller (1967), observed that there was general agreement with the view that grammatical knowledge did little to improve speaking and writing and that '. . . the teaching of grammar has been chiefly a waste of time' (p. 68). However, the seminar was split on the question as to whether knowledge about language should be taught explicitly and if so at what stage. Linguists, on the back foot, found it hard to argue for the utility of linguistic knowledge but wanted to defend it as a humanistic study. Almost overnight, the teaching of grammar disappeared from many English classrooms. After all, if language was an instinct (Pinker 1995), and human beings were born with an encoded blueprint that allowed for the generation of an infinitude of correct sentences according to need, as the transformational grammarians insisted, then 'grammar' could be considered caught and not needing to be taught.

I have suggested that Murray's first approach to writing, namely his account of narrative theory, is underpinned by a progressive discourse, where stories are seen as 'small generalizations about Life' (98) – a phrase that unconsciously resonates with Robert Frost's famous definition of a poem as a 'momentary stay against confusion'. But there is another discourse at work in Murray's approach to writing. We find it in his second approach, which Murray sees as derived from the work of such linguists as Labov and Halliday. In the argument I am developing here, this view of writing can be related to a model of English which emphasizes the acquisition of textual and sub-textual skills.

In terms of this model, the classroom writing focus switches to the achievement of a range of textual competencies, at word, sentence, paragraph and whole text level – and sometimes beyond. At its worst, this model offers a field day for skills acquisition advocates, for framers and fixers of discrete and often decontextualised learning outcomes which are non-problematically describable and measurable. At its best, this model recognizes the socially constructed demands for 'literacy' of a particular sort in a range of contexts. In one expression of the model, the Australian-based genre theorists turned their attention to the context of the school and declared that the pathway to empowerment lay in the mastery of six 'genres': report, explanation, procedure, discussion, recount and narrative (Cope & Kalantzis 1993, p. 9). In another expression of this approach, proponents of the 'new' rhetoric looked to the wider social stage and associated writing mastery with the ability to utilise knowingly and cunningly the language necessary to achieve a desired effect in a particular social context on a particular audience. The old triangle of text maker, audience and purpose – what Richard Andrews has termed the 'classic communication triangle' (Andrews 1992, p. 2) – was back. Arguments about genre were central to this model. But I think proponents of it would agree with Cope and Kalantzis (1993) that any definition of genre entails a recognition that textual form varies according to social purpose. 'Texts are different because they do different things. So, any literacy pedagogy has to be concerned, not just with the formalities of how texts work, but also with the living social reality of texts-in-use. How a text works is a function of what it is for' (p. 7).

In keeping with his partial allegiance to this skills discourse of writing, Murray focuses on features of the text at sentence and whole-text levels – on grammar and discourse. 'We use language,' he says, 'to make a coherent and understandable whole' (98). The writer here, signaled by the first-person, plural 'we', is a universal but individual, every-writer with a message to communicate via the (assumed) transparent vehicle of language. The object of 'make' is a noun phrase which is highly nominalised – to draw a term from Hallidayan grammar. Tellingly, I think, the adjective 'understandable' not only compresses, but suppresses the sense that the writer's text is understandable by *someone* – an audience. Murray himself, however, has not ignored the need to recognize an audience for writing. The writing task for Gavin and Harry had both a topic and a designed audience – the boys' peer group. 'The stories were to be bound in a class book' (96). Without wishing to be unkind, I suspect the task involved the boys in writing a kind of quasi-real world genre, which has a life only within the walls of the classroom and not beyond it, and where the audience in fact is restricted to the classroom teacher. Such an approach to genre or, indeed, school writing in general, is hardly uncommon in English classrooms!

In terms of the skills discourse, meaning is relatively unproblematic so long as a writer has mastery of a range of skills at sentence and text level. Murray, while admitting that linguistic terms can be complex, makes use of the concepts of 'schematic structure' and 'cohesion' (in particular, 'reference' and 'conjunction') as a basis for both analysis and diagnosis as he addresses himself to what is wrong (and right) in the boys' stories. What has also appeared here is a rationale for the overt use of grammar, or more broadly, knowledge about language, in the classroom. In the American context, Martha Kolln and others have followed this rationale, arguing for a rhetorical grammar, used for a different purpose '... from the remedial, error-avoidance or error-correction purpose of so many grammar lessons. I use rhetorical as a modifier to identify grammar in the service of rhetoric: grammar knowledge as a tool that enables the writer to make effective choices' (Kolln 1996, p. 29). In the Australian context, Murray's statement that an 'autobiographical narrative falls into a characteristic pattern or structure' (99) anticipates the view of Jim Martin and others of a genre as 'a staged, goal-oriented social process' (Eggins & Martin 1997, p. 243)–a view which was highly influential in the Genre School's challenge to the progressive model during the early 1990s, especially in Australia. Even those who within the Genre School questioned certain aspects of the approach (for example, its emphasis on product rather than process, its rigid formulation of schemata, its tendency to slip into a transmission model of education), strongly advocated the place of grammar in the classroom.

> We believe it is absolutely essential that teaching grammar must be a fundamental part of an effective genre-based approach to reading and writing. Without grammar, we will not be able to deal with the language issues which are so much a part of the concrete-abstract knowledge continuum. Grammar also enables us to break out of the reductiveness of the genre as end-product problem. Finally, it gives both teachers and students a way of talking about and dealing with language as an object that can be manipulated and changed to do particular things both in communication and expressing and organising knowledge. (Callaghan, Knapp & Noble 1993, pp. 201–202)

Traditional, decontextualised grammar teaching separates form from function. At their best, 'Genre' and other skills-based approaches to writing view the formal qualities of a text, at whatever level, as related to textual function, and understanding of and mastery of textual function as central to a wider sort of pragmatic, social competence. This competence, I will argue in the next section, is an important quality of the writer as user and innovator of language situated in a rhetorical space.

Singularly absent from Murray's approach to writing is a model of English that emphasises critical practice, where 'critical' is consonant with approaches to reading and writing such as *critical literacy* (for example, Lankshear 1995, Morgan 1997) and *Critical Language Awareness* (for example, Fairclough 1992, Janks 1994). If the Genre School put the focus back on the production of texts, it is arguable that critical literacy put the focus back on reading and away from writing. The reader who took centre-stage was a somewhat different sort of reader from the relatively stable entity of the other three models I have described. This reader was to be viewed as a cultural product, 'inscribed' by a range of discourses (not necessarily compatible with one another) and positioned by his/her discursive frames to respond in one way or another to the 'preferred' position offered by a text. The text was also destabilised. It was no longer a container of meaning (as per the New Criticism), nor a constrainer of meaning (as per the progressive model), but rather a space within which a play of meaning might be enacted by the deconstructive, 'writerly' reader. Meaning became a function of discourse (always with a capital 'D'), and individual texts lost their discreteness and became meaningful only in an infinitely complex network of intertextual relationships between utterances (Bakhtin 1986). The cultural context had become pre-eminent. So, increasingly, had technological mediation. The notion that 'literacy is a social practice' became a slogan, and then a mantra. And with the increased presence of ICTs as mediating textual practices, a growing emphasis was put on literacy, in all its forms, as technologised.

Key concepts in a critical writing pedagogy are 'ideology' and 'hegemony' – both contested terms. For my own part, I define an ideology as an elaborate story told about the ideal conduct of some aspect of human affairs. As I see it, its power lies in its 'truth' value, which is determined by the size and nature of its subscription base as much as by some notion of 'explanatory force'. In short, the truth of an ideology is determined by the number of people subscribing to it. The related term, 'hegemony', can consequently be defined as the state of affairs which exists when the subscription base of an ideology is broad in terms of numbers and reinforced 'vertically' by the social status of its subscribers (Locke 2004a). Or to put it more stridently, 'Hegemony is secured when the virulence of oppression, in its many guises (e.g. race, gender, class, sexual orientation) is accepted as consensus' (Kincheloe & McLaren 1994, p. 141).

Let's recall that Kevin Murray asked Gavin and Harry to write a story. Harry's story was warmly endorsed by Murray. What young boy would not be flattered by the comment: 'I have already added it to my stock of street-smart-kids-versus-the-Establishment stories'? If I might play critical discourse analyst here, it appears that Murray is telling us that in one sense Harry did not make up his story at all. In using the collective noun 'stock', he is suggesting that there are many versions of this story and that (in a way not specified), Harry has added to it. What an emphasis on critical practice does is draw attention to the writer, not as an individual agent who creates stories (original genius belongs with the cultural heritage model) but as a medium through whom a particular story is told. This particular 'story' (or discourse), I might suggest safely (speaking as a law-abiding, non-Australian), resonates with a construction of authority as something at which one can quite justifiably thumb one's nose. In terms of this discourse, a certain kind of outlawry is admirable. Putting it another way, there is a particular Australian discourse that positions readers to admire both Ned Kelly (in one of his versions) and street-smart Harry.

One aspect of the job of the writing teacher in the critical literacy classroom is to draw young writers' attention to the social consequences of privileging in their own writing particular discourses or 'stories', in the sense that I have used that word in the last paragraph. Just as the critically literate reader is also a writer, so the critically literate writer is also a self-reflexive reader of the position(s) he/she is offering a prospective reader to take up. A second aspect of the job is to ensure that writers are aware that the language they use *is not* a transparent medium of communication, but rather an opaque instrument that inevitably constructs its 'object' in a particular way. What Allan Luke says about the relationship between reading and metalanguage (or grammar) for critical readers, applies equally to critical writers.

By 'critical competence' then, I refer to the development of a critical metalanguage for talking about how texts code cultural ideologies, and how they position readers in subtle and often quite exploitative ways. My argument is that in order to contest or rewrite a cultural text, one has to be able to recognise and talk about the various textual, literary and linguistic, devices at work. (Luke 1992, p. 10)

So, 'grammar' retains its place in the critical literacy classroom, but with a different kind of justification, not so much to support pragmatic writing competence as to serve the purpose of linguistic analysis in the service of a critical awareness of the job all texts do in positioning readers to see the world in particular ways.

What makes a piece of writing work?

In the preceding section, I have given thumbnail sketches of four versions of English and, by extension, the writing classroom. My purpose in doing so has been to emphasise that writing is *not* the same thing in all approaches to the teaching of English/literacy. In this final section, I want to do two things. I want to argue for an informed and critically eclectic approach to writing, which does not confuse the models I have just described, but rather looks at ways in which they might lend different emphases at different times to the teaching of writing in the English classroom. Secondly, I want to share a marking rubric, developed in the New Zealand context, which I will use to revisit the question first raised by Murray twenty years ago: does a piece of writing 'work'?

In advocating an eclectic approach, I want to recognize that classroom practice seldom reflects a 'pure' model of the subject, grounded in only one of the versions of the subject discussed in the previous section. A range of factors contribute to the formation of an English teacher's professional knowledge and classroom practice. These include the critical orientation of their various degree courses, emphases in their initial teacher education, their history of professional development, the theoretical underpinnings of official curricula and assessment documentation that constrain them, the modelling of other teachers, the pedagogies embedded in textbook and other resources and last, but not least, their worldly understandings and abilities as related to the production, consumption and dissemination of texts developed in the wider social context (Locke 2004b).

I argue that our goal as English/literacy teachers of writing can be embodied in the figure of the *critical user and innovator of language in a rhetorical space*. In aiming to 'produce' such a person, I believe we can draw on all of the versions of writing discussed previously.

However, my preferred starting point is the notion of pragmatic competence, which I have previously related to an emphasis on skills acquisition. This competence would not be narrowly defined (in terms of, say, the mastery of a narrow range of decontexualised skills) but be broadly based in the ability of the writer to see herself as occupying a rhetorical space imbued with social purposes and expectations. In other words, pragmatic competence is social before it is textual.

The notion of a 'rhetorical space' involves a number of important recognitions. The first of these is that a speaker is always, as Bakhtin noted, a respondent:

> He is not, after all, the first speaker, the one who disturbs the eternal silence of the universe. And he presupposes not only the existence of the language system he is using, but also the existence of preceding utterances – his own and others' – with which his given utterance enters into one kind of relation or another (builds on them, polemicizes with them, or simply presumes that they are already known to the listener). Any utterance is a link in a very complexly organized chain of other utterances. (Bakhtin 1986, p. 69)

As Bakhtin further noted, the notion of being respondent not only involves a relationship to 'preceding utterances'; it also includes a relationship to those to whom one's utterance (written or spoken) is potentially addressed. We have moved here beyond the literal space of the Greek forum, to think of the rhetorical space as metaphorical – as having a temporal or historical dimension. This first recognition might be thought of as *about* audience, even though members of this audience may no longer be living. The second recognition, again using a spatial metaphor, recognises the discursive positions available historically in relation to the topic at hand. In writing about writing, I am aware of myself in relation to *other* positions that are available on this topic. In writing this chapter, I can think of myself in dialogue both with other writers (past and future, including the other contributors to this book) and with the positions they adopt.

This rhetorical framing of the writing act, as I have discussed elsewhere (Locke 2004a), has a number of assumptions:

- People construct texts to achieve a desired result with a particular audience
- Textual form follows function
- Texts are generated by contexts
- Texts assume a social complicity between maker and reader
- The expectations of participants in such acts of complicity become formalised in the conventions of genre
- These conventions relate to such language features (at least in print texts) as layout, structure, punctuation, syntax and diction. Knowledge about language (or grammatical knowledge) is justified as it supports the attainment of competence in relevant language features.

Within this framework, literature is not such much devalued (though it has been arguably 'decentred') as revalued. That is, the makers of 'literary' texts are seen, along with other text producers, as rhetorically positioning themselves and their audiences.

Furthermore, the 'literary' canon can be dusted off and refurbished, seen as a dynamic, constructed entity but no less valuable for all that. Indeed, within this framework, the canon and its associated idea of cultural heritage are viewed as having a historically situated function. The critically rhetorical user and innovator of language has no issue with the idea of culturally endorsed models worthy of emulation. He/she simply recognizes that the grounds for such admiration are contestable.

How does the concept of 'genre' relate to the approach I am arguing for? Certainly, a number of commentators have taken issue with aspects of the approach to genre advocated by what I have been calling the Australian Genre School (e.g. Richardson 1994, Sawyer 1995, Dixon & Stratta 1995). The last named, for instance, took the Genre School to task for the way it identified and numbered genres, the notion of a 'staged' structure, its tendency towards normativity and transmission teaching and for its disjunction from 'real world' writing practices. Drawing on Freedman and Medway's (1994) more dynamic view of genres as typical rhetorical engagements within recurring situations, I define a genre as the formalisation of maker-reader complicities as reflected in a range of relatively stable textual features. Certainly, I don't view this relative stability as particularly related to a 'staged' structure. Rather the approach to structure advocated here views it as composed of genre-specific elements, some mandatory and some optional, that can be sequenced or organized in an enormous variety of ways. The approach I am advocating would therefore question Murray's claim for a four-stage, 'characteristic pattern' for autobiographical narrative (99). Rather it would view narratives as characterized by such elements as orientation, predicament, complication, resolution, turning point, climax, dénouement and so on, which have the potential for a multitude of structural arrangements.

In what sense is the critical user and innovator of language in a rhetorical space 'critical'? To answer this, and to connect this eclectic approach to critical literacy, I focus on the second bullet-point above – textual form follows function. A simple definition of the term 'function' is the work that the language in a text does at any particular point. However, the notion of 'function', developed initially by Halliday (see, for example, Halliday & Hasan 1985) and taken up by Fairclough (1992) and other critical discourse analysts, was connected with a view that this language 'work' was constitutive, that is, it constructed its object in discourse. The critically rhetorical writer is self-reflexively aware that the language he or she is using in the production of a text positions an audience to view the world in a particular way. Language knowledge, then, will go beyond the understandings and skills required to establish 'competence'. It will extend to an understanding of how the specifics of language usage function in a constitutive way (in line with the statement from Allan Luke above) and an *attitude towards* that understanding. (In an age of spin doctors, it is a forlorn hope that an awareness of the constitutive power of language necessarily goes hand in hand with a socially transformative agenda of an altruistic sort.)

How does all that I have been arguing relate to an emphasis on personal growth? Well, one thing you might say about this version of English is that it's remarkably thick-skinned when asked to leave the stage. The Genre School did not manage to dislodge it. Nor did poststructuralism, viewed by some as the philosophical handmaiden of critical literacy in the classroom. Progressive (or 'personal growth') notions like 'self-realisation' sound rather quaint when stacked up against a statement like the following from Ray Misson:

> Rather than conceiving us as putting these different ways of talking on as a covering to a stable essential self, rather like putting on clothes to dress ourselves appropriately for particular situations, poststructuralism radically argues that there is no self apart from these ways of talking. The discourses we partake in are what constitute the self. Therefore the self is a social construct (the constructivist position), rather than being a given essence of a person (the essentialist belief). (Misson 1998, p. 148)

I'm happy to accept that my idea of the critical user and innovator of language in a rhetorical space is a construction. However, my use of the word 'innovator' is a deliberate attempt to assert the legitimacy of terms like 'agency' and 'creativity' and 'imagination' – terms beloved of the personal growth emphasis in English. Like Bakhtin (1986), I see a place for 'individual style' (p. 63) and 'expressive intonation' (p. 85) in the shaping of utterances. Like Damasio (2000), in his attempt at explaining human consciousness, I want to retain the notion of the autobiographical self. I think I'm doing more than splitting hairs in suggesting that the 'self' is one and that 'subjectivity' is multiple.

The critical user and innovator of language in a rhetorical space is a kind of supreme fiction . . . an impossible ideal perhaps. What might a set of criteria look like, against which to assess the stories of Gavin and Harry? The sets of criteria in Tables 2 and 3 are rubrics for a senior secondary qualification in English developed in New Zealand but in part modeled on the Victorian Certificate of Education (VCE) English Study Design as developed in 1989 (see Locke 2003b). Words in bold in the level indicators are instances of subject metalanguage. The left-hand column is a set of generic criteria that apply to any piece of writing. The right-hand column is an attempt to translate these generic criteria into genre-specific level indicators. In practice, rubrics like these are made available to students at the beginning of a unit of work or writing task. I should point out that I am not suggesting that the use of these rubrics replace the kind of formative assessment practice advocated and modeled by Murray in his article. Rather I am offering the rubrics as an example of an approach to assessment that to some extent dovetails with the eclectic approach I have been advocating. It also embodies a way of 'objectifying' criteria of judgment. (At this point, you might like to assess Gavin and Harry's pieces of writing yourself, using the rubrics.)

	Generic schedule	Level indicators
E E+ [1–2]	Incorporates straightforward messages in the production of a text. Has a limited sense of the text's intended audience and purpose. Some evidence of a developing viewpoint.	• **Story** revolves around one or two simple **events** • Little sense of **theme** or **character** differentiation • Some suggestion of **setting** with little relevance to **action**
D D+ [3–4]	Incorporates a number of linked ideas in the production of a text, especially at the paragraph level. Has a sense of the text's intended audience and purpose or purposes. Indicates a viewpoint.	• **Events** are linked plausibly with one another • Has distinguishable **characters** and **motives** • A limited attempt at illustrating a **theme** or **idea** • Selects and describes an appropriate **setting**
C C+ [5–6]	Incorporates and develops with some coherence a number of main and subordinated ideas in the production of a text. Shapes the purpose of the text to a sense of the intended audience. As part of a developed personal viewpoint, has some awareness of contextual factors affecting the impact on readers of the text produced.	• **Events** are convincingly linked • A clear sense that the **narrative** is serving to illustrate one or more **ideas** or **themes** • **Characters** are clearly defined and motivated • **Setting** appropriately and clearly evoked
B B+ [7–8]	Incorporates and develops coherently and in a controlled and deliberate way a number of main and subordinated ideas in the production of a text. Consciously shapes the purpose of the text to a sense of its intended audience. As part of a clear personal viewpoint, has an awareness of contextual factors affecting the impact on readers of the text produced.	• **Narrative** convincingly embodies one or more **unifying ideas** or **themes** • Deliberately evoked and **motivated characters** drive the **action** and highlight aspects of **theme** • An appropriate **setting** directly and indirectly evoked
A A+ [9–10]	Incorporates and develops with flair, imagination and coherence, a number of main and subordinated ideas in the production of a text. Has a clear set of purposes and a perceptive knowledge of the intended audience, which is used to position them in a deliberate way. Has a clearly articulated viewpoint and a critical awareness of contextual factors affecting the impact on readers of the text produced.	• **Narrative** subtly and cleverly embodies a complex of **unifying ideas** or **themes** • Well-etched, contrasting and convincing **characters** act as an effective **vehicle** for **action** and **theme** • **Settings** are confidently evoked and illuminate the action

Table 2: Writing: Prose Narrative (Content and Context)

	Generic schedule	Level indicators
E E+ [1–2]	Can employ some language features (layout, structure, punctuation, diction and syntax) in a straightforward way. Has a limited sense of how these features function in terms of the chosen genre.	• **Plot** consists of a few simple **events** somewhat carelessly linked • Inconsistent **pace** • Inconsistencies in **point of view** and handling of **tense** • A limited sense of the required **style** • Frequent **mechanical errors**
D D+ [3–4]	Can employ a range of features (layout, structure, punctuation, diction and syntax) in ways that are appropriate to their function in the chosen genre.	• **Plot** has clear, **linear sequence** of **cause and effect** • Some inconsistencies in **pace** • Some lapses in an otherwise consistent **point of view** • Has glimpses of what a **'literary' style** entails • A number of **mechanical errors**
C C+ [5–6]	Can deliberately and in a controlled way employ a range of features (layout, structure, punctuation, diction and syntax) in ways that are clearly appropriate to their function in the chosen genre.	• **Plot** consciously planned, e.g. incorporating **predicament, complication, resolution, key choices, climax** • Consistently **paced** • Consistent **point of view** • Has a sound sense of what a **'literary' style** entails • Occasional **mechanical errors**
B B+ [7–8]	Confidently and competently employs a range of features (layout, structure, punctuation, diction and syntax) in ways that are both effective and clearly appropriate to their function in the chosen genre.	• A number of **devices** used to consciously structure a well-paced **narrative** • **Point of view** confidently handled and sustained • **Style** is confident, inventive, fluent with a wide **vocabulary** • Few **mechanical errors**
A A+ [9–10]	Shows confidence, competence and flair in employing a range of features (layout, structure, punctuation, diction and syntax) in ways that are striking, innovative and clearly appropriate to their function in the chosen genre.	• A consciously unified **plot** shows an ability to **manage time** though the confident use of **single** or **multiple points of view** and other ways • **Style** is individual, inventive and innovative with wide-ranging **vocabulary** and **syntactical variety** • Almost free of **mechanical errors**

Table 3: Writing: Prose Narrative (Conventions of Language)

Table 2 focuses on the Content and Context of a piece of writing. It is probably a little unfair to Gavin and Harry to be assessing them against a senior school rubric. However, I'm using the procedure to show how the rubrics work and also to show how the graded nature of achievement-based assessment can be an aid in formative assessment. In assessing Gavin's story against Table 2, I find myself seeing his work as revolving around one or two simple events, having little sense of theme or character differentiation, and having some suggestion of setting with little relevance to action. Overall, Gavin's story is in the 'E' category. I would describe Harry's story, in contrast, as convincingly embodying one or more unifying ideas or themes, with deliberately evoked and motivated characters who drive the action and highlight aspects of theme, and as selecting and describing an appropriate setting. I'd put Harry in the low 'B' category.

Table 3 focuses on the Conventions of Language of a piece of writing. In assessing Gavin's story against Table 3, I'd suggest that the story plot consists of a few simple events somewhat carelessly linked, there is inconstant pace, a limited sense of the required style, and frequent mechanical errors (all 'E' level). However, the story has a consistent point of view ('C' level). Overall, Gavin's story is pretty much in the 'E' category. Again in contrast, Harry's story has a clear, linear plot sequence of cause and effect ('D'), some inconsistencies in pace ('D'), a sound sense of what a 'literary style' entails ('C'), occasional mechanical errors ('C'), and a confidently handled and sustained point of view ('B'). Overall, I suggest, he makes it into the 'C' category.

Such rubrics are not the last word in addressing the Murray's question, 'Does it work?' However, they do have certain advantages. Firstly, because of the 1–10 scale, they allow for textual elements to be described along a gradient. Such a procedure is clearly useful for formative assessment purposes. (Students receiving such a rubric after having a piece of writing marked would have a clear sense of where they need to develop.) Secondly, the use of discrete performance indicators reflects a position that writing is not just one thing. These rubrics transparently construct the act of writing, and it is this transparency which allows them to be contested and modified. In other words, they spell out what the assessor thinks writing *is*. Thirdly, rubrics like these highlight the fact that a piece of writing is seldom at a uniform standard across a range of performance indicators. Harry illustrates this dramatically in respect of Conventions of Language.

Finally, how might English/literacy teachers help Gavin, Harry and other young writers? One starting point is to reflect on writing task design (and its contextualization) and its relationship to motivation. In general, human beings don't have to be motivated to talk. Now, while acknowledging that learning the skills of writing requires effort, I don't believe this sufficiently explains why so many of our students find writing a turn-off. In terms of the four versions of English and their related constructions of writing discussed earlier, my experience tells me that the answer to the question of motivation lies in the second and third of these: the pragmatic rhetorical approach with its emphasis on competence and the progressive or personal growth approach with its focus on self-realisation through meaning-making. The cultural heritage approach is more likely to intimidate than to motivate. The critical approach, I think, is also not a source of motivation, but rather tempers and channels motivation once it is aroused.

As a classroom teacher, then, I would want to ensure that Gavin and Harry have the opportunity to engage in writing tasks that have relevance *for* rather than *to* them. I say this, because it is part of a teacher's 'inspirational' work to establish relevance in the minds of students when it may not be apparent to them. As a secondary teacher, one of the first things I asserted to a new class was a definition of rhetoric as the art of making language work for you. I would tell them that virtually everything in my program was aimed at serving that end. If I'd asked my students to write on 'An Exciting Day' for their peer group, as Murray's students were asked, I would have seen them as entitled to have asked me to justify the relevance of the task. It's hard to believe, reading Gavin's story, that he felt remotely excited about the task he was asked to perform; he hadn't committed and one suspects that in the absence of commitment, remedial work with him would have been a waste of time.

As for the place of knowledge about language in the English/literacy classroom as an aid to the improvement of student writing – in many respects, the jury is still out on this one. The formal teaching of syntax does not appear to have enhanced the quality of student writing, though certain kinds of instruction in sentence-combining (similar in some respects to what Murray suggests in respect of 'conjunction') do appear to have had some positive spin-offs (Andrews et al. 2004a, 2004b). My provisional position on this question is that an approach to knowledge about language that begins with a focus on the context/text relationship and which shows students what they can achieve *with* as well as *in* language is the place to start.

References

Andrews, R. (1992) *Rebirth of rhetoric: Essays in language, culture and education*, London: Routledge.

Andrews, R., Torgerson, C., Beverton, S., Locke, T., Low, G., Robinson, A. and Zhu, D. (2004a) The effect of grammar teaching (syntax) in English on 5 to 16 year olds' accuracy and quality in written composition, in *Research Evidence in Education Library*, London: EPPI-Centre, Social Science Research Unit, Institute of Education, retrieved November 15, 2004 from http://eppi.ioe.ac.uk/reel.

Andrews, R., Torgerson, C., Beverton, S., Locke, T., Low, G., Robinson, A. and Zhu, D. (2004b) The effect of grammar teaching (sentence combining) in English on 5 to 16 year olds' accuracy and quality in written composition, in *Research Evidence in Education Library*, London: EPPI-Centre, Social Science Research Unit, Institute of Education, retrieved February 1, 2005 from http://eppi.ioe.ac.uk/reel.

Andrews, R., Torgerson, C., Beverton, S., Locke, T., Low, G., Robinson, A. and Zhu, D. (In press) The effect of grammar teaching (sentence-combining) in English on 5 to 16 year olds' accuracy and quality in written composition, in *Research Evidence in Education Library*, London: EPPI-Centre, Social Science Research Unit, Institute of Education.

Bakhtin, M. (1986) The Problem with Speech Genres, V. McGee (trans.), in C. Emerson and
M. Holquist (eds), *Speech Genres And Other Late Essays: M. M. Bakhtin*, Austin: University of Texas
Press, pp. 60–102.

Brooks, C. and Warren, R. P. (1976) *Understanding Poetry* (4th edn.), New York: Holt, Rinehart and
Winston.

Callaghan, M., Knapp, P. and Noble, G. (1993) Genre in Practice, in B. Cope and M. Kalantzis (eds),
The Powers Of Literacy: A Genre Approach To Teaching Writing, Pittsburgh: University of Pittsburgh
Press, pp. 179–202.

Cambourne, B. (1988) *The Whole Story: Natural Learning and the Acquisition of Literacy in the Classroom*,
Auckland, N.Z.: Ashton Scholastic.

Cope, B. and Kalantzis, M. (1993) Introduction: How a genre approach to literacy can transform the
way writing is taught, in B. Cope and M. Kalantzis (eds), *The Powers of Literacy: A Genre Approach to
Teaching Writing*, Pittsburgh: University of Pittsburgh Press, pp. 1–21.

Cope, B. and Kalantzis, M. (eds) (2000). *Multiliteracies: Literacy Learning and the Design of Social Futures*,
London: Routledge.

Damasio, A. (2000) *The Feeling of What Happens: Body, Emotion and the Making of Consciousness*,
London: Vintage.

Dixon, J. (1975) *Growth through English (Set in the Perspective of the Seventies)*, Edgerton: NATE
(Oxford University Press).

Dixon, J. and Stratta, L. (1995) What does genre theory offer? in W. Sawyer (ed.), *Teaching Writing:
Is Genre the Answer?*, Springwood, N.S.W: Australian Education Network, pp. 77–91.

Eggins, S. and Martin, J. (1997) Genres and Registers of Discourse, in T. van Dijk (ed.), *Discourse as
Structure and Process*, London: Sage, pp. 230–56.

Fairclough, N. (ed.) (1992) *Critical Language Awareness*, London: Longman.

Freedman, A. and Medway, P. (1994) Introduction: New Views of Genre and their Implications for
Education, in A. Freedman and P. Medway (eds), *Teaching and learning genre*, Portsmouth, N.H.:
Boynton/Cook Publishers Inc. pp. 1–24.

Halliday, M. A. K., and Hasan, R. (1985) *Language, Context and Text: Aspects of Language in a Social
Semiotic Perspective*, Geelong, Victoria: Deakin University Press.

Gee, J. (1996) *Social Linguistics and Literacies: Ideology in Discourses* (2nd edn), London:
Taylor & Francis Ltd.

Green, B. (1997) Rhetorics of Meaning or Renovating the Subject of English Teaching? *Changing
English* 4(1), pp. 7–30.

Janks, H. (1994) Developing Critical Language Awareness Materials for a Post-Apartheid South Africa,
English in Aotearoa 22, pp. 46–55.

Kincheloe, J. and McLaren, P. (1994) Rethinking Critical Theory and Qualitative Research, in
N. Denzin and Y. Lincoln (eds), *Handbook of Qualitative Research*, Thousand Oaks, CA: Sage,
pp. 138–157.

Kolln, M. (1996) Rhetorical Grammar: A Modification Lesson, *English Journal* 85(7), pp. 25–31.
Retrieved 10 November, 2004 from
http://www.english.vt.edu/~grammar/GrammarForTeachers/readings/kolln.html

Knapp, P. and Watkins, M. (2005) *Genre, Text, Grammar: Technologies for Teaching and Assessing Writing*.
Sydney: University of New South Wales Press.

Lankshear, C. (1994) *Critical Literacy*, Belconnen, ACT: Australian Curriculum Studies Association.

Lemke, J. (1998) Metamedia Literacy: Transforming Meanings and Media, in D. Reinking,
M. McKenna, L. Labbo and R. Kieffer (eds) *Handbook of Literacy and Technology: Transformations
in a Post-Typographic World*, Mahwah, N.J.: Lawrence Erlbaum Associates.

Locke, T. (2000) English in the New Zealand Curriculum: Benchmarks and Milestones, *English in
Australia* 127–128, 60–70.

Locke, T. (2003a) 13 Ways of Looking at a Poem: How Discourses of Reading Shape Pedagogical
Practice in English, *Waikato Journal of Education* 9, pp. 51–64.

Locke, T. (2003b) Establishing a Counter-Hegemonic Bridgehead: The English Study Design Project, in B. Doecke, D. Homer, and H. Nixon, (eds), *English teachers at Work: Narratives, Counter Narratives and Arguments*, Kent Town, S.A: Wakefield Press/AATE, pp. 227–241.

Locke, T. (2004a) *Critical Discourse Analysis*, London: Continuum.

Locke, T. (2004b) Reshaping Classical Professionalism in the Aftermath of Neo-Liberal Reform, *English in Australia* 139, pp. 113–121.

Luke, A. (1992) Reading and Critical Literacy: Redefining the 'Great Debate', *Reading Forum New Zealand* 2, pp. 3–12.

Martin, J. (1993) A Contextual Theory of Language, in B. Cope and M. Kalantzis (eds) *The Powers of Literacy: A Genre Approach to Teaching Writing*, Pittsburgh: University of Pittsburgh Press, pp. 116–136.

Misson, R. (1998) Post Structuralism, in W. Sawyer, K. Watson and E. Gold (eds) *Re-Viewing English*, Sydney: St Clair Press, pp. 144–153.

Morgan, W. (1992) *A Post-Structuralist English Classroom: The Example of Ned Kelly*, Melbourne: Victorian Association for the Teaching of English.

Morgan, W. (1997) *Critical Literacy in the Classroom: The Art of the Possible*, London: Routledge.

Muller, H. (1967) *The Uses of English: Guidelines for the Teaching of English from the Anglo-American Conference at Dartmouth College*, New York: Holt, Rinehart & Winston.

Murray, K. (1999) Responding to Students' Writing: A Do-It-Yourself In-Service Kit, in B. Doecke (ed.), *Responding to Students' Writing: Continuing Conversations*, Norwood, SA: AATE, and also Ch. 6 in this volume.

Pinker, S. (1995) *The Language Instinct: The New Science of Language and Mind*, London: Penguin.

Roberts, P. (1997) Literacies in Cyberspace, in J. Wright and J. King (eds), *Set Special: Language and Literacy (No 3)*. Wellington/Camberwell, Vic: NZCER/ACER.

Richardson, P. (1994) Language as Personal Resource and as Social Construct: Competing Views of Literacy Pedagogy in Australia, in A. Freedman and P. Medway (eds), *Learning and Teaching Genre*, Portsmouth, N.H.: Boynton/Cook Publishers, pp. 117–142.

Sawyer, W. (ed.) (1995) *Teaching Writing: Is Genre the Answer?*, Springwood, N.S.W.: Australian Education Network.

Notes

1 These terms come from the systemic functional grammar associated with M.A.K. Halliday. 'Cohesion' is 'the set of linguistic resources that every language has ... for linking one part of a text to another' (Halliday & Hasan 1985, p. 48). These resources are listed as reference, substitution and ellipsis, conjunction and lexical cohesion. Murray (1999) defines 'reference' as 'a term describing how people, places and things are introduced into a text and how a writer keeps track of them once there', and 'conjunction' as 'the way writers link sentences together to show ideas in their correct relationship with each other' (p. 25).

2 Murray, writing in 1984, is drawing on a looser set of genre categories than that which would later be developed by the Australian Genre School.

3 I am not arguing that particular 'models' or 'versions' English *produce* different versions of 'literacy', or vice versa. Rather, I am suggesting that certain versions of English parallel particular versions of 'literacy', and that the parallelism itself is discourse-related.

4 The connection between writing and thinking related to this discourse is spelled out in the following way by Brian Cambourne (1988) when he asserts that writing 'is probably the most powerful, readily available form of extending thinking and learning that the human race has available to it. There is no other technology that has quite the same potential for ordering and developing human thinking' (p. 184).

5 For a more recent approach, identifying five 'genres' – describing, explaining, instructing, arguing and narrating – see Knapp and Watkins 2005.

6 This is discourse with a small 'd', to use Gee's (1996) distinction, that is an abstract noun denoting language in use as a social practice with particular emphasis on larger units such as paragraphs, utterances, whole texts or genres.

7 A 'process by which processes are converted into nouns or noun phrases'. Nominalisation occurs when the sentence 'A woman was raped in Kingsland' is changed to 'A rape occurred in Kingsland' (Locke 2004, pp. 49–50).

8 For an account of some of the debates, see Cope and Kalantzis (1993). For a critique of the Genre School's approach to writing, see Sawyer (1995).

9 In fairness to Martin, while earlier work (1993) refers, for example, to 'the canonical structure of the report genre' (p. 122), later work (with Eggins, 1997) emphasizes that the 'relationship between context and text [as reflected in an unfolding of stages] is theorized as probabilistic, not deterministic . . .' (p. 236).

10 Readers are referred to Wendy Morgan's excellent text, (1992), *A Post-Structuralist English Classroom: The Example of Ned Kelly*, Melbourne: Victorian Association for the Teaching of English.

11 In writing this paragraph, I am aware of having entered into a relation with an essay by Bakhtin. I am also aware of being in relation to you, the reader, who has just glanced at this endnote to see if it clarifies in some way the point I have just made.

12 Hasan, in Halliday and Hasan (1985), talks about text-types as having a generic structure potential, with 'obligatory' elements and 'optional' elements, with potential for both the placement of elements and their recurrence (pp. 55–56, 64, 108).

Chapter 6

Responding to Students' Writing

A Do-It-Yourself Inservice Kit

Kevin Murray

Kevin Murray's 'Responding to Student Writing: A Do-It-Yourself Inservice Kit', was first published by the Victorian Association for the Teaching of English in 1984, and reprinted in 1999 in Responding to Students' Writing: Continuing Conversations *edited by Brenton Doecke.*

What factors other than spelling, punctuation and grammar make a student's writing good or bad?

Let us compare two stories by two boys from the same Year 8 form who write about an identical experience – a football match at the M.C.G. which they had attended together. The writing topic was 'An Exciting Day' and the intended audience was the boys' peer group. The stories were to be bound in a class book.

First, read the stories for yourselves. They are typed exactly as they are written. Which in your opinion is the better story?

Many English teachers feel a bit guilty that their judgements in this matter are more intuitive than objective. There is nothing wrong with this. All literary response is personal before it is analytic. Some of James Britton's early research showed that intuitive 'impression marking' of senior essays by a team was more reliable than any single marker using a battery of pseudo-scientific scales and check-lists. But the fact remains that many of us feel inadequate when a young writer asks 'Exactly where did I go wrong?' or 'Tell me what I did right so that I'll be able to do it again'.

Correcting the spelling and punctuation errors will not get us very far here. Harry's problem with direct speech (The old bloke said, 'I was sitting in his reserved seat' – lines 15–16) does not detract from his sure command over language to capture the meanings he wants to get on to paper. In this story at least he has made the language do exactly what he wanted it to do.

Gavin's spelling errors, 'stiring' and 'baracks', (but 'getting'!) are minor compared

A DAY AT THE FOOTY *by Gavin N.*

1 The most exciting time of my life was when Richmond beat Colling-
2 wood by 9 points at the M.C.G. on Saturday from 2 o'clock til 4.36
3 p.m. It was Saturday 21st June 1980.

4 Before the match started Harry and I caught the train from Syndal
5 to Richmond. The train took about 35 minutes and when we got
6 there I got in for free because I had a free pass that I got from my
7 sister.

8 It was about lunch-time when Harry and I got there so we had a pie
9 to eat. The reserves were on and I forgot who won.

10 Finally the seniors came out that is Richmond and Collingwood.
11 The game started and the ball was kicked down to Colingwoods
12 forward line and Ross Brewer mark the ball in front of goals about
13 20 metres out. Ross Brewer kick the goal and the score was, no score
14 to Richmond and one goal to Collingwood. The match were on and
15 goals were coming from each team.

16 Finally the siren went and Richmond won by nine points.

17 Harry baracks for Collingwood and I was stiring him and he was
18 getting mad.

A DAY AT THE FOOTY *by Harry R.*

1 It was a Saturday when my mate Gavin and I went to the football.
2 When we got there the reserves match was on. It was half-time.

3 The match was between Collingwood and Richmond. Collingwood
4 won that match but the firsts were the ones that counted. Gav and I
5 decided to get a seat in the members before the match started.

6 The old bloke that was on the gate looked pretty blind and half deaf
7 so we decided to just run through and not stop. We didn't see the
8 policeman around the corner but he saw us and he belted after us.

9 We heard loud foot-steps behind us and when we looked around there
10 was this big blue creature behind us. We hit the toe and lost him.
11 After that we decided to look for a seat.
12 We found one and sat down and watched the footy.

13 Ten minutes later an old bald bloke came along with the same copa
14 that was chasing us before.
15 He didn't notice us but we knew him. The old bloke said 'I was sitting
16 in his reserved seat' we didn't stay and argue, we ran like hell.

17 Then the policeman knew us straight away and started to chase us.
18 We were too quick for the blue dummy and lost him around the corner.
19 After that we thought there was to much running to do in the members
20 so we went back to the Collingwood cheer squad and abused the ump.

with his failure to transmit any excitement to the reader. As Elizabeth Dines has said, 'These are relatively superficial aspects of language compared with the central task of helping children to say what they want to say – or organise intended meanings' [*Australian Journal of Remedial Education*, Vol. 12, No. 2, 1980: 15].

Here are two approaches to describing quality in writing which may help you penetrate beneath the surface errors of 'correctness'.

First, the theory of narrative developed by the Narrative Working Party, a branch of VATE. Broadly this group believes that the telling of stories performs a crucially important function for the human race – through anecdote and narrative we are constantly selecting significant incidents from the daily flood of events and holding them up for consideration – both by ourselves and our listeners. By telling others what happened, we come to understand what happens. Stories are small generalizations about Life which we then try out on others to check whether our findings match their perceptions. Given this view, the test of a quality narrative lies not so much in the bare events alone but in the valuation or significance imposed on the events by the writer, e.g. 'My father smiled. I'd never seen him so content'. It is the second statement, not the first which carries the important message to a listener or reader. We nod and say, 'So that's how he felt about his dad. Well! well!' Narrative traffics in values, not in facts.

A second approach to kids' writing is through discourse analysis which examines the ways we use language to string sentences together to make a coherent and understandable whole. Grammar deals with sentences as the largest unit (syntax); discourse analysis looks at meaning and how a writer sustains his thought across extended pieces of spoken or written text (semantics). This more rigorous approach is based on the work of such linguists as William Labov and Michael Halliday.

Now let us apply each of these viewpoints to our two stories:–

Gavin's Story
1. Narrative Working Party
William Labov uses an interesting rule of thumb to test narrative. If your response is 'So what!' it's crook. Using this test, Gavin's story fails. After a start which promises much ('The most exciting time of my life was when Richmond beat Collingwood . . .') he fails to focus our attention on any significant event. We are left with a bare and pointless narrative, shorn of the essential evaluation.

Search the story for evaluation. Are the bare facts infused with the writer's personal attitudes at any point?

2. The linguistic approach
Linguistics focuses more closely on the formal analysis of the language on the page. Its analytical procedures and technical terms are complex. However here are several commonly used linguistic instruments applied to the stories.

The schematic structure

Like an essay, a sonnet or a Western movie, autobiographical narrative falls into a characteristic pattern or structure.

1. The scene is set in time and place.
2. A chronological sequence of events is presented.
3. The critical event emerges and is focussed.
4. The critical event and its aftermath is evaluated or commented on.

Gavin carefully sets his scene in lines 1–3. Too carefully in fact. Did you sense there was something astray at this point? Why the overkill of detail? Why 2 o'clock till 4.36 p.m? Why the date? The train trip took 35 minutes etc.? More worrying is the helpless admission, 'The reserves were on and I forgot who won' (line 9). Compare this uncertainty and lack of confidence with his friend Harry's more certain touch at this point, 'Collingwood won that match but the firsts were the ones that counted' (lines 3–4). He not only gives the factual result but also evaluates that fact by noting the relative unimportance of reserve games.

Phase 3 of narrative structure begins on Line 10 with the senior game starting. Why do you think Gavin's story collapses after his description of the first goal? What do you think he intended with the final sentence?

Reference

This is a term describing how people, places and things are introduced into a text and how a writer keeps track of them once there. Immature writers often presume the reader knows as much as the writer and lapse into ambiguous reference, usually via unattached pronouns, e.g. 'The cup fell on the saucer and it broke'.

There are few errors of this kind in Gavin's simple anecdote – other than his assumption in line 12 that everyone knows who Ross Brewer plays for. We have to infer this from the score in line 14. 'One goal to Collingwood.'

Notice his careful naming of the teams in line 10. This is unnecessary as he has already done this in lines 1–2, but adults read so quickly and youngsters write so slowly. He probably forgot his earlier reference by the time he had reached line 10.

Conjunction

This refers to the way writers link sentences together to show ideas in their correct relationship with each other. For example, alternatives to the main idea are signalled by 'however', 'on the other hand', 'alternatively,' etc; time sequences (A and B); cause and effect (A so B, consequently, therefore); comparisons (A like B); additions (A and B, also, furthermore).

1. *Circle all the conjunction words and phrases used by Gavin. Does a pattern emerge?*
2. *(a) Gavin's story is simple so he does not need sophisticated connectives.*
   (b) Gavin's story is simple because he does not have sophisticated conjunctions at his disposal.

Which explanation do you prefer?

How should a teacher respond to Gavin's story?

It is the teacher's responsibility to respond as a genuine reader and tell Gavin gently but firmly that this is a flawed story. In Bernard Newsome's words, 'it leaves the reader no better, no worse off for having read it' (*Idiom* Vol. 15, No. 1, 1979: 23). This approach often surprises young writers. They think teachers only want to mark their work, not read it. The Narrative group, following the London school of thought led by James Britton, believes this is the trigger which will release good writing. Once pupils realise that there are real messages to be sent and real readers to receive them then mastery of the appropriate linguistic skills will emerge as a matter of course. One way to trigger this awareness is to write a genuine reply which responds to what the student is trying to say rather than how he is saying it. In Gavin's case it will also be necessary to discuss the story with him since there is so much which is still in his head and not on the page. Until he verbalises this explicitly the experience will not be truly available to him at all. The piece should be rewritten so that there is a better match between his intentions and their realisation. If the story is heading for publication rather than the 'dead-letter office' then rewriting is not the imposition it is normally felt to be.

The linguists favour a more direct approach. After having ascertained that Gavin fully understood the sort of writing he was being asked to undertake (i.e. personal, informal narrative versus impersonal formal exposition) attention would be paid to his difficulties with cohesion in general and conjunction in particular. One strategy might be to black out all the 'ands' in a piece of his writing and ask him (and the class) to fill the gaps with more appropriate conjunctions. Or duplicate a successful piece of class writing and ask the author to publicly explain his choice of certain link-words. This 'writing workshop' approach is based on the belief that analysis of students' actual writing is a more powerful learning experience than plodding through disembodied textbook exercises.

Pool ideas from your experience which might overcome problems of reference or conjunction.

Harry's Story

This is a successful piece of story-telling. How do we know? First Harry had the wit to realise that this bit of his experience was well worth recounting. I have already added it to my stock of street-smart-kids-versus-the-Establishment stories. On the other hand, Gavin, his mate in the same episode, seems unaware of its potential. Here is an extract from an interview with his teacher.

> T. Was that the day you tried to get into the Members Stand with Harry?
> G. Yeah.
> T. Was that fun?
> G. Yeah.
> T. Why didn't you put that into the story?
> G. I don't know.

This is not very informative but it does suggest that Gavin did not perceive or had rejected this particular escapade as grist to the narrative.

To have selected a single incident from a crowded world is one thing. To craft it well enough to preserve the bravado, excitement and jaunty defeat is another matter. There are probably a hundred ways of telling this story badly. Harry obviously has sufficient linguistic resources to avoid the main pitfalls.

Check Harry's control over the structure of narrative. Make a brief summary of the story, using the four stages of schematic structure (see above) as side headings.

Examine Harry's evaluation of the events. He does not explicitly state that he felt scared or harassed or that he has little respect for the law or old age. Where then do his values show through?

There are no major problems with cohesion. Except for one slip, the story contains clear sign-posts to guide the reader through the five characters involved (i.e. Reference) and it clearly indicates the causal relationship between the events themselves (i.e. Conjunction).

Reference – *check the reference-chains in the story. In Harry's story use the example of the Member and follow reference to the boys, the policeman and the gatekeeper. Notice where he shifts from nouns to pronouns, presuming that the reader can retrieve the identity of the participant without further cues.*

Notice his careful use of reference in lines 13–14. But were you confused in line 13 with the arrival of 'the old bald bloke'? Was this the same old man at the gate, looking for them? How could this new character have been introduced more clearly?

Conjunction – *circle all the conjunctive devices (but, later, then, etc.). Try to identify each one's function in the text, i.e. time sequence; causal or logical relationships. Compare Harry's conjunction markers with Gavin's.*

In general Harry shows greater control of narrative technique. Perhaps the most telling example lies in lines 7–8. 'We didn't see the policeman round the corner but he saw us and belted after us.' Here he detaches himself from the action to give us a view of the events not available to the boys themselves. The policeman has spotted them but they don't yet know. We tend to take this simple technique of parallel action for granted. 'Meanwhile, back at the ranch ...' expresses it well. But it is a strategy unavailable to many pupils in junior secondary forms. They are still tied closely to the events, relating them in a straight-forward 'and then' sequence, unable to decentre in order to describe the action from another vantage point. Harry can do it. We would need to look at more of Gavin's writing to see if he has yet reached this point in his writing development.

Can a teacher hasten the development of this particular strategy?

Can we throw pupils into narratives which demand its use?

How about presenting them with writing models which demonstrate its use?

Will time and maturity automatically take care of the matter?

Will the demands of a real audience spur young writers to use more complex linguistic constructions?

These are issues which can only be resolved by classroom teachers themselves. The research is still in its infancy. We can all be pioneers in this area.

One last question

What is your reaction to the style or register adopted by Harry?

The writing is certainly close to the informal spoken mode of the playground. 'He belted after us', 'an old bald bloke', 'We hit the toe and lost him'.

Should we tolerate such colloquialisms in the classroom? To condemn them out of hand is to settle for a sort of fastidious linguistic table-manners.

The real question to ask is whether the style is appropriate to the task.

Linguists of the Professor Michael Halliday school check three variables as pointers to appropriate register:

a) the subject matter or topic (the field of discourse);
b) the relationship between the writer and his audience – from formal to informal (the tenor);
c) the genre or form of writing being undertaken, i.e. essay versus story (the mode).

In Harry's case, an escapade at the football (field) written for his peers and a trusted adult (tenor) in the form of a narrative (mode) is a context which justifies an informal register. It would be inappropriate if he produced the same casual style when writing on the topic 'Respect for the Law' (field) for a teacher as examiner (tenor) in the formal essay mode. However mastery of narrative technique is probably a necessary stepping stone towards the development of the academic expository style.

We have spent a lot of time examining two simple anecdotes. The time will have been well spent if it has opened up more points of entry into children's writing than merely correcting the spelling. It is important that young writers observe the conventional forms of spelling and punctuation. It is even more important to help them use the potential of the language system to say what they want to say.

Chapter 7

(Trans)cultural Spaces of Writing

Alex Kostogriz

Culture is ordinary: that is where we must start.
Raymond Williams (1989)

Introduction

School life is a teeming beehive of literate activity. A defining characteristic of a school is that it is a place where students read, write and respond to a great variety of written and oral texts. This requires the development of a fairly sophisticated knowledge of how to navigate this literacy space, including particular sociocultural ways of reading, writing, speaking and knowing valued in schools. The literacy space of schooling constitutes discursive conditions that insure the legitimacy of certain meanings (understandings, values and beliefs) and the technologies of their reproduction. This involves developing the right 'word–deed–value combinations' to be considered as a successful literacy learner and an 'insider' to the discursive community of the cultural mainstream (Gee 1996). The space of school literacy privileges the culturally dominant literacy practices, thereby constituting both opportunities for access and a hurdle for non-mainstream students as they struggle to negotiate differences in textual meaning-making and cultural understandings. For them learning to navigate the literacy space of the cultural mainstream means not only learning how to get things 'right' and adapting to the new educational and sociocultural environment as soon as possible. It also means struggling to come to terms with their newly constructed cultural identities, changes in social status and constant negotiation between 'us' and 'them' in classroom learning practices.

Many literacy researchers and educators have emphasised the importance of recognising this struggle to make our educational system better prepared to deal with the increasingly diverse student population. Drawing on a sociocultural approach to language and literacy learning (e.g. Vygotsky 1978), they argue for the development of culturally responsive curriculum and pedagogy that would view cultural, linguistic and textual differences as a resource rather than a liability. According to Vygotsky, culture and language are central to learning, and students draw constantly on their lived experiences of culture and use home and community resources to make sense of their classroom learning. Hence, teaching how to navigate the literacy space of schooling successfully from this perspective involves the acknowledgment of multiple literacy practices and cultural 'funds of knowledge' that non-mainstream students draw upon as they engage with diverse texts at school (Moje et al. 2004). While some English language teachers value a new dimension that non-mainstream students bring to the classroom by approaching the same text differently, many educators who teach English to native speakers feel uncertain when ESL students appear in their class. One source of uncertainty is the contradiction between the multicultural politics of education and the monocultural ideology of literacy that is deeply rooted in a colonial history of English language education and sedimented in current teaching and assessment practices. Multicultural values are stalled, as it were, by the pressures to demonstrate rigid learning outcomes in English literacy by students from non-English cultural backgrounds.

The issues of students' identity and culture in literacy education are thus central for English teachers for the simple reason that classrooms can not be seen as monolithic cultural entities, in particular now when Australian schools are becoming intercultural 'contact zones' more than ever before. The culturally diverse composition of schools and classrooms is a sign both of the sociocultural fabric of society and educational globalization. As Western education and English language have gained the status of universal commodities around the world, we are witnessing growing enrolments of international students in Australian secondary schools, especially from the Asian region. Acquiring English language and academic literacy is seen by them as an empowering resource which affords educational, geographic and workplace mobility and provides access to powerful and lucrative positions in society. Economic globalization and the rise of networked economies have triggered worldwide demands in the area of English literacy, and the global spread of English in response to these demands is unprecedented in scale, especially over the last five decades. In this situation, as Crystal argues, the fact that English is a global language is 'the kind of statement which seems so obvious that most people would give it hardly a second thought' (1997, p. 1).

The rapid spread of English, however, has produced the language 'ownership' paradox in conditions where the users of English as a second or foreign language outnumber native speakers (Graddol 1999). A growing number of people in the world use English for a wide range of purposes that can vary from speaking English in multilingual situation as a tool of communication to its use for promoting economic development, encouraging trade and tourism, and contributing to academic exchanges and research activities. The ways that people appropriate the language are embedded in the local socio-cultural environments in which they operate. The different patterns of English language appropriation and the cultural diversity of language users make it problematic to enforce the cultural norms and linguistic standards of native English speakers. Rather, what needs to be recognised is that the wider English language spreads out, the more trends towards its diversification become accentuated. This linguistic phenomenon of fusion and fission often reflects a tension between the 'residual' forms of colonial re-production, particularly in and through language education, and the 'emergent' forms of new cultural identities and 'Englishes'. The patterns of English language appropriation in countries without a colonial past are also distinguished by a great diversity of sociocultural and political reasons for language use. International communication with neighbouring countries is one of the main reasons, and this quite often requires understanding and utilising Englishes rather than English. It is this concern that might lead us to give a second thought to the cultural politics of English in education as *the* global lingua franca based on a particular ideology of cultural meanings, linguistic standards and fixed textual genres.

But also in English-speaking countries, where conservative and liberal notions of multiculturalism, diversity and difference claim to provide final vocabularies for adjudicating cultural tensions in education, it is important to raise questions about the adequacy of teaching frameworks, methods and models of learning that construe singular cultural meanings and identities for those who are new 'latecomers' to the system. As many researchers and theorists have emphasised, the multicultural agenda in education is not feasible in conditions of the unifying top-down cultural politics of a permanent nation-state (e.g. Giroux 1996). This is particularly obvious in the tension between conservative and liberal frameworks of literacy education. By asserting the need for a unitary, national identity for all students, conservatives push forward the assimilationist agenda for migrant and minority students, insisting that they acquire mainstream cultural literacy which provides a basis for meaning-making in classrooms and beyond. Liberals rightly criticise this by emphasising the importance of other cultural identities and knowledge(s) for learning and thereby encouraging the construction of learning environments in which differences are valued and 'celebrated'. Yet, at the same time, they fail to see power-grounded relations among the cultural representations, identities and meaning-making resources of students in multicultural classrooms (Kincheloe, Slattery & Steinberg 2000). Neither the totalising power of a dominant culture nor the relations of power between dominant and subjugated knowledge(s) of students can be underestimated or wished away through a mere celebration of cultural difference.

This tension between a conservative emphasis on the need for assimilation and liberal, celebratory multiculturalism places many educators in an extraordinarily complex situation. On the one hand, they experience pressure to reproduce the dominant knowledge through curriculum design and implementation, as well as through literacy education which promotes the textual practices of powerful sociocultural groups. The successful acquisition of this cultural-linguistic capital by migrant and minority students is seen as an essential step towards accessing discourses of power that would ensure their future. On the other hand, many educators undoubtedly experience a certain amount of bad faith by going down this path, and they agonise over the culturally loaded nature of what they are doing. What happens when we as educators attempt to create a unified worldview, sanctioning some cultural meanings and marginalising others? What do we miss when we leave these meanings unexamined and instead focus on the development of technical skills in reading and writing? What are the consequences of promoting standard textual practices against which differences in meaning-making are seen at best as an error and at worst as a marker of learning disability?

This chapter will not provide answers to all these questions in a comprehensive way. Rather, my objective here is to make certain familiar practices in writing pedagogy strange again and to offer a transcultural model which might be more sensitive to the border-crossing practices and dynamic identities of non-mainstream students. In doing so, I am not proposing to discard the more familiar ways of thinking about writing, but rather to question them in a way that could expand the scope and critical sensibility of writing pedagogy in multicultural classrooms. By drawing on Bakhtin, I will sketch a dialogical perspective on culture, writing and meaning-making. This perspective might be helpful in thinking about possibilities of developing a transcultural understanding in dealing with differences. How we understand cultural differences in language and literacy education is central to what we do as educators in multicultural classrooms.

Problematising cultural monologism in writing pedagogy

When migrant and international students arrive in Australia, they face the challenge of simultaneously adapting to a new culture, language and educational system. The challenge is particularly great as they are often expected to produce written texts within a short period of time. Composing a text in English can be especially daunting for those who are not familiar with dominant cultural expectations or whose writing practices are different from the literacy practices valued at school. While some migrant and international students are able to rise to the challenges of school literacy in Australia relatively quickly, many of them have a difficult time adopting the stance and language necessary for successful learning. When addressing the problems these students encounter, many researchers into second language (L2) writing have concentrated on cultural-linguistic differences in the rhetorical patterning of written texts (e.g., Connor 1996, Olson 1995, Ramanathan & Kaplan 1996). Their goal has been to sensitise language educators to the preferred patterns of writing by culturally diverse students, thereby attracting their attention not only to the problems ESL students experience with writing but also refining an understanding of what counts as proper writing in English (L1).

Even though the initial aim of this research into writing might be well-intentioned, there is a certain degree of cultural essentialism in the studies, arguably leading to a deficit view of the Other. For example, the pioneering research of Robert Kaplan (1966) in this area not only articulated writing as a culturally diverse phenomenon but also paved the way to essentialising views of cultural differences as static, discrete and even opposite ways of writing and thinking. By analysing the organization of paragraphs in ESL student essays, Kaplan claimed that Anglo-European writing style is characterised by linearity, while Middle Eastern writers tend to use parallel constructions; Asian students prefer an indirect approach, marked by circularity coming to the point in the end; while users of Romance languages and Russian tend to digress and include 'irrelevant' material. Although researchers and language educators have come a long way from these deterministic representations of writing differences, the logic of rigid cultural binarism dies hard and the notion of Western superiority is still present in comparative-evaluative judgements made with regard to the 'less' logical or coherent writing of ESL students (Kubota 2001). It is not surprising then that, with the focus on rhetorical norms and linguistic expression, migrant and international students have been often positioned as linguistically (and cognitively) deficient. Constructed in this way, as Fox illustrates in her study, many ESL students feel 'ashamed about not being straight-line thinkers' (1994, p. 114).

For the last three decades or so, studies in contrastive rhetoric have enabled language educators to imagine what ESL education should be and, under the hegemony of process approaches to writing, literacy pedagogy has focused predominantly on remediating the cognitive processes of culturally different students and instilling greater respect for individual 'voice' and linear logic in composing. Making L2 writing similar to the strategies of native English-speaking writers has become the telos of writing development, emphasising the mastery of historically constructed rhetorical techniques and reflecting the prominence of universal Western rationality (i.e., logical and 'critical' thinking) and clarity (i.e., common sense). However, when we turn the cultural viewing lens back on these assumptions, it becomes clear that these are also based on the essentialised views of native speakers and 'good' writing. They reflect, as Atkinson (2003, p. 51) argues, the ideology of a relatively small segment of English-speaking people who have disproportionate power in defining what writing should be as well as those who come from middle class groups which 'place special emphasis on maintaining or elevating their socioeconomic status through educational "achievement"'. The assumptions of 'good' writing are embedded in the cultural politics of education that privileges textual practices and cultural values of powerful social groups.

Analysing the cultural patterning of writing pedagogy in the Australian education system, Michael Clyne (1999) argued that it has been heavily influenced by the British model of essay-writing. The 'essayist literacy' (Gee 1996) involves an emphasis on honing a deductive logic that would lead to the development of effective writing skills.

Such strategies as brainstorming, planning, drafting and reviewing are seen as essential phases in writing a clearly signposted and logical text. The task of the writer becomes then constructing an affective argument by combining in-the-head rationalism with hands-on experience and in line with the rhetorical norms of linearity and formalism. This framework represents the modernist views of learning that, to use Holzman's words, 'appear to be incapable of escaping Western culture's glorification of human cognitive processes . . . – the primacy of thought over action, the value of critical consciousness and critical faculties, knowing, knowing *about*, and *aboutness* in general' (1997, p. 45). This perspective on learning presents the mind of the writer as an entirely natural and independent processing machine that, in the 'Crusoe' tradition, constructs the cognitive world by dividing experience into atomistic parts, cognises the world with self-sufficient mental effort and, in turn, represents it as clearly and concretely as possible. The atomistic individual in this view will not oppose the principles of the rational order of modernity but will make logical and clear judgements by drawing on the conceptual framework produced by authority or in the 'consensus' of dominant culture.

The way that writing is presented and taught sends learners messages about who they are as writers, what is entailed in the act of writing, what they can do with writing, and what writing can do for them (Auerbach 1999). In fact, writing instruction often goes further than shaping conceptions about writing itself; it can also contribute to constructing learners' worldviews, identities and meaning-making possibilities. 'Essayist literacy', in this respect, is rooted in a *monological* tradition of Western modernism which emphasises individualism, universalism and rationalism. It is part of the Western scholastic tradition (Bourdieu 2000) which has tried to reduce knowing to the activity of the rational subject while ignoring its interaction with the world and the Other. When writing is seen as the mere expression of individual ideas, the process of writing becomes tantamount to a discovery-type activity in which the learner 'discovers' the self and her individual voice through the development and perfection of rational judgements. This emphasis on the workings of the individual not only evacuates the social from learning how to write but also portrays the preferred cultural patterning of writing as taken-for-granted. But most importantly cultural monologism in writing pedagogy misses the significant feature of literacy practices in multicultural conditions – that is, that textual practices are diverse, dynamic and changing. They are embedded in different sociocultural activities of people who can draw on two or more cultural literacy modes in one literacy event (Kostogriz 2005). The ways of writing do not exist in isolated cultural spaces. These spaces very often overlap and writing practices intermingle in complex ways. What happens in the intercultural 'contact zones' becomes then an area of particular interest for writing research and pedagogy that builds on a *dialogical* view of learning.

The recent study of Solsken, Willett and Wilson-Keenan (2000) unveiled how cultural monologism in literacy education excludes or marginalizes textual practices of migrant and minority students, thereby producing their identities as underachievers. When the dialogical learning on the boundary between two cultures is ignored, so is the role of home and community texts in minority students' classroom learning. Therefore, these researchers endeavored to reveal the importance of L2 students' family and community resources for literacy learning, focusing on textual hybridisation as a complex, intertextual process of meaning-making that is relevant to students' dynamic identities and cultural border-crossing. Through the microanalysis of the oral and written texts constructed by a female Latina student, these researchers have shown how the intermingling of home, school and peer language practices serves a variety of sociocultural agendas. They argued that textual hybridisation is connected to the construction of this girl's multiple identities: as a good student and literate member of the classroom community, by taking up the semiotic resources of classroom literacy practices; as a loving member of her family, by drawing upon her family/community semiotic resources; as a respected member of the peer group, by taking up the semiotic practices of other children; and to support the social cohesion of the group, by bridging the topics and genres of others, i.e., by intertextual hybridity.

However, Solsken et al (2000) observe that conventional views of literacy do not leave space to acknowledge or appreciate the richness and complexity of hybrid textual constructions. The girl's semiotic creativity, based on the syncretism of family stories and a variety of other practices, went largely unnoticed. Because her stories failed to approximate the conventional genres privileged in school, the girl was seen as a literacy-deficient student. In contrast, by bringing a culturally responsive perspective to the girl's participation in literacy events, these researchers were able to give an alternative vision of her literacy development. With a focus on meaning-making dynamics, rather than on textual form, she can be conceived of as an achieving, capable and creative student. Thus, a culturally responsive perspective on the textual hybridity of migrant and minority students has a direct connection to critical perspectives on literacy education that see in hybridity the potential to transform the knowledge, texts and identities of the mainstream curriculum.

A dialogical model of writing

One of the most significant sources for rethinking cultural one-sidedness in writing pedagogy can be found in the concept of dialogism which was productively elaborated by Mikhail Bakhtin, a Russian philosopher and literary theorist. For him, dialogue is not just a mode of interaction but, rather, a way of social life in which people establish multifaceted relationships between self and the Other, between a person and culture and between cultures. The dialogical model of life assumes that consciousness, meaning and understanding are never finalised but their dynamic formation depends on continuous interaction with difference – other voices, meanings and worldviews. From this philosophical position, dialogue creates the possibility of language and, at the same time, language itself has a dialogical and, therefore, social nature. Our oral and written speech, according to Bakhtin, is filled with the words of our others:

> In the make up of almost every utterance spoken by a social person ... a significant number of words can be identified that are implicitly or explicitly admitted as someone else's, and that are transmitted by a variety of different means. Within the arena of almost every utterance an intense interaction and struggle between one's own and another's word is being waged, a process in which they oppose or dialogically interanimate each other. (Bakhtin 1981, p. 354)

This means that every word participates in a history of rich intertextual relations in which it is linked one way or another to utterances previously spoken or sentences previously written by other people. People do not simply use language to construct their unique texts out of nothing. Words come *already* 'populated' with the intentions of others and carry historical traces of meaning. Consequently, the process of writing is a two-sided act, involving a dialogical tension between self and the Other. It is a contextually situated activity in which each sentence becomes a juncture of multiple historically constituted discourses. On this conception, the writer appropriates 'alien words' by evaluating them and populating them with her own intentions; but this is a complex social process in which a person who writes is both enabled and constrained by mediating discourses which sit in relations of power and interdependence with each other.

The writer, therefore, is engaged in a dialogical struggle which is marked by the ideological tension between centripetal and centrifugal discourses that operate within the heteroglossic cultural-semiotic space of language use. According to Bakhtin (1981), centripetal discourses are 'monoglossic' and normative. They tend to centralise or standardise language and fix or close meanings, ensuring the production of common understanding between people. Usually cenripetalism is also related to a wide-scale cultural, political or religious censorship that is trying to reduce diversity within the spatial boundaries of nation-states, regions or communities. Centrifugal discourses, on the other hand, keep language and culture alive by diversifying genres and resisting closure. Because these discourses gravitate towards the cultural periphery and articulate unofficial worldviews, they enable new meanings, identities and practices to emerge. Heteroglossia, according to Bakhtin, refers to the conflict between these two forces:

> The centripetal forces of the life of language, embodied in a 'unitary language', operate in the midst of heteroglossia. At any given moment of its evolution, language is stratified not only into linguistic dialects in the strict sense of the word ... but also – and for us this is the essential point – into languages that are socio–ideological: languages of social groups, 'professional' and 'generic' languages,

languages of generations and so forth … Alongside the centripetal forces, the centrifugal forces of language carry on their uninterrupted work; alongside verbal-ideological centralization and unification, the uninterrupted processes of decentralization and disunification go forward. (Bakhtin 1981, p. 271–272)

Once heteroglossia is incorporated into writing, the process of writing ceases to represent 'individual voice' and the author's intentions become expressed in a subjected way as the enactment of twofold direction in meaning-making. Bakhtin calls this phenomenon a double-voiced discourse which is 'directed both toward the referential object of speech, as an ordinary discourse, and toward *another's discourse*, toward *someone else's speech*' (1984, p. 185). Authorial writing, in this case, becomes dialogised in heteroglossic utterances, thereby permitting 'a multiplicity of social voices' and a wide variety of their links and interrelationships to different discourses and languages (Bakhtin 1981, p. 263). These distinctive links and interrelationships between utterances and multiple discourses and languages are an elemental feature of heteroglossic writing in which conflicting world views collide. Hence, in the process of writing, heteroglossia is the context-dependence of particular sentences and dialogism is the driving force of meaning-making. By its sheer location within a writing space created by heteroglossia, the writing subject is decentred and her consciousness is located in-between conflicting discourses, created by heteroglossia. In this matrix of dialogised heteroglossia, meaning-making lies on the interdiscursive and intertextual borderline and 'it is from there that one must take the word, and make it one's own' (Bakhtin 1981, p. 294).

From this Bakhtinian position, then, we might argue that the writing of ESL students is a meaning-making process which is not just about the reproduction of a unitary knowledge or recapitulation of fixed meaning (even though this is important for establishing or sustaining intersubjective links between the writer and the reader). Bakhtin also put emphasis on alterity – the transformation of meanings and under-standings based on rich heteroglossic potentiality and dialogical tension between dif-ferences in worldviews, understandings or cultural knowledge. The students' cultural otherness introduces strangeness that can take forms of opposition, disagreement or alternative evaluation, thereby bringing a 'surplus of vision' to otherwise taken-for-granted representations of things. This process was defined by Bakhtin (1968) as creative or 'conscious hybridisation' through which people transcend boundaries between two genres, languages, worldviews or cultures. While ESL students' learning to write in English is oriented towards shared meanings, there can be also many instances of creative hybridisation, especially in those genres that are 'conducive to reflecting the individuality of the speaker' (Bakhtin 1986, p. 63). The challenge for educators is then how to recognise cultural-semiotic hybridity and respond to differ-ence in writing.

Clyne (1999, p. 171, see also Ch. 8 this volume) examined typical responses of VCE/HSC examiners to essay-writing in content areas (e.g. History and English Literature) that were seen as digressions from linear progression. The most common comments were 'incoherent', 'confused and irrelevant', 'very jumbled', 'possibly foreign, certainly inarticulate in English', 'disoriented', 'repetitive', etc. It is clear that discourse structure and logical presentation were considered by the examiners as prerequisite features of acceptable academic writing and not so much the content. Meaning-making was reduced to clear and cohesive presentation – that is, to the expression of 'common sense'. In this respect, it can be argued that if 'clarity' substitutes meaning-making complexity and becomes the main indicator of understanding and a universal standard of literacy then, in Giroux's (1992, p. 24) words, this represents 'a troublesome politics of erasure'. That is to say, 'clarity' turns to be nothing else but the effect of power in cultural knowledge re-production. However, with the emphasis on meaning-making complexity, 'unclear' writing in many cases can be conceived as a reflection of dialogical tensions experienced by ESL students who are positioned on the boundary between cultures and within asymmetries of worldviews. The production of hybrid texts is characterised by meaning-making dynamics and uncertainty, for writing space is a site where multiple discourses clash, producing particular modalities of power dynamics. This particularity of hybrid constructions (Bakhtin 1981) attests to the fact that writing in multicultural conditions is mediated by multiple cultural-semiotic resources and ideological orientations, and they can *intersect* in writing events. The integration of competing discourses and knowledges produces 'texts within a text'.

Any text, according to Lotman (1988), has two major functions: the first function is the transmission of information in communication, and the second is the generation of new meaning. The first function is 'fulfilled best when the codes of the speaker and the listener most completely coincide and, consequently, when the text has the maximum degree of univocality' (Lotman 1988, p. 34). This requires the creation of an intermediate space – a metatextual level – that will furnish the prescriptive way of interpreting the text. In contrast, a text fulfilling its second function ceases to be a passive link (an instrument) in conveying some constant information. It exhibits the heterogeneity of its constituent elements; it turns out to be a 'thinking device' incorporating the junction of other texts or texts within a text. If we put these two functions together, it becomes apparent that meaning-making can not be simply assessed on the basis of its clarity (i.e. the ability to transmit 'common understanding'). What needs to be taken into account is also the ability to construct complex intertextual links that might as well lead to the meaning being transformed.

In Clyne's (1999) study, the examiners paid attention predominantly to the first function of texts – the clear transmission of information from the writer (author) to the reader. This assumption holds the view of the text as a 'container' – a structural-generic entity – to be filled with information. Therefore, students must demonstrate the knowledge of decontextualised parameters or a metatextual paradigm of how the text should be structured to get the message across in a clear way. This view overemphasises the knowledge of textual structures and homeostatic norms in order to encode information and thus privileges decontextualisation over situated writing action. Some of these themes are also prominent in genre-based literacy pedagogy (see Christie & Martin 1997). Teaching genres in regard to the first function of texts involves teaching those metalinguistic codes that would give an opportunity to create univocality in understanding. If the knowledge of a genre – a single 'text-code' – is deployed to the plurality of texts represented as a bundle of variants of that genre, then, according to Bakhtin (1984), the 'context is killed' in the singularity of metalanguage.

However, with the emphasis on the second function of written texts, hybridisation can be seen as the force opposite to the rigid, boundary constructing and self-identifying law of genre (cf. Derrida 1980). It reinscribes, remakes and redefines temporal and spatial construction of worldviews and their interpretative ideological uniformity. In our pre-service teacher education course, *Language and Literacy in Secondary School*, hybridisation of genres by student-teachers has constituted a powerful learning experience (see Doecke, Kostogriz & Charles 2004). Our students have been encouraged to actively engage not only in a diverse range of textual practices but also in producing texts that would combine a number of genres (e.g. narrative and academic writing). This kind of hybrid construction empowered teacher-students to interrogate their own literacy experiences as well as to construct new understandings of what counts as literacy. Through hybridisation of personal stories about 'literacy events' and a scholarly reflection on them, our students produced subtexts within the text. Writing in this way enabled dialogised heteroglossia to become a vehicle of meaning-making in professional learning, which is characterised by contradictions rather than by certainties. In reading and assessing these texts we paid attention therefore to their second, transformative function and not so much to the degree of their approximation to the standards of a traditional academic essay. This change in assessment focus revealed the complexity of meaning-making as our students tried to rethink the dominant view of literacy. By shifting their focus on family and community literacy practices, many student-teachers were able to problematise literacy education that is based on the textual practices of the sociocultural mainstream.

It became clear for us that productive meaning-making and learning can not evolve from a single cultural-semiotic space; for this to occur, at least two heterogeneous spaces are required. When a text, understood in such a way, interacts with difference, new meanings can be generated. The text needs, as it were, both an interlocutor within its frames (another text) and an interlocutor outside its boundaries (another consciousness) for meaning to be produced rather than transmitted. But this requires the transformation of learning environments and assessment practices that would enable the recognition of dialogicality and hybridization in writing as a valuable resource in learning rather than being conceived as a liability (e.g. a digression from linear and clear presentation). In writing pedagogy this is a matter of transcending patronizing attitudes to non-mainstream students by offering them opportunities of transculturation in meaning-making.

Towards a writing pedagogy of thirdspace

A thirdspace perspective on writing development acquires a particular significance for literacy practices in multicultural classrooms. With the emphasis on difference in the New Literacy Studies (Gee 2000), many researchers have attempted to overcome cultural dichotomies by developing a thirdspace perspective on the interaction between institutionalised literacy (e.g. school) and local textual practices (e.g. home and community) to address social, cultural and political issues involved in the literacy education of migrant, minority and socially disadvantaged students (Kostogriz 2005, Moje et al. 2004, Pahl 2002, Wilson 2000). The idea of thirdspace (Bhabha 1994, Soja 1996) is being deployed in these studies to propel a socially critical project of literacy education in 'new times' characterised by the struggle between the monocultural politics of literacy and local sociocultural diversity. By emphasizing the recognition of ever growing diversity of sociocultural and textual practices, multiplicity of text forms and multimodality of meaning-making practices, many sociocultural researchers conceive literacy in multicultural conditions as a set of practices that can not be reduced to the dominant culture. Yet they are also attempting to overcome the limits of local ethnic or social communities, by exploring cultural-semiotic hybridity which occurs in relations of power between the dominant and the subjugated, disrupting both homogenic-nationalist and ethnocentrist discourses. In a way, this is an attempt to transcend the logic of cultural binarism in education by promoting the value of intercultural dialogue and critical literacy for the construction of new learning environments.

This task might again draw fruitfully on Bakhtin's analysis of the dialogical in the production of transcultural consciousness. Bakhtin explicitly challenged the 'monological' notion of a cultural space as fixed and homogeneous through his exploration of contradictory tensions between semiotic fixity and motion. He sees the failure to engage in a genuine dialogue with the Other precisely because both self and the Other do not transcend the narrow preoccupation with self-consciousness, enclosed within itself and completely finalised. Bakhtin identifies this as an extreme form of monologism that 'denies the existence outside itself of another consciousness with equal rights and equal responsibilities' (1984, p. 292). In its pure form, the monological approach perceives the Other as an object of rational contemplation that does not have any particular value and hence does not require recognition as being unique. Such misrecognition, from a Bakhtinian perspective, can be surpassed only when the self is conceived as an open unity, as unfinalised. The ongoing dialogue between cultural differences triggers a semiotic motion across real and imagined boundaries created within and between cultures, social groups and ethnic communities. To be in a dialogue with the Other would mean to the individual consciousness getting out of itself and, in the space of 'outsidedness', meeting another consciousness (Bakhtin 1986). The space between self and the Other becomes a space of in–between–ness produced by the very act of inner distancing and pushing 'one's consciousness to the limit of Otherness in order to meet the external, "alien" Other' (Gurevitch 2001, p. 90). This model of dialogical interaction acquires particular significance in multi-cultural conditions because it imagines a thirdspace space on the fault line between two cultures as a simultaneous co-being of differences – the transcultural co–being in which asymmetries of power can be transcended only through a critical reconstruction of self.

If we deploy this ethical model to writing pedagogy, it becomes clear that traditional classroom practices are largely informed by monological perspective on difference. Many ESL students have been conceived through the lens of dominant culture as passive and dependent learners who are less capable of critical thinking and raising intelligent questions in writing than native English-speaking students (cf. Biggs 1996). As Zamel (1997) argues, the cultural determinism of Western language educators with regard to the Other colours the way in which they see both their students and the academic wor(l)ds they encounter. Cultural monologism assumes a unified writing culture of schooling and does not allow problematising the cultural values of the teachers and assumptions that underlie writing assignments and assessment criteria. What we need, as Bakhtin would put it, is to find ourselves in the Other by finding the Other in us in order to generate a critical stance on cultural determinism in writing pedagogy. When it comes to languages and culture, we need to relinquish the myth of cultural purity to recognize the performance of hybrid identities by ESL students in writing. As Clifford once argued, 'cultures do not hold still for their portraits' and 'writing culture' is alive (1986, p. 9), historically dynamic and changing. In dialogical encounters between 'writing cultures' students are changed as they participate in academic literacy practices of the mainstream and, in turn, the ways this literacy is conceived, taught and assessed should also change to reflect the growing presence of culturally different students in the classroom. Transcultural thirding in writing pedagogy can be possible only in dialogical relations between self and the Other; when both the native and the foreign are able to transcend their cultural one-sidedness.

The challenge educators face is therefore how to inject a third dimension into teaching, making it responsive to students' identities and their cultural and linguistic border-crossing in the construction of textual meanings. Handling cultural bumps in classrooms is an onerous task that is often beyond a teacher's control of such issues. In recognising the power of cultural centrepetalism in broad society and in education, one of the student-teachers in our study poses a number of baffling questions:

I will be working within a system that expects a certain standard and measurement of competence. So the questions I ask myself are, to what degree will I impose the dominant mainstream view of competence? Will I be able to detach myself from my expectation, and consider diverse students and what they bring to the classroom? Will I look outside the 'square'? (Doecke, Kostogriz & Charles 2004)

In grappling to answer these questions, her understanding of political constraints on professional practice, however, is transculturally mediated and broader than the one-sided perspective on cultural difference. She finds a new mode of dialogical consciousness that empowers her to conclude: 'I suppose being conscious and aware of these issues puts me one step closer to the type of teacher I hope to be'. This student-teacher, who is from a family of migrants, became acutely aware of how her parents were marginalised because of their uncertain grasp of English literacy and, when she went to school, of how schooling failed to provide a space for cultural and linguistic difference.

There are no simple solutions in transforming curriculum and assessment practices to empower the writing of non-mainstream students. While the 'genre approach' to teaching writing in Australia is a progressive movement in this respect, there is a need to take it a step further. Genre-based pedagogy provides access to cultural knowledge that enables ESL students to navigate mainstream literacy practices as well as to master main text-types. This knowledge, however, should be reassembled to bring about the active engagement of non-mainstream students in literacy learning, so that they could draw on their 'funds of knowledge' (Moll 2000) in dialogical understanding of how texts work and to examine relations of power in textual representations. A disordering of dominant knowledge in and through writing is particularly relevant for non-mainstream students as they explore concepts in such content areas as Science, Mathematics, History and Literature. Because students are situated in the network of different discourses and textual practices, they can approach the same text in different ways depending on the particularity of intertextual and interdiscursive connections they construct in reading or writing (see Moje et al. 2004). The development of a thirdspace perspective in this process is crucial; productive learning in multicultural classrooms depends on co-existence of differences and these should not be mapped in terms of either an absolute oppositionality (where one position demolishes the other) or a neat succession (a stage-like change). A writing pedagogy of thirdspace sees learning as a dialogical inquiry, occurring in an interaction of rival ideas and meanings and leading to the more open-minded, more self-critical production of new meanings.

In this view, the task of the teacher is again to ensure that making sense in the literate and textual activities of the classroom is based on intertextuality and intercontextuality. This becomes critically important because intertextuality and interdiscursivity lie at the heart of any social interaction (Fairclough 2000), including dialogical learning in the classrooms. When students have an opportunity to dialogise their own and other cultural experiences, when sociocultural heteroglossia becomes an inseparable part of classroom activity, a new, less rigidly structured pedagogical practice can be created. Teaching from a thirdspace perspective encourages the 'sociocultural forum' (Gutiérrez, Rymes & Larson 1995) as a transformative, dynamic and productive force in learning. It helps teachers define what counts as valued knowledge in the classroom and provides students with a real possibility to critically construct, contest and transform meaning.

To reorganise traditional pedagogy into a space of sociocultural pluralism, then, means moving from the domesticating representations of cultural knowledge and ways of re-producing this in written texts and toward the intellectually empowering practices that would integrate multiple cultural resources, voices and 'ways with words'. This shift from the monocultural to transcultural and pluralistic model of teaching is needed for the intellectual development of learners pertinent to their participation in the multicultural and multiliterate life of contemporary society. Because thirding for many non-mainsteam students is a life choice which ensures the survival of the marginalised and the disadvantaged, nurtures resistance and provides openings for border-crossing, a writing pedagogy of thirdspace aims to emphasize the importance of interrelationship between the new emergent cultural identities, literacy practices and learning in order to foster a dialogue between differences in schools and beyond. And, if we agree with Gee's (1996, p. 68) statement that the 'English teacher stands at the very heart of the most crucial educational, cultural, and political issues of our time', then a thirdspace perspective on writing can be a bottom-up attempt to subvert the broad politics of unconditional acculturation. Through the dialogical practice of teaching, learning and living with difference(s) we can recover a meeting point – a thirdspace – to create democratic learning environments such as needed in multicultural conditions.

References

Atkinson, D. (2003) Writing and Culture in the Post-Process Era, *Journal of Second Language Writing* 12(1), pp. 49–63

Auerbach, E. (1999) The Power of Writing, the Writing of Power, *Focus on Basics* 3, December Issue.

Bakhtin, M. (1968) *Rabelais and His World*, (trans.) H. Iswolsky, Cambridge, MA: MIT Press.

Bakhtin, M. (1981) *The Dialogic Imagination*, (ed.) M. Holquist, Austin, Texas: University of Texas Press.

Bakhtin, M. (1984) *Problems of Dostoevsky's Poetics*, (ed. and trans.) C. Emerson, Minneapolis: University of Minnesota Press.

Bakhtin, M. (1986) *Speech Genres and Other Late Essays*, (eds) C. Emerson and M. Holquist, Austin, Texas: University of Texas Press.

Bhabha, H. (1994) *The Location of Culture*, London: Routledge.

Biggs, J. (1996) Western Misperceptions of the Confucian-Heritage Learning Culture, in D. Watkins and J. Biggs (eds), *The Chinese Learner*, Melbourne: CERC & ACER, pp. 45–67.

Bourdieu, P. (2000) *Pascalian Meditations*, (trans.) R. Nice, Cambridge: Polity Press.

Christie, F., and Martin, J. R. (eds) (1997) *Genre in Institutions: Social Processes in the Workplace and School*, New York: Continuum.

Clifford, J. (1986) Introduction: Partial Truth, in J. Clifford and G. Marcus (eds), *Writing Culture: The Poetics and Politics of Ethnography*, Berkley: University of California Press, pp. 1–26

Clyne, M. (1999) Writing, Testing, Culture, in B. Doecke (ed.), *Responding to Students' Writing: Continuing Conversations*, Adelaide: AATE, pp. 165–176

Crystal, D. (1997) *English as a Global Language*, Cambridge: Cambridge University Press.

Derrida, J. (1980) The Law of Genre, *Glyph* 7, pp. 202–232

Doecke, B., Kostogriz, A. and Charles, C. (2004) Heteroglossia: A Space for Developing Critical Language Awareness? *English Teaching: Practice and Critique* 3(3), pp. 29–42

Fairclough, N. (2000) Multiliteracies and Language: Orders of Discourse and Intertextuality, in B. Cope and M. Kalantzis (eds), *Multiliteracies*, Melbourne: Macmillan, pp. 162–181

Fox, H. (1994) *Listening to the World: Cultural Issues in Academic Writing*, Urbana, IL: NCTE.

Gee, J. (1996) *Social Linguistics and Literacies: Ideology in Discourses*, 2nd ed, London: Taylor & Francis.

Gee, J. (2000) The New Literacy Studies: From 'Socially Situated' to the Work of the Social, in D. Barton, M. Hamilton and R. Ivanic (eds), *Situated Literacies*, London: Routledge, pp. 180–196

Giroux, H. (1992) *Border Crossings: Cultural Workers and the Politics of Education*, New York: Routledge.

Giroux, H. (1996) *Fugitive Cultures: Race, Violence, and Youth*, London: Routledge.

Graddol, D. (1999) The Decline of the Native Speaker, in D. Graddol and U. Meinhof (eds), *English in the Changing World*, *AILA Reviews* 13, pp. 57–68

Gutiérrez, K., Rymes, B. and Larson, J. (1995) Script, Counterscript, and Underlife in the Classroom: James Brown vs. Brown vs. Board of Education, *Harvard Educational Review* 65(3), pp. 445–471

Holzman, L. (1997) *Schools for Growth*, Lawrence Mahwah, NJ: Erlbaum.

Kincheloe, J., Slattery, P. and Steinberg, S. (2000) *Contextualising Teaching: Introduction to Education and Educational Foundations*, Boulder, CO: Westview Press.

Kaplan, R. (1966) Cultural Thought Patterns in Inter-Cultural Education, *Language Learning* 16(1), pp. 1–20.

Kostogriz, A. (2005) Dialogical Imagination of (Inter)Cultural Spaces, in J.K. Hall, G. Vitanova and L. Marchenkova (eds), *Dialogue with Bakhtin on Second and Foreign Language Learning: New Perspectives*, Mahwah, NJ: Lawrence Erlbaum, pp. 189–210.

Kubota, R. (2001) Discursive Construction of the Images of U.S. Classrooms, *TESOL Quarterly* 35(1), pp. 9–38.

Lotman, Y. (1988) Text within a text, *Soviet Psychology* 24(3), pp. 32–51.

Moje, E., Ciechanowski, K., Kramer, K., Ellis, L., Carrillo, R. and Callazo, T. (2004) Working toward Third Space in Content Area Literacy, *Reading Research Quarterly* 39(1), pp. 38–70.

Moll, L. (2000) Inspired by Vygotsky. Ethnographic Experiments in Education, in C. Lee and P. Smagorinsky (eds), *Vygotskian Perspective on Literacy Research. Constructing Meaning through Collaborative Inquiry*, Cambridge, MA: Cambridge University Press, pp. 256–268.

Pahl, K. (2002) Habitus and the Home: Texts and Practices in Families, *Ways of Knowing Journal* 2(1), pp. 45–53.

Olson, D. (1995) Writing and the Mind, in J. Wertsch, P. del Rio and A. Alvarez (eds), *Sociocultural Studies of Mind*, Cambridge: Cambridge University Press, pp. 95–123.

Ramanathan, V. and Kaplan, R. (1996) Audience and Voice in Current Composition Textbooks: Implications for L2 Student Writers, *Journal of Second Language Writing* 5(1), pp. 21–34.

Soja, E. (1996) *Thirdspace: Journeys to Los Angeles and Other Real-and-Imagined Places*, Cambridge, MA: Blackwell.

Solsken, J., Willet, J. and Wilson-Keenan, J. (2000) Cultivating Hybrid Texts in Multicultural Classrooms: Promise and Challenge, *Research in the Teaching of English* 35(2), pp. 175–197.

Vygotsky, L. (1978) *Mind in Society: The Development of Higher Psychological Processes*, (eds and transls) M. Cole, V. John-Steiner, S. Scribner and E. Souberman, Cambridge: Harvard University Press.

Wilson, A. (2000) There is No Escape from Third-Space Theory: Borderland Discourse and the 'In-between' Literacies of Prison', in D. Barton, M. Hamilton and R. Ivanic (eds), *Situated Literacy*, London: Routledge, pp. 54–69.

Zamel, V. (1997) Towards a Model of Transculturation, *TESOL Quarterly* 31(3), pp. 341–353.

Chapter 8

Writing, Testing and Culture

Michael Clyne

Michael Clyne's 'Writing, Testing and Culture', was first published in The Secondary Teacher, *the journal of the Victorian Secondary Teachers' Association (VSTA), in 1980.*

'Writing, Testing and Culture' Twenty Four Years On

The reappearance of the following article, while flattering, is the source of considerable embarrassment to the author. The intention of the original article was to draw the attention of teachers and assessors to the cultural bias of essay-writing norms. The foundations laid in the Kaplan (1972) article cited below have been to the construction of the sophisticated field of 'contrastive rhetoric' which has developed vigorously all over the world. (For an indication of this, see Kaplan 1988, Connor and Kaplan 1987, Clyne 1994, pp. 160–175, Mauranen 1993, Duszak 1997, Liddicoat 1997). Among the important studies are those elucidating the 'back to the baseline' type discourse structures in Japanese, Chinese and Korean motivated by indirectness, politeness and historical tradition (e.g. Hinds 1980, 1983, Liu Mingchen 1990, Kirkpatrick 1992, 1993, Eggington 1987). Some of the parameters in the following paper have been applied in a study of academic discourse and discourse expectations of German-speaking and English-speaking scholars (Clyne 1987, Clyne, Hoeks and Kreutz 1988). Others have examined the impact of culture on the essay-writing of non-native speakers – a contrastive study of English discourse by Chilean and Vietnamese students, which is in many ways vastly different, has enabled Farrell (e.g. 1995) to critique the role of the education system.

Writing, Testing and Culture

Essay-writing plays an important role in our education system. Its place in evaluation of student performance is so central that it seems impossible to imagine assessment without it.

Given this emphasis, we need to be careful that the structures we demand for essays don't have built-in biases for any social groupings.

My research, unfortunately, would indicate that important biases can discriminate against students from a number of backgrounds.

I believe that the essay-writing requirements in the Australian education system are based solidly on British cultural patterns. Consequently, many people brought up in multi-cultural Australia meet the essay-writing demands of our schools with some degree of unfamiliarity.

Let us first consider the notion of cultural patterns in a more general framework, taking as examples: degree of linearity, verbality and formalism, and the rhythm of discourse.

(i)   Some cultures are more linear in orientation than others. For instance, spontaneous queue-forming is more developed in Britain than in continental Western Europe. So are linear rules of argumentation in meetings, such as the stipulation that only one motion can be before the chair at a time, and the rule that the successful amendment becomes the motion.

In his pioneering study of the essays of foreign students in the United States, Kaplan (1972) postulated four kinds of discourse structures which he identified with speakers of particular languages (rather than with cultures) and contrasted with linearity, which he identified with speakers of English. As we will see, the situation has turned out to be somewhat more complicated.

(ii) The Anglo-Celtic rules for conducting meetings of all kinds are examples of culturally-conditional formalism. So are rules for the writing of academic treatises and essays in non-language subjects within the education system, where presentation may override the knowledge which is the object of the essay. Such rules are difficult for people from other cultures to acquire. Many migrants in Australia, who have reached a high level of competence in other aspects of English, find meetings of school parents' and citizens' associations, trades unions, and even gardening clubs as incomprehensible as a game of cricket. Adolescents and mature age students who received most of their education in a non-English-speaking country often fail here in subjects of which they have a good knowledge, because they do not abide by formal rules reflecting features of a culture that is not their own.

(iii) The rhythm (tempo) of discourse is more or less flexible, or structured differently, in different cultures (Kaplan 1972). Turks, who are accustomed to long monologues with no interruptions and plenty of narratives, are not able to function successfully in a society with short exchanges (Barkowski et al. 1976). Japanese-English bilinguals speak in shorter turns and listen more in Japanese conversations than in English ones (Elzingam 1978). Restrictions on discourse tempo (e.g. hurrying up business by moving that 'the motion now be put', slowing it down by referring it to a sub-committee) are characteristics of meeting procedures in

English-speaking countries that are unusual in most continental countries and many ethnic groups in Australia (Clyne and Manton 1979).

(iv) Some societies are more verbal, others more literate. While German students (especially North German ones) and those from many other European countries and the U.S. are required to project themselves verbally, some of the most capable students in Australia, who write very well, are often not able to express their thoughts verbally. This may be related to a '(pseudo)egalitarian' principle in many Australian secondary schools by which the brighter pupils should keep quiet and give the others a chance. It may be partly due to the emphasis placed on writing in class and examinations.

We have found (Clyne, Hoeks and Kreutz 1988), through a survey of linguists and sociologists, that there is a canon of good academic discourse for Australian scholars, which involves linearity, symmetry, the early positioning of definitions and of advance organizers indicating the path and organization of the text. Such a canon does not have a parallel for German scholars, for instance. In fact, interruptions to the linearity of a text are necessitated in most continental European cultures to facilitate the inclusion of a culturally desirable theoretical or ideological dimension, supplementary information or polemic with another school of thought.

School Essays

Let us take the matter back a few steps in the education system. In schools in English-speaking countries, a great deal of emphasis is placed on the techniques of essay writing, not only in the first language classes – as is the case elsewhere – but also in other subjects. The presentation of answers in examinations and class exercises is of great significance in all humanities and social sciences in English-speaking countries, and much time is spent in teaching these techniques. In continental European countries, the emphasis in examinations in such subjects is on testing specific and general knowledge. This is often done orally or through direct short-answer tests.

A number of essay-writing manuals used in English-speaking countries were examined. The following formal rules emerged: An essay must start with an introduction, which defines the terms of the topic or question and the scope of the essay (See Chessell 1976, Edwards 1975, Kinsella 1967) and which usually assumes that the reader (examiner) is ignorant of the material being presented. The essay must end with a logical conclusion which satisfies the reader that he/she has learnt something (Edwards 1975, p. 11). Edwards' typical study manual on essay-writing, as well as essay guides by Chessell (1976), Anderson (1971) and Kinsella (1967), implicitly advocates relevance as the primary virtue to be sought after in constructing an essay. The use of the manuals is encouraged to deduce the aim of the essay strictly from the wording of the topic or question (Edwards 1975, Chessell 1976). In the body of the essay, the student is advised to develop the key ideas 'making sure that the end of one paragraph leads on properly into the beginning of the next one' (Edwards 1976, p. 15). Kinsella warns that, by introducing facts or ideas that do not contribute to a linear progression, you would be violating the important principle of paragraph unity, which holds that every idea and fact in the paragraph should contribute to the development of a single topic, no matter how interesting or significant the 'digression' might be.

In the German-language manuals it is the transmission of knowledge that is given the greatest emphasis. The essay can assume the sharing of thematic knowledge (Hoppe 1976). However, the Prague School concept of proceeding from the known to the unknown, from theme to theme, is observed also in Central European essays (Edler 1976). Topics in German-language countries tend to be broader (e.g. 'Brecht's Plays' rather than the discussion of a quotation about them). While in English-speaking countries it is important to stick only to 'relevant' points, avoiding mention of anything else, the emphasis in Central Europe is on demonstrating knowledge, though the central argument needs to be clearly presented and a logical progression from introduction to conclusion is required (Killinger 1969). Thus, digressions are employed frequently. All this may entail repetition of the main points in German essays, whereas in English ones, redundancy is undesirable (Chessell 1976, p. 120). This partly accounts for differences in length between English and German essays or versions of the same text.

The Victorian Higher School Certificate Examiners' Reports of 1972, 1974, 1976 and 1978 for all subjects were consulted for references to essay-writing techniques. There was hardly a subject that did not comment on discourse structure. Examiners generally argued for 'relevance' and against the demonstration of knowledge if such knowledge, however correct, constituted a 'digression' from the essay topics. We have space for only a few representative examples:

- 'Clearly many candidates had either a general knowledge of the topic ... or a thorough specific knowledge ... But just having such information is not what is required by most H.S.C. essays ... those who write controlled relevant essays will always be appropriately advantaged.' (18th Cent. History 1978, p. 135)
- 'Irrelevant padding simply has to be eradicated.' (Biblical Studies 1972, p. 32)
- 'Neither great length nor knowledge of the most recent material necessarily makes a good essay.' (European History 1978, p. 216)
- 'The examiners can only give marks for material that is relevant to the questions.' (Greek History 1978, p. 277)
- The Politics examiners (1978, p. 365) put it even more strongly: 'Lack of relevance remains the major cause of failure'.
- According to the European History Report (1972, p. 107): '... inability to be successfully relevant was, as always, most examiners' major complaint'.

- In spite of the culturally-bound nature of discourse patterns, Victoria's Hebrew candidates (1972, p. 143) 'who did not address themselves specifically to the question being asked lost marks'.

Linear progression is implicitly recommended and digressions are strongly criticized. Art examiners commented on students who 'were unable to make up their minds about specific questions and simply rambled on' (1977, p. 24) and who wandered 'off the point ... introducing irrelevant ideas and illustrations' (1978, p. 25). Australian History examiners censured 'students side-tracked into pages of narrative' (1972, p. 30). A Biology Report (1972, p. 37) found that 'rather than answer in structural terms, many resorted to circular arguments ...' English Literature examiners (1972, p. 93) felt that summing-up 'final paragraphs mostly came too late to redeem the plodding and haphazard impression created by the rest of the answers', while in Geography (1972, pp. 129–30) 'many answers included potentially useful material, but failed to demonstrate its relevance to the central issues'.

A word of advice was given by the 18th Century History examiners (1972, p. 68): 'Plenty of essay-writing practice during the year will train students to marshal their ideas in an orderly fashion'.

First Examiners' comments on 400 H.S.C. (Year 12) History scripts were perused, sometimes with recourse to the actual essays. (The comments are an internal communication between examiners.) The general picture is the same as that emerging from the Examiners' Reports. Most of the comments were on discourse structure, although there were also many on the content (e.g. well-informed, too general, too specific, inadequate material, no supporting evidence). Failed essays, those on the borderline (4 out of 7), or those obtaining 5 out of 7 despite a good knowledge of the topic, frequently received comments on the organization rather than the content of the essay, e.g.

1/7 Incoherent
Confused and irrelevant
Very jumbled
Possibly foreign, certainly inarticulate in English.
2/7 Irrelevant
Rambling
Disoriented
Incoherent.
3/7 Padding
Disorganized
Repetitive
Mostly irrelevant
Gross repetition.

4/7 Information away from the point
Not all relevant
Marginal
Poorly organized.
5/7 Rambling but makes good points
Poorly organized
Extremely well-informed but does not follow the requirements.

A random selection of essays by 37 Year 12 students from Melbourne schools was collected, complete with teachers' comments and marks. Eleven were European History essays from a high-status Catholic boys' school; thirteen English Literature essays were from a co-educational state high school, and thirteen English essays (on set books) from a medium-status Protestant boys' school. The structure of the essays was analyzed by a research assistant who had experience as both a secondary school teacher and an examiner of HSC English and German (as well as by myself). As each class was taken separately, and essay structures were compared in teachers' evaluation, we have not attempted to investigate the socioeconomic and ethnic backgrounds of the pupils. (However, they had received all, or virtually all, their schooling in Australia.)

Of the History essays, the only one that departed significantly from a linear structure received the lowest mark 13/20. Another, in which the beginning of each paragraph reads like a new introduction, also detracting from cohesion, was given 15/20. All the comments were at least partly on the discourse structure, and marks ranged from 13 to 19 out of 20.

The two English essays with the highest marks (16/20 and 15/20) were the most linear in structure. The two other fairly good results (15/20 and 13/20) were for essays with a high degree of linearity. One essay that was passed with 12/20 is, in the words of the teacher, 'faulty in presentation', but the middle part becomes 'relevant' in retrospect through a good conclusion. Three essays with numerous digressions were given 5, 8 and 9 out of 20 respectively. Three with parallel structures ('you go one way, then the other') received 8, 7 and 10 respectively (the last albeit containing some good material), while circular-structured essays gained 7 and 8 out of 20, respectively.

In English Literature, too, essays with a very linear structure were awarded 17/20 and 15/20. An answer with one major digression received 15/20, and an essay with two major digressions 13/20. An otherwise good answer which changes orientation towards the end obtained 13/20, an essay with about six minor digressions 11/20 (teacher's comment: 'Pretty waffly'). A factually sound answer which both digressed and was circular was given 11/20. The two essays that were failed were one that did not discuss the question and drifted away from the main argument in the middle (9/20) and one where the central argument is frequently interspersed with trivial generalizations (8/20).

In all three batches of essays, as in the examinations, it is clearly the discourse structure that is of vital importance. In a number of instances, one is led to the impression that the content is merely an excuse for giving the student 'something to express'. The prerequisites for something to be deemed acceptable, logical or cohesive are influenced by a cultural discourse pattern.

I have begun to collect a corpus of assignments written by later year secondary school pupils in Germany. The comparability with the Australian assignments is not great, probably because the essay genre does not play such an important role in the education system of the German speaking countries. So far we have some 12th Year History assignments from a Gymnasium in Braunschweig, 11th Year German essays from one in Ostfriesland, and 12th Year Geography tests from the Braunschweig Gymnasium. Both schools are co-educational and, of course, selective.

The history assignment was a summary (Protokoll) of a particular period of modern German history discussed in class. Of the seven assignments, four were partly or wholly in note or point form (i.e. with incomplete sentences). Most of them were organised under headings and subheadings, in a form similar to that of mass-circulated newspapers. The emphasis of both pupils' work and teacher's corrections was on content learning and the reiteration of knowledge rather than on discussion and analysis. The teacher's corrections were minimal and involved, first and foremost, content deficiencies, and also lexical and grammatical errors and style. There were no comments on the formal (point form) or on discourse structures.

The German assignments were students' responses to a TV play, entitled 'Darf eine verheiratete Frau fremdgehen?' – 'Is a married woman permitted to be unfaithful (to her husband)?' The freedom of format was quite striking. In fact, the exercise was described by different pupils as 'Essay', 'dialectic essay', 'argumentation', 'home-work', and 'scheme of an antithetical plan'. At the most, four of the 20 assignments would qualify to be described as 'essays' in Australia. Ten were partly in point form and two of these in note form (i.e. with incomplete sentences). Half of the essays stressed the thesis and antithesis and gave mainly lists of arguments. Some of the students devoted much space to their own views: others did not mention these. Six of the essays contain no paragraphing. Generally, the question is neither defined nor argued, and material in the topic sentence is not developed. There are varying degrees of attempts at linearity from the topic sentence of one paragraph to that of the next. The preoccupation with 'dialectics' reflect the importance attached to philosophy in the German education system.

From the teacher's comments and marks, it may be deduced that her expectations highlighted content (i.e. number of powerful, complete and original arguments), relevance to the question, and sub-discourse aspects of language (lexical choice, syntactic correctness, spelling, punctuation). The highest mark was given to the longest essay, which contained the most arguments and the greatest degree of linearity, but also a large amount of repetition. The lowest mark was attributed to lack of originality and poor linguistic competence. The teacher stressed, however, that this essay did adhere adequately to the subject. Linearity was not given prominence in the marking, but the antithesis required by the 'dialectical essay' was a major criterion.

In the thirteen Geography tests, discourse structure and linguistic expression varied vastly, but marks were allotted consistently on content. Expression was not commented on, and there was only one remark concerning 'relevance' (involving a weak test paper): 'You ought to refer to the essential things!' General comments on other papers were 'You seem to lack all foundations of geography' and 'There are indications in your work that you could do better!'

All in all, performance and expectations confirm that the German education system is concerned primarily with content and hardly at all with formal discourse structures (especially in non-language subjects). This does not mean that linearity is necessarily not regarded as an additional virtue, but it is relatively unimportant in Germany compared to Australia, whereas particular and general knowledge is of more dominant significance. Although I have not checked the results of university students in Australia who received most or all of their secondary education in continental Europe, I know of many such people who fail because they do not write essays 'according to the requirements'. With the use of essays for Higher School Certificate examinations increasing rather than decreasing in at least some states, and the rise in the number of overseas-educated mature age students, it may be timely to investigate whether our examination techniques may be discriminatory.

I am not arguing against essay-writing requirements in examinations but in favour of a recognition of the cultural foundations of the techniques and expectations.

If culture-specific discourse structures play as important a role as is suggested in our data, they should occupy a prominent place in teaching programs for both ESL and other second and foreign languages, including languages for special purposes.

The essay-writing requirements in our education system are based on British cultural patterns of linearity, formalism, and discourse rhythm. These are also reflected, for instance, in rules for the conduct of meetings in English-speaking countries.

The presentation of answers in examinations and in class is of great significance, even in non-language subjects in English-speaking countries. Linearity and relevance, measured in terms of the wording of the topic, are important. In German speaking (and other continental) countries, however, the emphasis is on testing specific and general knowledge. Digressions and repetition are tolerated more. This is concluded on the basis of essay-writing manuals from English and German speaking countries, Victorian HSC Examiners' Reports, examiners' comments on 400 papers, and class exercises (complete with marks and teachers' remarks) from Australia and Germany.

Students who have received most of their education in continental Europe may be discriminated against through our essay-writing requirements and the same may well apply to those who were educated in Asian countries.

References

Anderson, W.E.K. (1971) *The Written Word: Some Uses of English*, London: Oxford University Press.

Barkowski, H., U. Harnisch and S. Kumm (1976) 'Sprechhandlungstheorie und Gastarbeiterdeutsch', *Linguistische Berichte* 45, pp. 42–56.

Brunner, E. and Dorstal, E. (n.d.) *Der Deutsche Aufsatz*, 2 vols, Wunsiedel.

Chessell, P. (1976) *Essay Writing: A Guide* (with photos by H. Birnstihl and cartoons by R. Tandberg), Melbourne.

Clyne, M (1987) Cultural Differences in Academic Discourse: English and German, *Journal of Pragmatics* 11, pp. 211–47.

Clyne, M. (1994) *Inter-Cultural Communication at Work: Cultural Values in Discourse*, Cambridge: Cambridge University Press.

Clyne, M. and Manton, S. (1979) Routines for Conducting Meetings in Australia: An Inter Ethnic Study, *Ethnic Studies* 3 (1) pp. 25–34.

Clyne, M., Hoeks, J. and Kreutz, H.J. (1988) Cross-Cultural Responses to Academic Discourse Patterns, *Folia Linguistica* 22, pp. 457–74.

Connor, U. and Kaplan, R.B. (eds) (1987) *Writing Across Culture*, Reading, MA: Addison-Wesley

Duszak, A. (1997) *Cultures and styles of academic discourse*, Berlin: De Gruyter.

Eder, A. (1976) Texttheoretisches zum Aufsatzunterricht, *Wiener Linguistische Gazette* 12, pp. 25–56.

Edwards, H. (1975) *Writing Better Essays: Study Manual*, Geelong: Clarke Learning Associates.

Eggington, W.G. (1987) Written Academic Discourse in Korean, in U. Connor and R. Kaplan (eds), *Writing Across Languages: Analysis of L2 Text*, Reading, MA: Addison-Wesley, pp. 172–89.

Elzinga, R.H. (1978) Temporal Organization of Conversation, *Sociolinguistics Newsletter* 9 (2) pp. 29–31.

Farrell, L (1995) "Doing well . . . Doing badly": An analysis of the role of conflicting cultural values in judgement of relative academic achievement, in A. Duszek (ed.), *Cultural Values and Intellectual Style*, Berlin: Mouton de Gruyter, pp. 1–32.

Hinds, J. (1980) Japanese Expository Prose, *International Journal of Human Communication* 13, pp. 117–58.

Hinds, J. (1983) Contrastive Rhetoric: Japanese and English, *Text* 3, pp. 183–95.

Hoppe, O. (1976) Thesen zur Aufsatzurteilung, *Linguistische Berichte* 45, pp. 70–6.

Kaplan, R.B. (1972) Cultural Thought Patterns in Inter-Cultural Education, in K. Croft (ed.) *Readings on English as a Second Language*, Cambridge, Mass. pp. 245–62.

Kaplan, R.B. (1988) Contrastive Rhetoric and Second Language Learning: Notes Towards a Theory of Contrastive Rhetoric, in A. C. Purves (ed.), *Writing Across Languages and Cultures*, Newbury Park pp. 275–304.

Killinger, R. (1969, 1972, 1975) *Sprachübungen für allgemein-bildende höhere Schulen*, 3 vols, Vienna.

Kinsella, P.L. (1967) *The Techniques of Writing*, New York: Harvard.

Kirkpatrick, A. (1983b) Information Sequencing in Mandarin in Letters of Request, *Anthropological Linguistics* 33, pp. 1–20.

Kirkpatrick, A. (1983a) Information Sequencing in Modern Standard Chinese, *Australian Review of Applied Linguistics* 16, pp. 27–60.

Liddicoat, A. (1997) Texts of the Culture and Texts of the Discourse Community, in Z. Golebiowski and H. Borland (eds), *Academic Communication Across Disciplines and Cultures* 2, Melbourne: Victoria University of Technology pp. 38–41.

Liu, Mingchen (1990) Qi, Cheng, Hé, Jié, *Australian Review of Applied Linguistics, Series S*, pp. 38–69.

Mauranen, A. (1993) *Cultural differences in academic rhetoric*, Frankfurt: Lang.

Chapter 9

Becoming a *New* New Critic

Assessing Student Writing

Wayne Sawyer

Introduction

In his strand keynote address at the 2003 IFTE conference, Andrew Goodwyn discussed the present state of the profession in England under the combined imperatives of the National Literacy Strategy (NLS) and the Framework for English, the latter an outcome of the National Curriculum of 1997. Goodwyn's research tells of a profession which is seeing its subject re-defined in ways that many of its members wish to resist. Yet he also pointed to a gap between experienced teachers with a sense of the recent history of the subject and new teachers who had never known that the subject they taught could be anything other than that which was defined by the national imperatives of the NLS and the Framework (Goodwyn 2003a). It is, of course, this new generation of teachers who will inherit the subject and possibly re-define it in significantly different ways. This theme continues in another report on this research where he highlights the much more positive attitudes towards complying with government prescriptions among younger teachers and student teachers, concluding that 'clearly they are likely to develop a different professional identity from their more experienced colleagues' (Goodwyn 2003b, p. 132)[1].

My concern in this chapter is less with the professional identity of English teachers than with a kind of collective forgetfulness that can overcome us whenever 'the next big thing' is dropped upon us, leading us to sometimes lose sight of the value of what we already do and know – and what that means for a generation of teachers who thus have quite a different experience of the subject, especially of the subject as driven by political imperatives.

Here my focus is on classroom writing, and, specifically, how English teachers could approach assessing their students' writing. Since the mid-90s, the main concern in assessment discussion has been debates prompted by system wide requirements, such as standardised testing and end-of-schooling credentialling. This almost invariably means concern with variations on criterion-referenced or standards-referenced *systems* and their role in being able to measure performance, often, though not always, for the purposes of ranking. Rubrics are designed so that pieces can be designated as 'sophisticated', 'highly achieving', 'moderately achieving', etc. What is lacking, I believe in this discussion of assessment is a focus that existed in earlier work on:

- the degree of detail that makes a work 'sophisticated'
- how to provide that detail as feedback to the student.

Without such a focus, 'sophisticated', 'poor', etc., can remain vague and contestable terms, despite the rubrics which appear to make unproblematic, objective distinctions.

The equivalent kind of testing regime to that discussed by Goodwyn which exists in NSW high schools, for example, is contained in the Year 10 'English/literacy' School Certificate test and the English Language and Literacy Assessment (ELLA) in Years 7 and 8. Only the Year 10 test is compulsory for all school systems, but, in effect, most students in the nominated Years undertake the tests. I have written elsewhere about problems with ELLA in particular (Sawyer 1999a, 1999b). Briefly, the main problems identified with the writing test included:

- a '0/1' marking scale on items of grammar which did not discriminate between the student who made one error and the student who was incorrect every time – hence belying ELLA's claim to being 'diagnostic'
- a total emphasis on 'text-level processes' in terms of whether the piece conformed to a particular definition of 'text-type' (i.e. whether it is of a particular 'genre' as defined by adherents of the more reductive 'Sydney' version of the 'genre schools'. For discussions of the genre/text type issue and the 'Sydney school', see Hasan 1995, Sawyer 1995, 2002, Richardson 2004). The 2004 ELLA for Year 7, for example, marked a student down if his/her narrative (different 'text types' are targeted each year) did not contain a 'Complication' or 'Resolution', according to the definition of narrative as composed of an 'Orientation/Complication/ Resolution' (NSWDET Educational Measurement Directorate, 2004).

In some ways, ELLA has improved in terms of its marking procedures. An earlier obsession that students should be able to demonstrate a capacity to handle the whole gamut of simple, compound and complex sentences, for example, rather than using only some of these (students were actually marked down for writing only in complex sentences) appears to have been dropped. Importantly, the number of items marked only as '0/1' has been reduced in relative terms. Students who may have little idea about correct use of conjunctions (such as ESL students) and students who make one error will both still score '0', but on the whole there appears to be much more room for professional marker judgment compared to the earlier days of ELLA (NSWDET Educational Measurement Directorate 2004).

Nevertheless, with the Year 10 School Certificate marked in similar ways, the main focus of 'English literacy' as it is publicly assessed in NSW remains largely mechanistic. As Richardson argues, 'The influence and impact of the Sydney genre school in dislodging expressivist pedagogies ... in Australia has been profound. English literacy documents in all States and Territories unilaterally treat genres as unproblematic' (2004, p. 124). To return to Goodwyn's point from my first paragraph – what is the subject going to look like to a generation of English teachers who have only known a public assessment regime of this sort (and despite 'literacy' being ostensibly an across-the-curriculum phenomenon, it is still the English teacher who is called to account in practice for 'literacy' results, particularly in Year 10)? Moreover, how is this view of the subject compounded when systems imperatives drive professional development?

I would like to proceed by providing an historical overview of an era in which the assessment of writing was discussed in terms of the detail of a student's piece and in terms of the feedback to be provided.

The 1980s

In some ways, the 1980s were the heyday of research on assessing student writing in terms of raising questions about how to describe student achievement and give feedback to students to help them improve their work. In Australian and the UK, particularly, seminal works on assessment were produced in that period: Brian Johnston's *Assessing English*, Andrew Stibbs' *Assessing Children's Language*, Andrew Wilkinson et al's *Assessing Language Development* and the work of Dixon and Stratta in *Achievements in Writing at 16+*. Indeed, I believe Wilkinson's Crediton Project remains one of the most important works ever undertaken in assessment because of its detailed, comprehensive, longitudinal nature – and one which remains in the front rank today, despite the fact that it was produced over two decades ago.

What did this research offer to teachers? Following are some examples to remind us of this work.

Stibbs

Andrew Stibbs first published *Assessing Children's Language* in 1979 when he was Advisory Teacher for the County of Cleveland in the UK (the edition referred to here is that of 1981). The book was the product of two years' work among a working party of the North East and Cleveland Durham branches of NATE, with material provided by schools in that area.

In a chapter on 'What we are assessing', Stibbs provided a long example of a student's writing, which begins as follows (spelling and punctuation errors are as per original):

Lost in the Fog

The chilling night air felt dampening on my warm brow, I walked on past a what seemed to be a thousand acre field of under ripe beetroots. The evening mist began to fall, slowley at first, then before I knew it I was stranded, the place I knew not. My view was obscured by the dazzeling on coming head lights The time was getting late, the exact time I could'nt tell for sure onething I knew was it the fog did'nt lift soon, that would be the end of my late fridays. I walked on, only to find myself lying flat out in the middle of a laural bush. At the time I could'nt remember what I had done, it seemes to all come back to me know, yes, A car, a Volo I think, came shooting oup the road, I steped back and there I was flat out. I must have triped ofer a man hole cover or somting, yes, because I can remember putting my hand on some thing cold, with little lumps on, it did'nt occure to me at the time least ways untill I got home that I sat on somthing else as well. (Stibbs 1981, pp. 11–12)

Stibbs goes on to analyse the teacher's response to this piece (the teacher's corrections have been omitted from this copy), which consist of responding only to the observable surface features – particularly spelling and punctuation. He also shows the extent to which the teacher – even in his/her own terms – has missed the opportunity for genuine diagnosis. (Stibbs asks his readers whether the writer can, for example, spell 'remember' or not? Is 'dazzeling' a cause for praise or criticism?) More importantly for my purposes here, however, is Stibbs' commentary on the mood of this section (addressed to the reader, not the student):

'Lost in the Fog' creates an eerie mod and an anticipation of events to come. It uses vague words and phrases like 'seemed', 'before I knew', 'obscured', 'knew not' and 'could'nt' (sic) 'tell for sure' which help the reader share the narrator's disorientation. (p. 16)

I would agree that the writer creates a sense of disorientation. However, I would argue that the writer uses very precise vocabulary to create this mood rather than accepting Stibbs' slightly negative comment about 'vague words'. There are other examples: 'At the time I could'nt remember what I had done', 'I can remember putting my hand on some thing cold, with little lumps on', 'I sat on somthing else as well'. This disorientation is, in fact, continued into the current moment when the narrator attempts to recall events through such phrases as 'it *seemes* to all come back to me know', 'A car, a Volo, *I think*', 'I *must have* triped', '*yes*, because I can remember'. These successive phrases convey an impression that the narrator is grasping after certainty, but remains stranded in a moment of uncertainty and suspense with 'it did'nt occure to me at the time least ways untill I got home that I sat on somthing else as well'. (In fact it is one of the complete story's faults, I feel, that we never find out what this 'somthing else' is.) Moreover, this sense of eerie foreboding is underlined by the way the piece presents a series of objects and events that appear to be at a point of change and that dominate this section: 'under ripe beetroots', 'the evening mist', 'began to fall, slowley at first', 'the time was getting late'.

In the story the narrator finds him/herself in a launderette alone, sleeps there overnight and awakens to recognise the locale and steps out of the launderette with the closing words: 'it was only tem minutes walk, so home I went. Expexting only the worst'. The teacher comments that 'Expexting only the worst' is 'Not a sentence', while Stibbs argues that it contributes to the 'appropriate tone' (p. 15). I would argue further that in a story structured around vagueness, uncertainty, mystery and suspense that the piece reaches its appropriate end by leaving the narrator and the reader in a state of unknowing. That it should be 'the worst' is perhaps doubly appropriate (and, incidentally, with respect to the teacher's comment, the student has demonstrated throughout that he/she can write in correctly structured sentences).

Stratta and Dixon

In the early 1980s, John Dixon and Leslie Stratta produced for the UK Schools Council a series of monographs in which they analysed writing submitted in coursework folders for 16+ GCE/CSE[2] examination. Each monograph presented a different genre of writing, such as 'Narratives based on personal experience' and 'Narratives based on imagined experience'. My interest here is in these two genres specifically. In their work on analysing these narratives, Dixon and Stratta (1981, 1982) produced a series of criteria against which to measure development. These 'staging points' of writing development arose out of their answering the following questions about the relevant coursework writing:

- What resources are used in setting and situation? (1982, i.e. for imagined experience only)
- What kinds of ordering occur in the narratives? (1981, 1982)
- What sort of readers are assumed in the narratives? (1981, 1982)
- How comprehensive a viewpoint is presented by the writer? (1981) What significance is there in the point of view presented? (1982)
- What are examples of significant uses of language? (1981, 1982)

In the 'personal experience' monograph, they present one example of a piece written by a student about an Easter Geography excursion in Amsterdam in which two students after a fairly boring morning's wandering inadvertently become involved in a violent protest against the demolition of houses to make way for a new Metro (1981, pp. 10–13). Dixon and Stratta's analysis of this piece includes the following observations (addressed to the reader, not the student):

> *What kinds of ordering?* . . . in the opening paragraphs two opposing outcomes of the day are foreshadowed . . . This brief prefiguring of the experience is a favourite device of the author . . . One effect of such foreshadowing is to fill a rather mundane sequence of morning events with ominous meaning . . . The second innovation is the use of contrasting themes: morning and afternoon begin to stand for 'ordinary' and 'violent' . . .

> *How comprehensive a viewpoint?* . . . The narrator, initially detached, moves steadily closer to the thoughts and feelings of the two girls . . . even in evoking a climax of panic, the writer can achieve a precise reflective observation on the girl's inner state of mind . . . Equally, retrospective awareness is held in check

> *What significant uses of language?* . . . There is a continuity, a flow of consciousness from the sensory detail to her mental comment (now) and on back to the visual image, now reinforced figuratively as she sees him crumpling . . . it involves using a complex combination of appositional phrases and further clauses with extended phrases and clauses of manner, each with precise selection of words (1981, pp. 13–15).

Thus, as with Stibbs, we find the student writing being analysed in significant linguistic terms. These discussions each go far beyond concern with text-level processes or easily observable surface features to attempt to say something of significance about the achievement of each piece.

The Crediton project

Wilkinson, Barnsley, Hanna and Swan in the Crediton project produced what still remains today a remarkable study of the long-term writing development of students. In order to gain their picture of writing development over time, the Crediton team set over a hundred students from three schools four written tasks. The students were given the tasks as part of their normal school work over a period of three months and the pieces were assessed in three age groups: ages seven, ten and thirteen. The tasks were:

1) Autobiographical narrative
   The happiest/saddest day of my life (7/10 year olds)
   The best/worst experience I have ever had (13 year olds)

2) An account of a process
   How to play . . .
3) Fictional story
   Based on three visual stimuli, of which one was to be chosen as the basis of a story
4) Discussion of an issue/point of view/persuasion
   Would it work if children came to school when they liked, and could do what they liked there?

From this sample, the team attempted, in effect, to describe the characteristics of writing at these three age levels. From their analyses of the pieces produced by students in response to the four tasks, the following four dimensions of growth were derived:

- *Cognitive model* (based on language development in terms of sub-sets of 'Describing', 'Interpreting', 'Generalizing' and 'Speculating'). This model was used on tasks #2 and #4.
- *Affective model* (based on development in terms of sub-sets of 'Self', 'Other People', 'Reader', 'Environment' and 'Reality'). This model was used on tasks #1 and #3.
- *Moral model* (based on attitudes/judgments about self/others/events). This model was used on tasks #1, #3 and #4.
- *Stylistic model* (based on language development in terms of sub-sets of 'Syntax', 'Verbal Competence', 'Organization', 'Cohesion', 'Writer's Awareness of the Reader' and 'Effectiveness' as well as a series of specific sub-sets for each task). This model was based on all four tasks.

The researchers commented (to the reader) on the *affect* of one particular thirteen-year-old's piece as follows:

> It shows the affective beautifully controlled through the careful selection of images, the presentation of character, and narrative comment. The writer seems not only to be coming to terms in poetic art-form with the emotional meaning of the loss of a mother and father, and the feelings of a devoted husband over the loss of a wife, but inserts the symbolic in the form of a father-figure who brings a calm supportiveness to the boy at the same time that he brings word of the father's death. Even his father's death can be seen as symbolic in its appropriateness. (Wikinson et al. 1980, p. 150)

They comment on the *style* of another girl's narrative in these terms (again addressed to the reader, not the student):

Nina has access to a variety of subordinations when necessary. However, here she selects a series of simple structures of the S.V.O. (Subject, Verb, Object) type which are in keeping both with the idiom of the spoken language, and the tenseness of the situation being evoked. Competence in style in this particular is a matter of being able to select from a repertoire as appropriate. Thus the long last speech is in contrast to the laconic final sentence ... The choice of individual words and phrases is careful ... There is sensitivity to the way words would be spoken 'What do you mean, we do' with the implied stress 'we'. The title 'who cares' is picked up skilfully in the final words of one of the speakers ... This last is also a feature of organization. The obvious narrative line, the murder of the woman, is rejected, and instead we hear about it incidentally through the dialogue. Thus the chronology ... is interrupted by retrospections ... The opening seizes the attention and focuses on the control issue. The conclusion – 'the car drove into the night' symbolizes the indifference which the dialogue has argued out, and the title indicated ... (Wikinson et al. 1980, p. 176)

Once again, the writers are taken very seriously. We have close reading and sophisticated analyses that respect the achievements of the writers and go far beyond concern with text-level processes or easily observable surface features.

Johnston

My final example of this kind of close reading of student writing from the 1980s issues out of Brian Johnston's important Australian book, *Assessing English*. In this book, Johnston sets out ultimately (in the words of the sub-title) to 'help students reflect on their work'. He covers areas of reading and oral language assessment, school reporting and assessment structures and a number of other topics on assessment.

With regard to writing, Johnston includes among his strategies one he calls 'showing how you read' based on his response to a piece written by a Year 9 boy. In essence this is a running commentary on the student's piece as he reads. The commentary is directed to the student:

OF AN UNMENTIONABLE THING	
Though I hate to dare admit it. It did happen. I didn't know now. All I know is that it is terrifying.	*O.K., first paragraph short. Short sentences got me very interested. It's very easy to understand and you've implied that it will be hard to believe what I'm going to read, and that it was confusing to you and that you still haven't put it together, but that it was terrifying. So I'm looking forward to the second paragraph.*

I think it started off in a dark, dingy, smoke-ridden cellar. This cellar was used as a sort of bar, but it was virtually unknown, and few of those who knew it did not shun it.	*That's good atmosphere there. 'I think' seems a bit weak, but, again, I'm not sure. It's adding that little bit of uncertainty.* *'Few of those who knew it did not shun it'. In other words, most of those who knew it did shun it. Right, that's the effect it had on me at first.*
I was there in search of a story for my paper. Neither me nor my editor knew what the story I was after was about, but in this area lately there had been many reports of something that prowled the dark lanes and alleys bringing great fear and a feeling of evil and doom. No one knew what shape this evil took. Most who had encountered it said they had felt its presence of doom, and seen an indistinct blur. It was always encountered at night in dark alleys or lanes . . . (Johnston 1987, p. 55)	*Great! This is very sustained, casting a lot of ominous questions in my mind . . .* *Right . . .*

Johnston's approach is quite different in many ways from the British writers so far discussed, but it shares, I would suggest, one key assumption which I will consider below.

The mindset of the literary critic

One approach that all of these writers share is, as I have already observed, that of taking students' writing very seriously in order to subject it to this degree of analysis/discussion. Johnston, for example, suggests quite seriously that this approach be taken by teachers to each piece of writing through audiotape and even times his reaction to this piece in order to test its feasibility for a real class of over 25 students (it took seven minutes for the complete piece to be read and commented on) (Johnston 1987, p. 56).

However, what these writers also have in common is what I would call an essentially *descriptive* mode in their approach to these pieces. I often ask groups of teachers and student teachers to write responses to Stibbs' 'Lost in the Fog' piece discussed above. I choose not to give them the text, but instead read it aloud. Invariably, reactions are largely positive, but, equally invariably, they fall into recognisable categories of response – and if I were to categorise teacher responses to any piece, typically they, too, would fall into something like the following categories. Some readers:

- give marks (6/10)
- make running annotations and corrections

- offer positive judgments ('very good')
- offer negative judgments ('poor')
- give a very general description of the piece ('it creates atmosphere'/'uses contrast well')
- respond as a reader, rather than teacher ('I really enjoyed . . .')
- give general advice for the future ('be more descriptive')
- give quite specific advice for the future ('if you were to use more . . ., then the effect would be . . .')
- offer quite specific description of what they have done in the piece ('in the opening, your use of words suggesting obscurity created an atmosphere of suspense'/'the contrast between light and dark suggested . . .').

My suggestion here is that of these categories, the most *useful* to the writer are those which are most specific. There may be very good reasons why you would want to praise a writer in very general terms ('positive judgment'), but here I am interested in a hard-nosed judgment about what is most *useful* to the writer and I suggest that the categories 'give quite specific advice for the future' and 'offer quite specific description of what they have done in the piece' are the most useful. In each case, the teacher makes *conscious* and *concrete* the *value* and *effect* of certain writing strategies, and therefore makes them available not just for re-use, but for development.

This means adopting an essentially descriptive mode towards the student's writing based on close reading of their text. The phrases 'descriptive mode' and 'close reading' apply to the work outlined above from the 1980s, but they also describe a particular stance when assessing students' writing: the mindset of the literary critic.

Essentially, all literary criticism is a descriptive act in trying to display some variation of, for example:

- 'what is there on the page', including the structures involved in a text
- 'how I am reading '
- the ideological values implicit in a text
- the historical moment reflected or created by the text
- etc.

In using the phrase 'close reading', I am invoking the ghost of a particular school, that of New Criticism, which has been justly condemned for ignoring the historical contexts in which texts are created and read, in effect for treating texts as isolated objects free of authors, readers and socio-political events (see, for example, Eagleton 1983, pp. 46–53). However, I would argue that the discipline of close reading is a strong, positive legacy from New Criticism (given that the value of close reading is recognised as a condition for producing multiple readings of texts rather than a 'correct' reading).

I would further argue that what Stibbs, Dixon and Stratta and the Crediton project (Johnston is treated further below) are doing in the extracts above are committing something very close to New Criticism.

As a tool for *teaching* the texts of *authors brought into the classroom*, New Criticism has received a bad press precisely because it has tended to evoke the image of the teacher-as-lecturer declaiming on the one correct reading of the text and, moreover, on that text as isolated from author, reader and context. However, I believe that a New Critical-based model as a *tool for assessing the written texts of the students within the class-room* has certain advantages. Gilbert, Kamler, Lensmire and others in recent years have reminded us often of the need to question the notion of 'personal voice' in students' writing, which can have the effect of making the *writer* synonymous with the *text*. While the details of their arguments differ, they agree on the need to treat student writing in a way that sees it as distanced from the writer him/herself. Following this, they also agree on the need to treat writing systematically *as text* (see Gilbert 1989, 1990, Kamler 2001, 2003, Lensmire 1998). Despite their being 'growth model' gurus, and hence allegedly perpetuating a Romantic, unconstrained-personal-voice approach to writing (cf. Christie et al. 1991, p. 17, Christie 1993, pp. 76–102), the work of Dixon and Stratta and Wilkinson as outlined above shows a tendency to treat texts in just the opposite way. It shows a tendency to treat texts as *artefacts*, with all of the connections carried by that word to notions of 'art' and 'artifice'. It is an approach which may have strong advantages in encouraging writing as 'something that can be taught systematically and textually' (Kamler 2003, p. 35) when used as an assessment tool.

Johnston's approach is quite different, though still displaying the essentially *descriptive* mindset of a literary critic. His particular brand of 'literary criticism' is much closer to the kind of reader response criticism demonstrated by someone like Stanley Fish. When Fish reads the *Religio Medici* of Sir Thomas Browne, for example, one sees the reading mind in a temporal sequence. Here is an extract from Browne's text:

> That there is but one world, is a conclusion of faith … *Moses* (hath) decided that question, and all is salved with the new terme of creation, that is a production of something out of nothing; and what is that? Whatsoever is opposite to something or more exactly, that which is truely contrary God: for he onely is, all others have an existence with dependency and are something but by a distinction; and herein is Divinity conformant unto Philosophy, and generation not onely founded on contrarieties, but also creation …

and here is Fish reading it

> Browne's strategy is simple … but nonetheless effective. The form of his sentences, in conjunction with a series of prominently displayed logical connectives – 'that is',

'whatsoever' . . . – suggests that the reader is experiencing a progressive clarification of the word and concept 'creation' . . . But each attempt at redefinition and refining serves largely to introduce new problems . . . and there is a growing disparity between the triumphal march of the surface rhetoric . . . and the reader's deepening confusion. 'And what is that?' asks Browne obligingly, as if to acknowledge the difficulty of comprehending a 'production of something out of nothing'; but his answer – 'Whatsoever is opposite to something' – is unhelpfully tautologous, and its elaboration – 'that which is truely contrary unto God' – returns us in a circle to the original question, 'and what is that?'

At this point, the simple declarative 'for he onely is' will be welcomed with relief, if only because it is at least intelligible; but it also implies the futility of the process it interrupts: for if the existence of anything other than God can be affirmed only by linguistic and perceptual distortion, 'are something but by a distinction', the attempt to locate or specify 'that which is truely contrary unto God' is prima facie absurd. Nevertheless, we go on, carried forward by the current of prose into a flood of closely packed quasi-philosophical terms – 'Divinity', 'conformant', 'Philosophy', 'generation', 'contrarieties', 'creation' – which only increases the confusion of the preceding sentences. The reader is exactly where he was at the beginning of the sequence, still waiting for the clarification he has so often been promised. (Fish, 1972: 354–55)

I am not suggesting that either Johnston in this instance or his young writer throw up the complexities which Fish finds in Browne, but the impulse is the same – we see the reading/responding mind in action as it attempts to make sense of the text. It is, again, an essentially *descriptive* act that produces a degree of specificity which not only takes the young writer seriously, but enacts for him or her the issues that are raised for the reader by the piece itself. Once again, this model of literary criticism, when used as a driving impulse for assessment, tends to treat texts as artefacts removed from any personal authorial voice and, thus, again, may have strong advantages in encouraging writing as something to be taught systematically as text.

The effectiveness of assessment

Research shows that students rarely respond effectively to the comments teachers make on their work. A recent review of this literature by Belanger (2004) shows that students fail to understand comments; that feedback generally has a negative effect on students' attitudes towards writing; that teachers' questions frequently confuse students; that students do not read and/or do not act on teachers' comments and that the grade or mark dominates most students' responses. There is comfort to be had, however. The literature also shows the effectiveness of manageable suggestions for improvement; that feedback which is 'focused' is effective; that comments referring to specific skills that were taught in class were read and understood and, importantly, that students became engaged with teacher responses when they could see that their teachers were engaged with their ideas, not just with mechanical errors (Belanger 2004, pp. 43–46). My argument is that the descriptive impulse, the mindset of the literary critic that was demonstrated in the 1980s, has the potential to pick up all of the positives in this research literature because it is a means by which teachers can clearly show students that their work is being taken seriously. More importantly, however, it is about focused, close reading on ideas and on language use.

At this point, I need to face the obvious objection of: a class of 25–30 students, at least a couple of pages each in a piece. Am I seriously suggesting that teachers should be able to give to students the kind of feedback reflected in the detailed comments made by Stibbs, Dixon, Wilkinson et al. and Johnston? Will a teacher ever get past the first assignment? Johnston suggests one solution – the tape recorded response takes seven minutes. His is still a valuable insight in providing a model of oral response to student writing (and also, incidentally, of encouraging teachers to give oral feedback during the writing, rather than just relying on written summative comments after the event). There are other solutions, as well, that make this approach quite manageable in class:

1. *Do not focus on the whole piece.* Respond to those sections of a piece where a worthwhile description can be made. This may only be a paragraph. This is a particularly useful strategy when a particular aspect of the craft has been taught in class, and where you can focus on responding to a small section of the piece which demonstrates that skill.
2. *Do not respond in the same detail to each student each time.* At each 'marking session', isolate a different group of 4–6 students for this kind of detail, keeping good records over the year in order to reach every student equally.
3. *Do not do it in writing.* Oral feedback – including while students are working on a piece – is just as effective, provided it is *specific*, focused and *understood*. In fact, it can be more useful since the student can respond back, ask questions and seek further specific suggestions on the spot.
4. *Use one model text for everybody.* Giving feedback to a piece of writing is a teaching moment. Use a piece from the past, a piece of your own or a volunteered piece from the class to describe in the way Stibbs, Stratta and Dixon, Wilkinson et al. and Johnston do. One text analysed in front of the whole class provides a good teaching moment and valuable feedback that can be applicable to all.

One effect of re-visiting 'the mindset of the literary critic' would be a move away from an obsession with 'text-level processes' as defined in 'Sydney school' genre theory and away from concern with a very limited set of possible 'genres'. It would open up a broader sense of exactly what it is that *can* be addressed in writing pedagogy – be this overall textual structure, powerful uses of language in specific local points in a text or the use of a range of traditional 'literary' devices such as point of view for specific effects. We could revive a language for discussing stylistic and cognitive *development* in writing. We could move on from a view of writing as defined by the 'Sydney school' of genre theorists towards a much broader view as contained in the work of Nancie Atwell, who sees the pedagogy of writing including notions of 'craft' as well as the traditional 'conventions' that include spelling, punctuation and grammar. In Atwell's broad pedagogy, the latter are seen as important and taught thoroughly, but so are areas of 'craft' such as:

- narrative voice
- showing and telling
- the effects of particular vocabulary – such as modifiers, passive and active constructions – on style
- stylistic precision
- reflecting on audience needs and concerns
- focusing content
- openings
- purposes and characteristics of specific genres (in the broadest sense, including areas such as parody)
- embedding context
- narrative structures such as flashbacks and foreshadowings
- organising information and argument
- crafting realistic dialogue
- poetic techniques
- maintaining momentum/pace
- developing characters
- developing themes
- point of view
- plausibility (Atwell 1998, pp. 162–184)

New Criticism has attracted a lot of criticism because it treats the text as reified aesthetic object, but as an impulse underpinning the assessment of writing this is exactly its strength – the valuing of the 'art of writing' in the very sense in which we use that term in the visual arts to refer to 'craft' and 'technique' (Misson 2004).

Conclusion

What I have argued for here is the impulse towards *description* in the assessment of writing – a drive that is concerned to detail *what* has been built and *how* it has been built, which is essentially a drive towards literary criticism. I would not want to take the argument for adopting a New Critical approach to any great extreme – obviously not pursuing, for example, the ingenious readings of a William Empson who illustrated in increasingly complex ways the ambiguities of his chosen texts (Empson 1947). Nevertheless, the essential twin impulses of New Criticism for close reading and for focusing on the text in isolation do force a linguistic move that is very similar to the move from 'voice' to 'text' which is called for in modern approaches to writing education. It has been my argument that along with this move comes an accompanying impulse towards treating the student's piece as *artifice* or *craft*. One consequence of this latter step is an opening up of pedagogy not just to explicit, direct teaching, but to a much broader sense of what 'explicit, direct' teaching can encompass, as exemplified in the work of Nancie Atwell, rather than in the narrower range of 'Sydney school' genre theory. This descriptive impulse is also present in the reader-response-oriented approach taken by Brian Johnston, which exemplifies its own kind of close reading.

In terms of assessment specifically, the mindset of the literary critic which I am suggesting teachers adopt does not necessarily determine in advance what is to be rewarded, but, in taking an essentially descriptive approach, rather seeks to show 'what is there'. In this sense, it may or may not pose something of a challenge to the notion of criterion-referenced assessment and pre-determined rubrics. That would depend on the breadth of such rubrics.

To re-visit the value of such an approach I would like to finish with another short piece from the 80s – from Andrew of Year 9:

> Deep in the dungeons he stands, chained to cold jagged stone wall. He looks up into the corner to see a tiny hole, where the light shines onto a corner. The light is flickering on off, on off from the gulls. As he watches, the light fades away, slowly until he can see no more.

As Johnston and Watson argue, what is important in this situation is not just that Andrew knows that the teacher likes the piece, but that 'he leave knowing that he has drawn a strong *contrast* between the freedom of the gulls and the confinement of the dungeon, using the light as a connecting device' (1983, p. 7). To have described in this way what one has done is one way of making it conscious in order to be able to repeat it and, more importantly, to develop it in the future.

References

Atwell, N. (1998) *In the Middle: New Understandings about Writing, Reading, and Learning*, Portsmouth, NH: Boynton/Cook.

Belanger, J. (2004) 'When will we ever learn?': The Case for Formative Assessment Supporting Writing Development, *English in Australia* 141, Spring, pp. 41–48.

Christie, F. (1993) The 'Received Tradition' of English Teaching: The Decline of Rhetoric and the Corruption of Grammar, in Bill Green (ed.), *The Insistence of the Letter: Literacy Studies and Curriculum Theorizing*, Pittsburgh: University of Pittsburgh Press.

Christie, F., Devlin, B., Freebody, P., Luke, A., Martin, J.R., Threadgold, T. and Walton, C. (1991) *Teaching English Literacy: A Project of National Significance on the Preservice Preparation of Teachers for Teaching English Literacy* – Volume 1, Canberra: Department of Employment, Education and Training.

Doecke, B. and McKnight, L.(2003), Handling Irony: Forming a Professional Identity as an English Teacher', in B. Doecke, D. Homer and H. Nixon (eds), *English Teachers at Work: Narratives, Counter Narratives and Arguments*, Kent Town, SA: AATE and Wakefield Press.

Dixon, J. and Stratta, L. (1981) *Achievements in Writing at 16+. Paper 1. Staging Points Reached in Narratives Based on Personal Experience*, London: Schools Council.

Dixon, J. and Stratta, L. (1982) *Achievements in Writing at 16+. Paper 2. Narratives Based on Imagined Experience: Possible Staging Points at 16+*, London: Schools Council.

Empson, W. (rev. edn 1947) *Seven Types of Ambiguity*, New York: New Directions.

Fish, S. E. (1972) *Self-Consuming Artifacts: The Experience of Seventeenth-Century Literature*, Berkeley, Los Angeles, London: University of California Press.

Gilbert, P. (1989) *Writing, Schooling and Deconstruction*, London: Routledge.

Gilbert, P. (1990) Authorising Disadvantage, in Frances Christie (ed) *Literacy for a Changing World*, Melbourne: ACER.

Goodwyn, A. (2003a) The Professional Identity of English Teachers, Paper given at the Conference of the International Federation for the Teaching of English, Melbourne, July.

Goodwyn, A. (2003b) 'We teach English not literacy': 'Growth' Pedagogy under Siege in England, in B. Doecke, D. Homer and H. Nixon (eds) *English Teachers at Work: Narratives, Counter Narratives and Arguments*, Kent Town, SA: AATE and Wakefield Press.

Hasan, R. (1995) The Conception of Context in Text, in P. H. Fries and M. Gregory (eds), *Discourse in Society: Systemic Functional Perspectives. Meaning and Choice in Language: Studies for Michael Halliday*, New Jersey: Ablex.

Johnston, B.(1987) *Assessing English: Helping Students to Reflect on their Work*, Milton Keynes: Open University Press.

Johnston, B.and Watson, K. (1983) A Model for Evaluation in the English Classroom, *Developments in English Teaching* 2(1), July.

Kamler, B. (2001) *Relocating the Personal: A Critical Writing Pedagogy*, Albany, NY: SUNY Press.

Kamler, B. (2003) Relocating the Writer's Voice – From Story to Voice and Beyond, *English in Australia* 138, Spring, pp. 35–40.

Lensmire, T. (1998) Rewriting Student Voice, *Journal of Curriculum Studies*, 30(3), pp. 261–91.

Locke, T. (2003) Establishing a Counter-Hegemonic Bridgehead: The English Study Design Project, in B. Doecke, D. Homer and H. Nixon (eds), *English Teachers at Work: Narratives, Counter Narratives and Arguments*, Kent Town, SA: AATE and Wakefield Press.

Locke, T. (2004) Reshaping Classical Professionalism in the Aftermath of Neo-Liberal Reform, Joint issue of *English in Australia* 139, and *Literacy Learning: The Middle Years* 12(1), February, pp. 113–21.

Misson, R. (2004) What are We Creating in Creative Writing? *English in Australia* 141, pp. 32–40.

New South Wales Department of Education and Training (NSWDET) Educational Measurement Directorate (2004) *English Language and Literacy Assessment (ELLA) Years 7 and 8, 2004: Writing Task – Marking Procedures*, Educational Measurement Directorate.

Richardson, P. (2004) Literacy, Genre Studies and Pedagogy, in W. Sawyer and E. Gold (eds), *Re-Viewing English in the 21st century*, Melbourne: Phoenix Education.

Sawyer, W. (ed) (1995) *Teaching Writing: Is Genre the Answer?* Sydney: Australian Education Network.

Sawyer, W. (1999a) ELLA: Please Explain, *The Australian Journal of Language and Literacy* 22(1), February, pp. 40–48.

Sawyer, W. (1999b) Testing the Benchmarks: Literacy and Year 7, *English in Australia* 124, pp. 8–15.

Sawyer, W. (2002) Simply Growth? A Study of Selected Episodes in the History of Years 7–10 English in New South Wales from the 1970s to the 1990s, Unpublished PhD thesis: University of Western Sydney.

Stibbs, A. (1981) *Assessing Children's Language: Guidelines for Teachers*, London: Ward Lock Educational and NATE.

Wilkinson, A., Barnsley, G., Hanna, P. and Swan, M. (1980) *Assessing Language Development*, Oxford: Oxford University Press.

Notes

1 For discussions of generational change in other national settings, see Locke (2003, 2004) and Doecke and McKnight (2003).
2 General Certificate of Education/Certificate of Secondary Education.

School
Writing

Chapter 10

Talking to Write

On Line Conversations in the
Literature Classroom

Prue Gill

Preamble

This chapter is about a way of being in the Literature classroom. It is not a how to, or a 'you should do it this way', rather, a reflection on the way that the use of on line discussion with students in my senior Literature classroom seems to be consistent with my desire to work reflectively, collaboratively, and with a focus on the relationship between language and ideas. I will start with an admission. I approached the concept of technology in the classroom with the reluctance of one who reckoned that teaching was primarily about human relationships, and the intervention of technology would inevitably mean some sort of loss in the human dimension of classroom and school communities. Many others felt the same way. We monitored the use of television, we snuck past pinball alleys as if they were sites of some dystopian nightmare, we celebrated the feel of the book in the hand, we were suspicious of the individualism nurtured by the computer screen, and perhaps (though we'd never have seen it this way) we were wary that in the plethora of media and screen opportunities for young people, as teachers we might lose our centrality in the teaching and learning process. It took an unhappy, wayward student who teetered constantly on the edge of being suspended, to change that for me. She taught me that there were some things that could happen well on line which could not happen in the ordinary classroom, or in any conversation we might have outside it.

Were you grumpy with me in class today, or was it something else?

I could send this email to her after a disastrous year 11 Literature class, in which scarcely a moment of time seemed to belong to anyone but her. In this question, I was taking no blame for her inattention, but I was asking her how it had seemed for her.

I'd come out of the class knowing that something had to change. No one in the room was unaffected by the distraction, no discussion was able to proceed unimpeded, no quiet reflection or reading was possible. It was difficult, too, to find a way to confront this face to face without exerting authority in ways I'd rather not. For a start, this student was lightning fast at escaping the room just as the bell was about to announce the end of the lesson. To chase her down the stairwell stretched my dignity, and anyway, I wanted some peace, and I wanted to square it off with other members of the class who bore astonished witness to her attention seeking.

I hardly expected a reply to my question so I was pleased when one came. It started: 'Sort of . . . but no, not you really, it's just that . . .'

That small contact was the beginning of a 'conversation' and relationship which developed over the rest of the year and beyond. Sometimes it was face to face, but whenever things got really difficult in this student's life, it was on line. As a consequence, I started to use email more regularly in situations that we might think of as pastoral care. And gradually I became aware that I was developing a particular 'voice' on line which gave a new dimension to my sense of self as teacher. I began to use this voice as a more significant part of the teaching and learning in my classrooms and I began to see that students, too, might find unexpected possibilities in extending their own habits of talk in the classroom. If, as Vygotsky suggests, 'a thought unembodied in words remains a shadow' (Schultz 2004), then perhaps thoughts written on line might help to shed some light. Or if, in Virginia Woolf's terms, 'nothing has happened until it has been described' (Nicholson 2000), then perhaps an on line discussion, leading to the sharing of writing on line, might constitute a 'new' space for teaching and learning, a border territory between talk and formal writing, in which students could put their ideas into words in a public way.

In this reflection I will explore the ways that on line discussion has extended the conversations I have with students, often about writing, and has strengthened the sense of each class as a small learning community which exists beyond the walls of the class-room. Many of the ideas expressed in this piece come from the students themselves. I have included their comments exactly as they appeared on line – grammar, punctuation and spelling errors included.

I want to add one further comment before I continue. I teach in a large private school for girls, a school which has been at the forefront in the development of a lap top program. Our students have their own lap top, their own school email address, and are automatically connected through a 'wire-less' system to the school intranet and the world wide web when they are in class. Hence an on line learning system – including class discussion lists and chat groups – is part of our daily life. Furthermore, as a teacher I am given excellent support and ready practical assistance in my use of technology. I acknowledge the problem raised by the inequities of educational provision in Australia at the turn of the millennium. But for the purposes of this pedagogical discussion about the role of technology in my teaching of Literature, I must say 'this aside . . .' if I am to explore some of the possibilities for teaching and learning that I am thinking about. Long experience in the government system leads me to think that I'd work in some of the ways I describe, whatever the teaching context, even though access to technology may be more restricted.

Valuing discussion: the politics of the literature classroom

Building an alive and challenging intellectual learning community in the classroom is integral to teaching, but in literature more than in some other subjects, discussion is central to learning, and it must happen well. As a way of illustrating that the quality of discussion in our literature classroom is of the highest significance, I read with students an address given as the PEN Lecture by A. L. Kennedy at the Edinburgh Book Festival in 2001. I give an extract here, by way of explaining a view I share about the teaching of literature:

> Fiction is always about people other than the reader – by agreeing to read it, we agree to collaborate with the minds and voices of the authors, to let them put their words into our mouths, our minds – one of the most intimate intrusions possible. In the case of the novel, we may sustain this intrusion for days, if not weeks. We do this because we tacitly acknowledge that their thoughts can be as important as our own and because they address us, uniquely, with the 'uncritical respect that you give to friends and relatives', if not lovers. We believe in the people authors make, whoever they are, we care about them, understand they are important, help to make them important, suspend our disbelief and take them into our imaginations and this is enjoyable and feels very natural and is an exercise which can begin to make it hard to murder or torture, or harm other people, even other people that we don't know, and which will also make it more difficult for us to stand by while such murders and tortures and harms are committed.
>
> And what else does fiction do? It makes us not alone. The writer writes it in the intimate anticipation of the reader, the reader finds it in a private, personal voice: one which mingles their own and the other's, the familiar stranger's: a music which is there whenever they want it – openly aloud or interior – and which has in it the faith to make words out of nothing. The reading and writing, especially of fiction, is an exercise in the practice of faith.

What I draw from Kennedy's words is her sense that the reading and discussion of literature can be both private and public in nature, and in being public, it is inevitably political. Through narrative, for example, we can tease out, identify with, or reject ways of negotiating the freedoms and constraints that are implicit in democratic process. Does Ellen compromise her new found sense of independence in her relationship with

Mr Jevons at the end of Patrick White's *Fringe of Leaves*, or will she be finally free to express her sensuality openly and with ease, to speak with her own voice? Do her actions reinforce or challenge prevailing social views about relations between men and women, freeperson and convict, black and white 'Australians' early in the story of white settlement? How does our discussion of these questions help us to think analytically and critically about the world we inhabit a couple of hundred years later? Can we use our understandings about White's protagonist to help us analyse the situation of the woman speaker in Gwen Harwood's sonnet 'In the Park', or the application of the law of provocation in the case of the murder of a woman by her husband, or the implications of the loss of the languages of minority populations. A shared narrative enables us to debate what we mean by justice or self determination. Using narrative we can talk about shaping futures. Or as A. L. Kennedy suggests, through narrative we are lead to realise that the thoughts of 'the other', and their particular standpoint, are as important as our own.

School curriculum is insufficiently informed, it seems to me, by the idea that democracies must be continually reinvented rather than taken for granted, or unquestioned. This view underpins my goal to ensure that everyone develops a voice in the class – everyone knows that others will be attentive to their views. I aim to engender an attitude to authority that is respectful, but questioning. I do not wish to be the central voice in the classroom. There are some issues on which we may collectively agree – there are others on which we will remain divided. This sense that we can consciously model values of democracy through classroom process underpins the voice I value in the classroom. Gunther Kress, in *Writing the Future: English and the making of a culture of innovation* (1995), argues for an English classroom that is not only deconstructive, but reconstructive. Like A. L. Kennedy, he suggests that the classroom can give students a conception of what it is to be a citizen of democracy, because at one and the same moment it can encourage them to consider their voice simply as one of many, and yet foster their agency as an individual. For these reasons, the clarifying of ideas and values that happens in the English and Literature classrooms, and the acknowledgement of the implications of particular stances or actions, can constitute the basis of an education addressing the important issues of our times.

Like Kress and Kennedy, I want the classroom to be a space where 'meaningful social interaction broadens people's sense of self beyond the "me" and "I" into the "we" and "us"' (Grossman et al. 2000, p. 8). I like the notion of interdependence that is implied by the term 'community' and want to think of the class as constituting a group who 'participate together in discussion and decision making, and who share certain practices that both define the community and are nurtured by it' (Grossman 2000, p. 9). And so I think that part of my role is to help students develop confidence in using language to pinpoint and develop their ideas, to extend their ways of seeing, to 'broaden their sense of self', to 'nourish the collective identity or rescue the memory of the community that generates it' (Galeano 1992, p. 169; see also Knight 2004, p. 78).

Talk, writing, and talk about writing, are thus not ends in themselves but can be a way of helping us to construct our futures – both public and private.

The nurturing of talk

One of the luxuries of teaching senior students is that it is quite easy to break down some of the formal and artificial barriers that commonly exist in schools. My students wander into class – sometimes a little early, sometimes a little late. They bring their recess talk with them, and I like that. They flick in and out of personal chat as they prepare for what we will be doing in Literature. It may take 10 minutes to set up the class (which, admittedly, is 75 minutes long). In the context of the institution, that can make me uneasy, but I see such informality as a way of learning about each other, and hence as contributing to our ability to have a conversation about an idea or a text or a piece of writing. Strict boundaries are so 'naturalised' in schools, that it is easy to be nervous of blurring them. I have to remind myself how artificial the bell is, how artificial the notion that we're only working when we're doing something formal. I like to value the 'liminal spaces' – what I earlier refer to as 'border' territory – as being productive. I tell my students that my mother broke her hip, that I've spent the night in hospital, that I saw a good film, that I am outraged by something in the press. They do the same. And then when they email me they often add – 'hope the weekend is good', or ask 'how's your mother?'

And so often we move into the content of the class in a ragged manner. And our typical literature class is based primarily on talk. Take the day we are studying the stories of Beverley Farmer. I am trying to get students to approach the stories via close analysis of short passages – to increase their confidence in moving from observations about the representation of a particular moment, to broader, more general conclusions about Farmer's writing and her positioning of us as readers. This is the approach they need to feel confident of in the all important final exam. I have allocated stories to pairs or groups of three students, and they are to make a class presentation on their story, via the analysis of an extract they've chosen themselves. I want them to draw on language and stylistic features in their discussion as well to discuss connecting or overarching ideas. We sit with our chairs in a circle, text in hand, and a pencil for annotations or jottings. It is students who lead the discussion.

'There's heaps of dialogue' we are told,
'she often uses Greek language as well'
'and she uses Greek English like "you hev" and "womans never paint their
    hairs here"'
'that's cute, and what about "you mek fool"!'

My role is to ask the questions that help them move from passage, to story, and then across the collection of stories. 'How might the capturing of the Greek/English difference affect the story?' I ask. I push them to locate the evidence for the assertions they make in the words of the text, in the tone or mood or rhythm or metaphor or image. 'Where do you see this?' ... 'can you show us?' ... 'what makes you say that?' ... 'what is the implication here?' ... 'if you follow that line where do you end up?' ... 'what conclusions are you beginning to draw?' I want them to be talking about language and meaning.

I also tell them, at the beginning of the discussion, that later on I will ask them to reflect on what they saw happening during the discussion, but this time on line. In an earlier class, I have given them an extract from Ron Ritchhart's *Intellectual Character: what is it, why it matters and how to get there*. Ritchhart offers a framework with which to understand intellectual 'character' as a broad repertoire of practices. He has reduced these practices to a small list, including curiosity, open mindedness, scepticism, strategic thinking, metacognition, and truth seeking. A group of teachers in a number of neighbouring schools have been teasing out how they 'interpret' these dispositions by making careful observations of classroom behaviours. Thinking it will help my students reflect on their own strengths as a learner, I have talked with them about this project, and I'm hoping that they can use the framework of intellectual dispositions to help them think about the classroom discussion. Where do they see these dispositions in action? For homework, the students are to think back over the discussion and respond to two questions posted on the on line discussion list:

1. *Could you think back over the discussion we had in class today, and jot down a note about a moment when you saw one of the dispositions of intellectual character (curiosity, open-mindedness, metacognition, truth/understanding seeking, strategic thinking, scepticism) at play? You might need to refer back to the reading I gave you.*
2. *Thinking about your own approach to learning, with which of these dispositions do you most identify, or alternatively, which do you think best describes your style? Justify your response.*

And so the process of the class is firstly to talk about writing (Farmer's), and to follow that with writing (in the informal manner of talk, on line) about their talking.

On line talk/writing

I use an email distribution list of class members to attach tasks or a resource, to ask students to bring a text to class, or do some prior reading, or preparatory thinking about a particular question. These are the sorts of things I used to do at the end of a class, and sometimes still do, but I often find myself sending these messages online. Such notices could equally well happen on a Literature noticeboard. I also use email to follow up students who are absent, or send them a note about what we covered in class, or remind someone that they've not submitted due work. Email distribution lists are not the key to pedagogical change, they simply make some things easy, and they help me to develop the conversational relationship. The following email, for example, was sent to the student mentioned earlier in this chapter:

> *Just checking in to see how the reading is going – since I'm on the email and I was thinking about you. I have to go now and do some reading of my own – yes, Fringe of leaves. Otherwise I won't be up to date for class tomorrow!*
> *See you then.*

Her reply was swift:

> *Fringe of Leaves is the hardest book that i have ever read. i really do not think that i can read it. i am only up to page 50 and i am really struggling. please can you help me. is there any way that you can get this book on tape? what do i do? i am really enjoying cats eye though, it is really good and i thought that i would hate it but once you get into it, it is really good. please write back*

I felt pleased by the positive tone and the query, and thought at the time, that it was unlikely we would have had this conversation face to face. There seemed fresh possibility about the fact that we were both out of our ordinary contexts. Later she asked more about a task I'd set:

> *i dont really understand how i should go about the significant moment component. i have done all of the rest but i dont know if i should include quotes or just make it dot points or a large summary?*

Teachers receive queries like this from students all the time, but not from all students. I'd not been asked a question of any kind by this student and I began to think she was not yet comfortable enough in the classroom to do so. In this case the email was significant in building a way of working together.

Email is personal, and usually private. The discussion list, on the other hand, is public, and therefore more daunting, and more interesting. In class discussions it is possible to be a listener only, to seek support for a view through body language, to moderate tone according to feedback, to slip back into the friendship group. This can't happen in a discussion list. Nevertheless, the questions I set at the end of the discussion about Farmer's stories were straightforward, and while it would have been simple for students to submit their response individually, I wanted them to 'hear' the ideas that others were expressing and in this way to develop a shared language about learning.

One student, writing of the long discussion we had teasing out our responses to Andoni, the husband in the story 'Pumpkin', says:

> *Mostly, I saw the disposition to be' truth-seeking and understanding' – that is, we all tried to work out the importance of using 'copper' instead of bronze, or the importance of the aside in the brackets in the 'A Woman with Black Hair' passage. I think during the 'Woman with Black Hair' passage we each tried to pinpoint why it made us feel the way it did . . . But its very difficult to pinpoint specific actions of thoughts because many of the things we discussed in class can be classified in several ways.*

Another student takes the same moment in the discussion but uses it in a different way:

> *I thought there was some strategic thinking involved when we discussed why Farmer used 'copper' to describe Andoni. Some people used chemistry knowledge about the properties of copper to theorize about this image. Maybe there were signs of metacognition when everyone gave their own opinions as to whether the descriptions within the brackets were Farmer's or phsyco stalking man's thoughts. People explored how the section made them personally feel; looked into their own minds.*

For a third student, a different disposition is at play.

> *During the discussion many people were obviously thinking critically about Farmer's work, and looking beyond what Farmer had written, especially about the imagery used in 'Pumpkin' and the narrative style of 'A Woman with Black Hair'. I think that people were generally open minded and willing to accept and discuss other people's ideas to try to understand both the meaning Farmer had intended and what the stories meant to us.*

Later, we could discuss the differences expressed in the reflections, and conclude that it was very difficult to make neat identification of intellectual qualities at play. But we decided to keep working with the ideas. The second question seemed easier for students to respond to, and they were quite eloquent when writing about a sense of their own learning styles. The following extracts are glimpses into their much longer comments, but give a sense of how prepared the students were to give attention to the theory. I was surprised by the emphasis on scepticism:

> *I think that my main approach is using curiosity, scepticism, and . . . truth seeking? I love to collect details, string them together and then argue about them (usually changing my mind about them halfway through). I think everyone uses scepticism we don't just accept things at face value but try to find out more. Unfortunately I'm not very good at metacognition . . . and sometimes I abandon logic for emotion and intuition.*

I definitely have a curious nature, but this is mostly due to the fact that I seem to be sceptical of almost everything. Despite this, however, I am moderately open-minded when it comes to certain aspects of my learning (e.g. new study/memory method) . . . Overall I believe all I really want to do is find the truth, in whatever I'm doing. That is usually why I'm so curious and ask too many questions!!

I think I am naturally very sceptical about most things, but I am also very interested in under-standing what I am learning, as I really don't like just accepting things just because that's the way they are. I think that being metacognitive would be very valuable, but I don't think this is really a skill that I possess, although I think Lit is a subject that really makes you do this. I think I am fairly open-minded, although it's very hard to really know of course.

That is a good point, I think to myself, and take note of it. We should talk about it further. How can we tell whether we are open minded or not? How can we recognise our own blind spots? Can we help each other become more aware of the assumptions beneath the conclusions we draw? Another student raises similar questions about the difficulty of self analysis:

I think I use a lot of strategic thinking and truth seeking in my work, especially when doing subjects like Literature and History where you need to examine writing critically and question work very carefully. I find that there is a lot of open mindedness required to properly do the tasks set, such as passage analysis. However, something like metacognition is difficult, because I think it requires you to examine yourself in a way that may be difficult. Reflecting on your way of thinking I believe is something easier to do when you can be more objective.

And this final extract focuses on the interplay of the dispositions:

I believe we display all of these charactaristics at various times – they are aspects of human nature so its a hard question to work out which best describe us. I reckon i'm quite a mixture of these qualities – some more that others sometimes – but fairly evenly distributed. I've got a good dose of the bad qualities too, like procrastination, not caring, grumpiness, lack of motivation – we cant forget these either because i think its harder to overcome these things than to develop the others. When i get over boredom and closed-mindedness, it automatically leads to the good intellectual qualities we have been discussing

These are thoughtful comments which show that the students took the task seriously. As I reread them now, I realise that the more interesting question would be to ask the students whether Ritchhart's framework or theory was helpful in thinking about themselves as learners. If yes, in what way? Did it alter their sense of intelligent behaviours? Did they find it enlightening, or confidence building or surprising or useful?

Nevertheless these personal reflections made public, journal style, served several purposes. The comments drew on a shared pedagogical language which we could then use through the rest of the year, and thus added a dimension to the discussions between us all in the literature classroom. They also affirmed the value of including student talk in my own thinking about teaching and learning. Both the theory and their response to it reinforce the potential of collaborative learning. But they also alerted me to the way I was phrasing questions on the discussion list. The level of reflection in the reply will in part depend on the wording of the question. I determined to build the language of intellectual character more consciously into our discussions, employing the terms in my own on line response to their writing, thus extending the terrain for discussion, and reinforcing the value of reflection about learning.

Developing analytical thinking on line

Another possibility offered by the discussion line is the way it can be used to extend and develop the conversation that we have in class. I asked a different class to work further on a poem we had read that day – Gwen Harwood's poem 'Barn Owl'. The task was to be done outside class:

> *Hello everyone*
> *Great discussion today about some of the details of Barn Owl – now for your theory of what the poem is 'about' – ie the big ideas dealt with. Try to give evidence, which shows HOW you are reading particular moments in the poem. I suggest about 100–150 words. Look forward to reading your comments.*

This is a fairly typical sort of homework or follow up task. The advantage offered by the discussion list, however, is that the responses are public, and the discussion line is saved for future reference. It provides a bank of ideas for students to draw from when they write their formal analysis for assessment. Here are some extracts of student writing – exploratory in tone still, since this was early in the year. Most write in the tentative voice of one who is still thinking the poem through. Nevertheless, they show how students feel confident to focus on very different aspects of the poem. One student writes:

> *A central theme in Barn Owl that I interpreted was the mindless cruelty of mankind. The child 'crept out' to kill a helpless owl, described as his 'prize who swooped home at this hour'. It is clear that the child has watched the owl before to know when and where it would return, and thus had intentionally planned to shoot it. It doesn't matter that in the end the child put his 'head upon (his) father's arm, and wept,' to show remorse, because the deed is already done; crying won't bring the owl back . . . Even in the poem the child is aware of (his) own 'cruelty', yet only when it is too late.*

For another:

> *Perhaps the child 'who believed death clean/ and final, not this obscene' is a reflection on the many young soldiers who too had to confront death – which leads to the question, how old is the main character? From lines such as 'a horny fiend, I crept' or 'old No-sayer', which are like childish imaginings, and also reference to baby's hair in 'wisp haired judge', I gathered them to be somewhere round 8 to 12. However, the age or the sex of the child wasn't important to me as I read – it was the journey that mattered.'*

And for someone else, the central idea is situated elsewhere:

> *The speaker in the poem uses the act of killing the owl as a gateway for him or herself from childhood into adulthood. The quote 'master of life and death' indicates that this action of killing is enabling the speaker to take control of his or her otherwise out of control life. The shift in the tone of the poem, from harsh and resentful at the start 'let him dream of a child obedient, angel mild – old No-Sayer', to vulnerable and innocent at the end 'I leaned my head upon my father's arm, and wept', shows the journey that the speaker is wanting to make, but in fact cannot as he or she is not emotionally ready for it yet. Instead of being empowered by the killing of the owl, the speaker ends up needing the support of his or her father more than ever 'My father reached my side, gave me the fallen gun. "End what you have begun"'.*

Here the students are grappling with the literary features of the work. They write of a central idea, of how the shattering of the child's innocence might metaphorically reflect the experience of young soldiers at war, of shift in tone. They point to the irony (without yet naming it) of the child's vulnerability at the end. Another student uses more structural analysis to lead to conclusions about the meaning of the poem:

> *It's written in a 6-line verse, with rhyming pairs of line 1–3, 2–4, and 5–6, however, because the events are written in chronological order, with a main character (the child), it takes on the air of a lyrical short story. This is further enhanced by the structure – a beginning (the child creeping along) a middle (the child shooting the owl) and a clear conclusion (father instructing him to 'finished what [the child] had begun'). There is also a character journey – the child learning about death and their own 'cruelty', though their confusion about what this journey will mean is apparent in the last two lines: 'owl-blind in early sun/for what I had begun.' This painful loss of innocence seems to be the poet's main message.*

My role is to tie up the conversation at the end. I make no comment on form or structure or grammatical ease, and individual contributions are rarely singled out. My aim is to respond to the sum of the 'talk', to the ideas raised. For the moment, students are liberated from a focus on writing skills:

Thanks for these insights, which really add to my way of thinking about the poem too. I like the way that you've commented on the paradox (not in those terms I know) of experience about life—that part of the gaining of knowledge is our awareness of what we don't know. The child does not discover the expected, rather the unexpected awareness of vulnerability, the need of the father at the very moment that independence is sought. And another paradox here is that while the ultimate power might be to take a life, in fact the death of the bird overpowers the child—whose misery is mirrored in the eyes of the bird.

I like too the way some of you have commented on structure, form, language—that it is a lyrical narrative, that mood changes, that there is a sense of progression, that using an unexpected word like 'stuff' makes a difference to our reading. It's great too that some of you contextualised your reading, so imagined that this may will be a comment on war—a mindless cruelty that is only understood after the event. I like the comment too, that the transition the child makes is irreversible—lovely.

Feel free to use any of the ideas you've read about in your own way, to help you come to your own reading of the poem.

In these comments I am teaching, modelling both analysis and written reflection. I reiterate the theory that we will read differently, can gain insights from each other, and that our own readings will be enhanced if we draw on these insights. I am both validating points made by the students, and putting them in new light—using, for example, a word like paradox in a way that they might easily model. But I do not wish to be the authority. I aim to keep questions open rather than tie them up, to encourage the students to keep thinking, since there is much more analytical work to be done.

Sharing more formal writing and teacher feedback

The idea of having a discussion about student writing, rather than 'correcting' writing, is a staple of English teaching, hardly new. A glance through the issues of *English in Australia* or *Idiom*[1], journals which have consistently aired the debates about responding to student writing, will attest to this. It is a recurring theme, too, in the STELLA website (see 'Language Modes in the English/literacy Classroom,' this volume). But it is not easily managed in the senior classroom environment, mainly because it takes lots of time, a scarce resource when the imperative of assessment drives the senior years. On the other hand, I have found that my online voice works conversationally at my desk or at home, and I can talk whenever I'm ready.

Part of the process of developing collaborative learning is getting the students to be less self conscious about sharing more formal writing. It is common for English teachers at senior levels to work with sample A+ material or to post outstanding essays on the school intranet so that students have access to them. But I want students to feel that it is not only exemplary or complete written work that is valuable to others. If they think of their written work as representing thought 'in progress' and if they value that progress, then they will gain from reading the work of others at all stages of development. It is often appropriate, too, to share the comments I make to one student, with others. Similarly, if I am asked a question via email, I often send my reply (along with a copy of the question) to everyone in the class. I want questioning and thinking to be celebrated.

When the formal written analyses on 'Barn Owl' were submitted, I felt that most students were writing much more confidently. The next extract was one I 'posted' as an online resource for other students to read. It was not the most sophisticated or complex, but showed a real development for the student who wrote it (my contribution and comments in bold – I use a coloured font for these online).

Strong language is used to convey the serious impact that this action has on the child's life. The owl is described as 'ruined', not just 'shot'. This word expresses not only the notion that the owl will invariably die, but the child's life is 'wrecked' now as well **at least for the moment.** *Wounds can heal, but by using this particular word a sense of finality is implied for all involved in the poem.*

Language is also often used in relation to 'eyes' and being 'blind.' The owl is depicted with 'daylight-riddled eyes'. It is at this point in the poem that the relationship between the child and the owl becomes unequal as the boy seems to hold an advantage over the bird. However, the child eventually describes himself as 'owl-blind'. This demonstrates that all along the child has himself been blind to the consequences his actions will lead to for both himself and the owl. **Good point**

I love your analysis here S, and your good use of text to back up your points. There is much more to be said – particularly in the relationship between father and child, the bid for independence, the blundering attempts we all make to 'prove' ourselves, especially to prove ourselves as independent in the eyes of our parents. But you could also talk more about the literary features, the power of the images etc – much in the way that you've done so nicely with your early comments about tone.

By sharing extracts like this, and my response, I hope that the atmosphere will be set for a face to face class conversation about writing – their own, and the writers whose work they study.

Interactive discussion

It is the potential to enhance collaborative learning through interactive on line discussion that I have found most surprising about on line work. One of the challenges for me has been to move students towards addressing their comments to each other, rather than implicitly directing them to me. I finally realised that once I set a new discussion thread going, I should not be enthusiastically tempted to respond to each new idea as it was posted. I had to discipline myself to let the student talk proceed unimpeded. I learned this lesson when I was technically thwarted from participating during one holiday period. I had taken a week of leave attached to the September school holidays in order to travel, and I planned to maintain contact with my year 12 students as they began to prepare for exams ahead, via a web based discussion group. Because of a hitch, all my attempts to log on to the school discussion list from internet cafes in out of the way places failed. Fortunately, my absence seemed integral to the success of the talk. Rather than writing to please me, or to ask questions of me as authority, the students really started to work with each other and even with students in the other Literature class. After initial concern expressed on the discussion line about my whereabouts – physically and virtually – they went on without me. These few comments were amongst the opening ones made:

> *Hey there everyone,*
> *Well, I just re-read The Bacchae today, and was a bit confused about something. At the start of the play, Cadmus is walking to go and worship Dionysus, however at it's ending, Cadmus is also punished for not worshipping Dionysus – though he DID recognise Dionysus as a God.*
> *Was he punished for – 1.) Just thinking that by worshiping the God would be to shed fame on the family. 2.) That his offspring were refusing to accept Dionysus and therefore he should be punished as well. Or 3.) Am I just totally missing the point ALL together? Cheers, and I hope everyone is having a well deserved rest.*

> *I'm not really with it with the Bacchae, but I don't think Cadmus did anything directly wrong, I think he was punished because of his grandson, you know how one person can shame the whole family, or destroy the family name, and how in Romeo & Juliet he says 'a plague on both your houses' by which he means a plague on both their families, even though not necessary everyone in the family did something wrong the whole family is punished for it.*

> *Hi everyone! Just in response to what L was discussing . . . Lise, I really like your idea about how Cadmus may have been punished because he had the wrong motivations for his worship of Dionysus. It definitely seems like he's a bit half-hearted about it all – he says to Pentheus, 'Even if, as you say, Dionysus is no god . . . lie royally' which might indicate that he himself has doubts about Bacchism and just how divine Dionysus really is. He accepts Dionysus however because, as you said, 'credit (will) come to us and to all our family', and also, it seems, to just follow the safe road – 'Don't stray beyond pious tradition'. So perhaps Cadmus was punished for his shallow devotion.*

This is the beginning of a discussion that went on for 28 pages during the school holidays, involving 14 voices, several from another class. For much of the time, there was no teacher participation at all, and as a consequence the students were writing for each other, without the need to please. Like conversation, the comments made in the course of the discussion were exploratory – jumping from idea to idea, slipping between texts, leaving some ends dangling, tying others up, making make excellent links across texts as they explored analytical concepts such as 'experience', 'colonialism', 'the other'. As I read the discussion now, some time later, I notice the way students are working together to nut out their interpretations, even across classes. There seems no need to gain a competitive edge. Their talk is filled with phrases such as:

'But I also think you and S are right in saying that . . .'
'I had a puzzle that I just found out the answer to so I hope if anyone was wondering this
will help . . .'
'But I just had another question which I hope someone can help me with . . .'
'does anyone know . . . when and how, and why, do you think this happened?'
'In our class we had a similar discussion about . . .'
'Tell me what you think . . .'
'Just writing(sic) to add my intelligent advice to this holiday chat!'
'Just another thought – has anyone had thoughts about . . .?'
'I hope this all makes sense . . .'

They offer each other advice:

Plus guys read over those notes that we took on that French Philosopher we watched the video a fair while ago – but he was on about natural desires and impulses and how animals surpass humans in that they act on these impulses. Also that they are forever naked and not aware of it therefore free from society's restrictions and experience. These ideas fit in with both Blake and White.

And some begin to show quite subtle connections, such as this student commenting on a character in *A Fringe Of Leaves*

Austin's commited reading of his Virgil obviously shows how although he cannot physically take part in the 'rural life', he still wishes to obtain knowledge of such a lifestyle. Interestingly when Austin reads aloud to Ellen a section of his Virgil, he comments to her something along the lines of 'one forgets how little you understand', yet it is Ellen who understands more about rural life, than he. I also find it interesting how Austin comments at a later point in the text that 'outside the pages of Virgil sheep and cows can be counted amongst the bores', but if he had a real appreciation of what Virgil stood for, and you could even go further to say a real appreciation of Ellen, he would not have voiced such an opinion.

It is commonly acknowledged in pedagogical discussions that students learn most effectively when they can relate new material to their existing knowledge – and that is what this group of students seem to be doing. They are grappling with ideas raised across the texts about social and cultural values, about change, about threats to old certainties. I am hoping too that they will see how ideas such as this can lead to long discussions about the shape and values of our own culture – the views that are privileged, or mainstream, the voices which fight to be heard. I want them to be sorting out how these ideas can help them think about how they might like to see their own society in the future.

I can see, also, the potential of the discussion line as a transition between classroom talk and essay writing. While the writing on the discussion list is very close to talk, it strikes me that there is a difference in the level of reflection that is shown when there is space for deep thought. The writing is different too – more alive and interesting than much of their essay writing, which often seems tongue-tied, and bound by mechanical adherence to form or their idea of 'getting it right'. I find myself asking the students to write in their essays with the engagement they show when writing on the discussion list.

Some tentative conclusions about changes in teaching practice

What are the things that have changed for me since I've been working regularly on line? The question is hard to answer in a neat way – since on line work is just one of a repertoire of approaches to teaching and learning. And because things often happen spontaneously, or simultaneously, or work in concert with each other – it is not easy to be sure of what leads to what.

One change is that my response to their writing is far more able to be framed in terms of a conversation, rather than in terms of correction. I write all my comments in another colour. I don't use the 'insert comment' facility in WORD, since that either underlines the comment, investing it with symbolic power I don't wish it to have, or offers a callout which gives insufficient space. I tell students to think of the coloured words as my voice. And when I 'intervene' in their writing because I have something to say – because I'm following through an idea in the work, or asking a question, or adding an aside – I am thinking of my intervention as an active part of the teaching and learning process, both for me and for them. Hence there is a shift in power relationship between me and the students – I know it remains, but I think in a lesser way. I am building my relationships through a 'voice' that I develop on line, and in a way that retains my centrality to the classroom, but perhaps diffuses my power.

An associated change lies in the conception of writing as work in progress rather than a finished product. There is potential here to release young writers from the tyranny of getting everything right. Ultimately, students may say that their writing is finished for now, but they acknowledge that some time in the future, they might do something different with the ideas in the piece.

Another change is that writing becomes public, and students don't feel shy or fragile or vulnerable about sharing their writing. In some ways, the very act of having the 'conversation' about the writing, validates the writing itself. The discussion becomes public, building the community of learners, sharpening analytical skills, building confidence in putting ideas into written words, exposing students to a whole range of ideas, from which they can draw to arrive at their own readings.

In this process I am also modelling – in that my response to the writing, in writing, becomes part of the teaching. All this has a transformative power I think – so that we are better able to think of the classroom as a learning community, of which I'm part.

In that sense, the relationships between teacher and student, and student and student, draw us all into a common task, and we work with each other. Students must adjust to the reduced emphasis on grading, ranking and practising exam tasks (although we do that too). For some, this is difficult and, given the culture of the final years of schooling, understandably so. It leaves me with questions too – could this approach in some way disadvantage them? I am hoping not, but I worry about it. Finally, I am learning a great deal myself about language and literature – specifically, their centrality to ideas, to culture and to an education which prepares young people to become active in shaping their private and their public worlds.

References

Galeano, E. (1992) *We Say No: Chronicles, 1963–1991*, M. Fried et al (trans), New York: W.W. Norton.

Grossman, P., Wineburg, S. and Woolworth, S. (2000) *What makes Teacher Community Different from a Gathering of Teachers?* An occasional paper, Centre for the Study of Teaching and Policy, University of Washington.

Kennedy A L. (2001) The PEN Lecture delivered at the Edinburgh Book Festival. http://www.a-l-kennedy.co.uk/PENhtm.

Knight, T. (2004) The Classroom: Democracy and Citizenship, *Curriculum Perspectives* 24(3), Sept. 2004, pp. 75–79.

Kress, G. (1995) *Writing the Future: English and the Making of a Culture of Innovation*, Sheffield: National Association for the Teaching of English.

Nicholson, N. (2000) *Virginia Woolf*, New York: Viking.

Ritchhart, R. (2002) *Intellectual Character: What It Is, Why It Matters, and How to Get It*, San Francisco, CA: Jossey-Bass.

Salmon, G. (2000) *E-Moderating: the Key to Teaching Online*, London: Kogan Page.

Schultz, R. (2004) Vygotsky and Language Acquisition. Accessed in March 2005 at: http://www.english.sk.com.br/sk-vygot.html.

Note

1 *English in Australia* is the journal of the Australian Association for the Teaching of English, and *Idiom* is the journal of the Victorian Association for the Teaching of English. Note in particular the special edition of *Idiom* titled: *Responding to Students' Writing*, 1996 (vol. 1).

Chapter 11

Temporary Validation

The Challenges of Remedial

'Literacy' Programs

Bella Illesca

Introduction

This morning I gained a glimpse of our working conditions through fresh eyes. Deborah, an American English teacher doing Emergency Teaching was appalled at the small, cramped space we had squashed ten big year 9 boys and 4 girls into for our remedial literacy lesson during period 2. I am so used to this room that I had forgotten that the small space we occupy was once the office between two portable classrooms. I no longer notice our drab surroundings: the dirty dishwater-coloured linoleum floor, the moth-eaten lace curtain covering an aluminium framed window, the outdated resources gathering dust, and the cold, damp, dullness of the room.

As the 14 Year 9 literacy students turned up and weaved their way over chairs and around each other to find a spot around the table in the centre, their legs became entangled with the chair legs, tables, books, extension cords and other students' feet. There was the usual crying out that was probably heard in the adjoining classrooms, 'Aaw come on Tim, move over!'; 'I hate this room'; 'Miss can't we go to the computer room?'; 'This is such a povo school!'; 'Why do the girls always get to sit next to the heater?' Bucket chairs are pressed hard against each other and once you're in you can't get out until the person who is by the doors moves with his/her chair. Keith arrived last and straddled Duke's legs as he stepped over him. Paul called out, 'Unwanted physical contact!' Deborah and I stood like soldiers on opposite sides of the room looking down at the 14 warm bodies in front of us. Willing them to settle down.

Deborah was so appalled by what she saw that she asked the kids to think about writing a letter to the editor or the school's principal complaining about the conditions. For the past few weeks we had been working on the film *Billy Elliot* with a computer based writing unit and attempts to get the kids to use pen and paper in this room had always been met with serious resistance. So, we had decided that when we were timetabled in this room we would focus on oral work such as screening sections of the film for discussion. I was pleased with Deborah's suggestion and I was interested to see how they would respond. In her animated way, Deborah explained the potential of letter writing and described how as a newly wed she had launched a letter writing campaign which had resulted in her being allowed to go to sea with her sailor husband. But even as she was relating what, to me, was an interesting story, the boys were interrupting her with fart noises. I glared. I tried other things to encourage them to pay attention to Deborah's anecdote. But nothing stopped them.

Her instruction to brainstorm, draw or make a list of dot points of their thoughts and feelings about working in this room were met with cries of, 'I can't', 'I don't have a pen', 'I don't know what to write', 'I need paper', 'What's the point?', 'You just said everything!' 'Why don't YOU write it?' and 'Hey, look! Nipple cramp!'.

Here are some of the points that the students produced (their original spelling retained):
* WE are crouded in a small room
* You get costrofopic
* Some people fart and it stinks
* I feel inbarasted to go in there
* We some times have to wright on our lap
* When its hot we cant open the windows because there broken
* You can't open the door fully because all the tables and the chairs are in the way
* When we walk through the other rooms to get in here it inbarracing
* Its hard to listen to our teachers because we can hear the teachers in the other rooms yelling
* No computers
* To squishie
* Depressed can't put books on table
* I don't feel like working
* Chars are not very conforable
* Get to hot in summer
* We work in cramped space and some people can't even get a table

By the end of the lesson, we had collected a list from each of them and they were told that if they wanted to they could continue with this in the computer room next lesson.

Journal Entry, 21 August 2003

The following chapter describes my professional learning while coordinating a literacy intervention program at a state secondary school. I had worked as a secondary English teacher at this school for several years, and had even acted as English Coordinator. While it might seem logical to invite an English teacher to coordinate a literacy intervention program, it proved challenging for me to reconcile my professional knowledge and experience as a teacher of English with my role as coordinator of this program. My sense of the rich possibilities of English language conflicted with the functional model of literacy that I was obliged to teach, and I was left with a feeling of bad faith as I worked with colleagues and students in an effort to improve the students' literacy skills. How could I justify drilling and skilling students who were already alienated from the English curriculum and schooling in general? Why were we resorting to such measures rather than endeavouring to make the English curriculum a richer experience for them? I have described my struggle with the culturally (and politically) loaded nature of such literacy intervention programs elsewhere (see Illesca 2004). My purpose here is to use the data I gathered as a practitioner researcher in order to provide a small window on how students who had been labelled 'deficit' experienced such a program.

The Policy Environment

This school was one of 118 Victorian secondary schools with 'poor' results, as measured against the *Curriculum and Standards Framework* (or CSF) (BOS 2000), a list of learning outcomes that all students across the state are supposed to achieve at certain stages in their schooling. Because the school was recognised as 'disadvantaged' and 'under-performing', it was to receive a portion of the $81.6 million state government funding to improve 'literacy and numeracy outcomes for students in years 7–10' (DE&T 2002, p. 1). I was aware that as a teacher who was agreeing to be a part of this state-wide program, I was also accepting the political, social and cultural parameters within which it was operating. This became evident to me when even before we began our work, a colleague and I were asked to write the school's 'Outcomes Compact', an accountability contract that would be signed by the school and the government. We wrote this document with increasing awareness of how we were taking on the same language of accountability and performance management that had framed the state government's own plan, a plan defined in terms of 'intended outcomes', 'performance measures', 'output measures', 'targets', 'reliable data' – all signs (as we were to find out in the early weeks of the program) that would mediate how we would see and act towards our students.

It was made clear to us by the school's 'Action Plan', the 'Outcomes Compact' and the regional administration that the success of the program would be measured by a combination of teacher judgement, staff opinion surveys, the CSF II and student attendance data. Significantly, the other 'measures of student achievement' would be standardised tests. In response to the school and the region's call for 'data' to identify the students 'at risk' who would be invited to participate in the literacy programs in Years 7, 8, 9 and 10, we were obliged to implement a comprehensive testing regime, including the DART at Year 7 and the Upper TORCH comprehension test at Years 8, 9 and 10. I will not go into detail about what each of these tests purportedly reveals about an individual student's 'literacy', merely make the point that such tests are based on a narrow version of literacy that constructs students in deficit ways – i.e. concentrating on what students *don't* know and *can't* do, and de-emphasising what they *can* do and what they *do* know. In accepting state funding we acquiesced to using standardised tests as an ongoing measure of student achievement, and we understood that it was important that the student 'data' at the end of the year should reflect 'improvement'. Within this performance management framework it was clear that the emphasis would be on teaching literacy as a discrete set of functional reading and writing skills, and inculcating students with the dominant culture's rules and codes for textual practices. This meant little or no recognition of the social, political and cultural environments that had shaped the experiences of these students and that continue to shape what they are struggling to become. The students were essentially reduced to numbers on diagnostic charts.

Although we had misgivings about the educational worth of using such tests as a selection process for students to participate in the program, the testing still went ahead and by late February the Year 7s had been DART tested, and the Year 8s, 9s and 10s had been Upper TORCH tested. Attempts to re-test the fourteen Year 8 students eventually selected to participate in the Year 8 literacy program were aborted on the grounds that they were 'unco-operative', 'difficult' and reluctant to be tested any more (so three of my colleagues reported during a literacy team meeting where they explained the difficulties they encountered when they tried to implement another test). Some of the kids in Year 8 had been tested many times. One Year 8 student who had also been involved in the Year 7 Restart literacy program in the previous year was emphatic: 'I ain't doin' another fuckin' test for youse!'

On the basis of teacher recommendations and a range of standardised tests, we eventually managed to select fourteen Year 9 students (four girls and ten boys) to participate in a withdrawal program, and this chapter will focus on this particular class.

Learning Quickly

About half of the fourteen Year 9 literacy students were those who had always struggled with schooling in some way or another, but had remained mostly invisible. These students were generally quiet and withdrawn; they rarely asked for teacher help and often coped by copying from a friend in order to keep up. Others tried to complete tasks to the best of their ability without assistance. The other half of the students were kids who were highly visible and impossible for teachers to ignore because they coped with their inability to 'keep up' in class by being continuously disruptive or easily distracted – this included being rude and aggressive, playing the class clown, or just not turning up to school. A number of the Year 9 students who scored 'poorly' on the standardised tests we administered refused to join the class because of the stigma attached to being withdrawn from normal lessons in order to participate in a remedial program. Students also explained that they did not want to miss out on their mainstream English class because they would be removed from their friends and teachers. On the other hand, at least one Year 9 student was compelled to participate because his parents were eager for him to receive additional literacy assistance.

The experience of participating in this literacy intervention program was a contradictory one for both students and teachers. The mood that I feel characterised the Year 9 literacy withdrawal class which we established at the start of the year was one of gloomy resignation (as one student remarked, 'at least we get out of German'), uncertainty, and in some cases relief. Several students who had spent years in either noisy or silent struggle were glad to finally be receiving attention and assistance with their school work. However, this emotional and academic support came at a significant social cost. One of the difficulties that they had to endure was the stigma of being in what was seen by students and teachers within the school as a 'remedial' program.

For many of these students schooling had mostly been about not fitting in. As they had travelled through school year after year, they had found themselves increasingly out of sync with the literacy practices the school system valued. These students had come to realise that their abilities did not match the state benchmarks for being considered 'literate', and that probably they would never be up to 'standard'. The irony was that although they were finally receiving the attention they deserved – concentrated teacher assistance, small class sizes, regular individual access to computers – they were being further displaced, labelled and marginalised by the very authorities they should have been able to trust: their parents, teachers, the school and the state.

In line with the school 'Compact', we started off the year by focusing on drills and skills approaches to reading and writing, such as comprehension exercises, spelling tests, cloze exercises and grammar tasks based on short stories. I was familiar with the research literature which argued that such functional definitions of literacy were only one aspect of literacy, and that to be fully literate meant engaging in other practices (see Freebody & Luke 1990). But initially I felt locked into administering such routines (we had, after all, written the school 'Compact' ourselves!).

However, we quickly experienced failure. The students rarely brought pens to class, and when they did they were reluctant to put pen to paper, as their spelling, punctuation and grammar could at times be so poor that they felt completely disabled. It was common for students to give up or refuse to complete exercises. The language drills and grammar exercises only seemed to emphasise their weaknesses, reminding them of what they could not do rather than building on their strengths and helping them to sense their potential. From the way that some students responded to different activities, we became more and more convinced that what these students needed was not ever increasing doses of phonics, or other decontextualised drills and skills, but immersion in a meaningful and rich curriculum that appreciated their values, experiences and voices.

As I worked with these students I came to know more about the lives they lived on the margin as they struggled to fit into the mainstream. During this time, I was repeatedly reminded of my past experiences as a teacher of English, where the richness and openness of the curriculum had provided me with sufficient scope to engage students with a range of language abilities from a variety of backgrounds in my classes. So, armed with this knowledge of the potential of English teaching, we set about redesigning and implementing a course that – to borrow the language of the Victorian

Curriculum and Standards Framework – allowed students 'to speak, listen, read, view and write with confidence, purpose and enjoyment in a wide range of contexts' (BOS 2000, p. 5).

As the year progressed, through observations and informal conversations with students, we found out what they might be interested in, and along the way we designed curriculum that took advantage of the access that we had to computers. We put together some web-based units of work focusing on the films, *Billy Elliot* (1999) and *I am Sam* (2002). In response to anecdotes that some students told and questions they asked, we put together a unit titled, 'Teenagers and the Law'. We also spent quite a few weeks on things they initially resisted, such as 'Poetry and Creative Writing' and text responses based on short stories. During Term 4 we worked on 'Resumé Writing and Interview Skills,' when we focussed on preparing resumes, developing interview skills, making phone calls to prospective employers and lining up work experience or paid work for the summer holidays. This unit culminated in an excursion to the local shopping centre, where students distributed their resumés to shops managers and then went to the cinema. Although this last unit was an exciting and rewarding time for students and teachers, the unit of work that proved to be the most significant turning point was the one based on the film, *Billy Elliot*. During this unit we were able to repair (or in some cases begin to establish) our relationships with the students, which had been severely undermined by our relentless focus on functional literacy, and in the process we restored our confidence in our own professional knowledge, skills and abilities as English teachers.

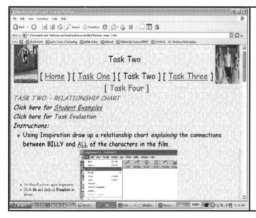

The *Billy Elliot* assignment was created using MS Frontpage. Students were asked to complete the following four assessment tasks:
- A 'Film Study' analysis.
- A 'Relationship Chart' using Inspiration.
- A 'Photo Album' using MS Powerpoint.
- A 'Letter Home' from Billy to his family.

Each task encourages the student to 'write about some challenging themes and issues', 'Adjust writing for a range of purposes and audiences' and 'Identify and control the linguistic structures and features of written texts that present some challenging themes and issues' (CSF II: 67) in the film, *Billy Elliot*.

Figure 1. Summary of the Billy Elliot assignment

The selection of this film to study was prompted by lingering concerns about the persistent sexist and homophobic attitudes held by some of the male students in the class. We did not expect to change their attitudes, but hoped that we would enable them to gain some awareness of the implication of their words and the consequences of their actions, and that perhaps they might begin to reflect on their attitudes beyond the classroom. *Billy Elliot*, the story about an 11 year old boy living in a tough and depressed North England mining town who wants to be a ballet dancer, promised to be a good vehicle for exploring some of these issues.

The remainder of this chapter consists of two pen portraits or case studies of students from this Year 9 class. I have constructed these pen portraits, writing in the first person singular, on the basis of conversations I had with the students during the course of the year, as well as samples of their work. I am not pretending to offer a complete account of these students – they are both flesh and blood individuals, who cannot be summed up by second hand definitions of them (cf. Bahktin 1984), least of all by the results they achieved on the standardised tests we originally administered. The pen portraits were written at the end of the year, when the program was winding up and we were evaluating what we had achieved. Each commences with a statement by the student about being involved in the program.

Pen Portraits
Rochelle

I want to do this literacy class again in Year 10 because it's easier. Like, 'cause I have problems in class. Like, I'm behind in everything . . . I'm slower at things than other people. I have dyslexia and it makes my words jumble up and I get behind in my writing. It upsets me because everyone is in front and I am still near the end. I just need more time to do the work. In this class everyone works at their own pace and I don't feel behind. In this class I have done all of the work. I get along with everyone. It's taken about 2–3 weeks in . . . at the start of term one I felt uncomfortable because there were so many guys in here, then it changed because everyone talked, you get to know each other and I went to Primary School with Duke and I've been good friends with Paul . . . If I had to go back to the normal class – I call it that because it's a different class to the other class – you don't get as much help as you do here. Like if you need help teachers come straight to you, in a normal class they just ignore you . . . because there are so many people in the class. It's okay but you don't get work done. There's no one to talk to in here. No people that I hang out with so I end up doing my work. I'm not liking the reading because I hate reading. I've never liked it because I'm so slow at I t . . . I've never been a reader . . . the best part that we've done is Billy Elliot because it's a good movie. I'm into dancing and stuff. I love 'Save the Last Dance.'

The ways in which teachers practise and think about students and their work are important social practices. They determine what is 'normal' and 'not normal' in schooling and shape the ways that students perceive themselves and their abilities (Popkewitz 1998). The language in Rochelle's portrait reflects the production and reproduction of certain ways of being a 'successful' student with which she clearly struggles to identify. The language she uses to describe herself as a learner – 'I have problems in class', 'I am behind in everything', 'I am slower at things than other people' – indicates not only that has she learnt to see herself as a 'failure' at school, but that she locates the difficulties she has in the classroom within herself rather than in the mainstream curriculum or the ways that schools operate to reproduce social and cultural advantage and disadvantage.

Rochelle's positioning of herself outside the mainstream, and her struggle to understand herself and those around her, is further compounded by her 'dyslexia', and her participation in a program that has categorised her literacy abilities as being deficient. Although Rochelle feels 'comfortable' in the Year 9 literacy class – she can work at her own pace, she doesn't feel 'behind' and has gradually got to know the 'guys' – she still sees the space in this literacy class as being different from other classes. There are enough differences between her mainstream classes and the literacy class for her to describe one as 'normal' and the other space as not 'normal'. Somehow, the class in which she feels comfortable and where she can do the work remains the 'not normal' class.

Rochelle worked quietly and on her own most of the time in this class. She had difficulty with spelling and reading – as she said, the 'words get jumbled up'. A sustained piece of writing was never more than a page long, and she admitted that in her mainstream classes she would spend most of her time chatting quietly and not doing the work because it was too hard. Rochelle was one of three Year 9 literacy students I had taught before. When I taught her in Year 8 English I would spend all my time keeping the boisterous boys on track by working closely with them for lengths of time, but I would often neglect Rochelle because she was quiet. When I would get to her she would dutifully show me her work and I would anticipate that she would eventually complete it. What I rarely had a chance to do was to talk with her in any depth about her work. Even when I did have the opportunity to talk with Rochelle, like many of her peers she was often so embarrassed and inhibited by the intimidating presence of some other students in the class – bullies or popular kids (or both) – that she didn't really share her thoughts. She needed the kind of support that required more than the occasional lunchtime session. Girls like Rochelle are regularly marginalised in their classes by the words and actions of both students and teachers. Even when we, the teachers, are aware of the gendered and unequal nature of our practices, it is difficult to counteract the effects of dominant social and cultural forces acting on a class, whether this be in the form of a group of bullies or popular kids in a classroom intimidating less powerful kids, or an education system that privileges the lives and experiences of certain groups of students over others.

My relationship with Rochelle developed quickly during the year that we both spent in the Year 9 literacy class. We were together for 8 periods a week, and the growing trust and familiarity between us made a significant difference to the way we talked about her work, what she was prepared to write, and her increasing confidence in her abilities. Our conversations usually started with, 'Miss, I don't know what to do', and then over the next 15–20 minutes we would talk about her writing and begin to work on it.

Rochelle had chosen to begin the Billy Elliot assignment with the 'Relationship Chart' activity which required her to use the software, 'Inspiration', to draw up a chart explaining the connections between Billy and all the characters in the film. As a class we spent a lot of time talking about the film in previous lessons and occasionally Rochelle had also voiced some ideas and opinions, but when I returned to check on Rochelle's progress she hadn't written anything because, as I saw it, she still did not appear to have the confidence to put it on paper. So I encouraged her to talk to me about the sort of things she was thinking about including in the 'Relationship Chart', and as she spoke about the characters in the film I typed her words into a Word document. We did this for about twenty to twenty-five minutes, and then I asked her to read and organise the notes that I had taken as she spoke. Rochelle printed the page of notes out and began to read, write and think about how she was going to organise her ideas onto the 'Inspiration' relationship chart. She worked on this for about a week by herself and sometimes with her friends and teachers. By the end of the year her ready smile, uninhibited conversation and regular output of writing conveyed an increased self confidence and belief in her abilities as a writer. As she remarked: *In this class everyone works at their own pace and I don't feel behind. In this class I have done all of the work.*

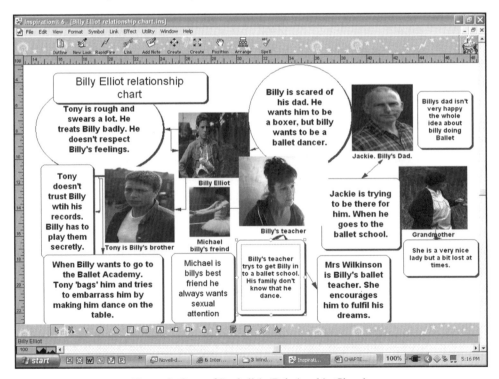

Figure 2. Copy of Rochelle's 'Relationship Chart'.

Paul

This class is good. It's helping me with my reading and writing and spelling. I would feel mad and probably try and leave school if I couldn't do this class. If I didn't have to do a language it might be alright, but it still might be a bit hard. But I would try hard. This is a helping class. The other normal English class . . . it's harder stuff — reading and writing — we read harder books and harder spelling words. The work we do in here is easy. What makes this easier? It's not too difficult — the reading and writing and stuff. Not as much people in here. You usually always get a teacher when you need one. Probably behaviour is worse in other subjects 'cause I'm with more people that I know and there's not as many teachers to tell you off. I really enjoyed the story writing, the resume, the work we looked for at the Shopping Centre and Billy Elliot was alright and kind of fun cause you got to watch the movie and the work wasn't too difficult.

Many of the Year 9 students described this literacy class as 'easy', 'good', 'helping' and even 'fun'. Their pleasure in coming to class is closely associated with the work being 'easy', and yet this comes across as almost something to be ashamed of, as if somehow their having 'fun' and completing tasks that they were able to do devalued the work that they were producing — in their eyes and in the eyes of their peers. For students like Paul and Rochelle who were already socially and economically disadvantaged, 'hard books' and 'hard spelling words' represented a curriculum that only served to further compound their sense of estrangement from 'normal' English. For them, mainstream schooling had just become about 'hard stuff' — dominant cultural norms and practices — that they could not access. Douglas McClenaghan writes that, 'what happens in schools and classrooms can be significant in students' networks and indicates possibilities for conceiving of school as a dynamic and enabling space' (McClenaghan 2004). What the teachers in this literacy program hoped to achieve with these literacy classes was to create such an environment, a space where instead of focussing on the gaps in these students' learning, we worked from their abilities and potential. Instead of making them do work that reinforced their powerlessness, we presented them with more accessible yet challenging literacy activities in the hope (and professional expectation) that they would find this work engaging, self-affirming and a basis on which they could use language to communicate in meaningful ways.

Initially, most of the boys responded negatively to the film, *Billy Elliot*, calling out that this was a film for 'poofs'. Led by Paul, they made fun of the characters' accents and made those who were enjoying the film feel uncomfortable. The girls had not seen the film, and were quietly enjoying it, but they became annoyed that the boys kept 'spoiling' it. (Another male student, Travis, privately confided that it was one of his favourite films.) Each time we screened the film, the first few minutes were accompanied by cries of, 'Not again!', 'Miss, I can't watch any more of this!' We tried to make the screenings special by setting up a data projector, and with some considerable effort, we finally got through the first screening. When we told the students that we were going to watch certain scenes again, we almost had a riot on our hands. We needed a lot of patience to persist when things looked bleak; the girls and some of the boys needed a lot of courage and confidence to express an interest in discussing and finding out more about certain aspects of the film and its characters. There were certainly points at which we felt like giving up, but gradually, the howls and protests died down and students were given some space to talk about Billy and other characters, to tentatively venture opinions, to ask questions and exchange thoughts. Although it took a while, they slowly accepted the film and allowed themselves to laugh at certain scenes, such as Billy's older brother playing air guitar in his underwear, or the moment when Billy calls his ballet teacher a 'blob'. Sometimes, the same students who were initially resistant to the film would arrive in class quoting lines from the script, anticipating dialogue or adopting the dialect in their own speech. Of course the boys still cringed, made silly noises and punched each other during the 'homosexual' scenes, but at least they were thinking, talking and engaging with the film.

Paul was one of those students whose main mode of operating in the classroom was through talk. He was in his own words 'a good talker', but someone who lost all confidence in his ideas and abilities when he had to put pen to paper. In many ways Paul was one of the dominant figures in the little community of this year 9 literacy class. And yet his perception of his own abilities with language – *The other normal English class . . . it's harder stuff – reading and writing – we read harder books and harder spelling words* – reflects the extent to which his identity as a student and a person have been shaped by a sense of what counts as good writing, and that the stuff which he produced did not count.

The *Billy Elliot* activity that Paul chose to begin with was the 'Photo Album' writing task (see Figure 3 for further details about the task). When assessing Paul's writing in this activity against the *English Curriculum and Standards Framework II (CSF II)*, it would be easy to focus on his lack of 'conventional punctuation and spelling to enhance accuracy and readability' and to criticise his work for not containing any 'complex sentences with embedded clauses' (BOS 2000, p. 67). However, to view his written work with a narrow focus on the mechanical aspects of language would be to ignore the rich and complex literacy practices that Paul engaged with when constructing his written response. In fact, even within the narrow confines of the CSF II, Level 5 learning outcomes it is clear that Paul has not only consolidated the CSF II Level 5 Writing Outcomes, but that he is at the point of achieving Level 6 outcomes. Indeed, he has produced a 'text' that in many ways is evidence of far richer literacy practices than those envisaged in the *Curriculum Standards Framework II*.

Paul's written work is not perfect or complete. When he was enthusiastic about a task he would produce it in record time and move onto the next one without looking back. Although we had difficulty getting him to proofread and redraft his own written work, he enjoyed helping others with their written work. Yet despite Paul's lack of attention to the drafting process, the 'Photo Album' activity demonstrates that he was capable of operating with a range of texts, and was able to differentiate between thought and speech to construct meaning. You could also say that he showed a sensitive handling of issues related to identity, sexuality and sexual awakening.

In Figure 3 we can see that Paul produced a text with MS PowerPoint that speaks to the reader at a number of levels. He uses words and images to begin an analysis of the nature of Billy's relationships with some of the key characters in the film. Paul also presented us with a narrative written from Billy's point of view that captured some of the 'challenging themes and issues' that Billy was confronted with in the film (BOS 2000, p. 67). In each PowerPoint slide Paul not only 'adjusted his style of writing' (BOS 2000, p. 67) to suit the task, but used images to enhance the narrative.

Paul also adds another layer of complexity to the images by creating speech bubbles that give the reader a further insight into the characters by capturing their personal voices. He thereby accomplishes another CSF outcome, namely that 'Students ... experiment with language for specific effects; for example, using slang in dialogue to give readers an insight into the characters' (Board of Studies 2000, p. 66). Paul's use of words such as 'fancy', 'fanny' and 'me' not only infuse the text with the feeling of another time and place. These words also give the reader a sense of the way in which Paul's own voice and humour have become interwoven into the text: although continents apart, Billy's dialect is not unlike Paul's own mode of speech, and in this text we find that Paul has appropriated language to explore different voices in a way that suggests 'language is a part of a social interaction whether with imagined others or with the meanings and uses of words that others have employed at other times and places' (Street 1997, p. 51).

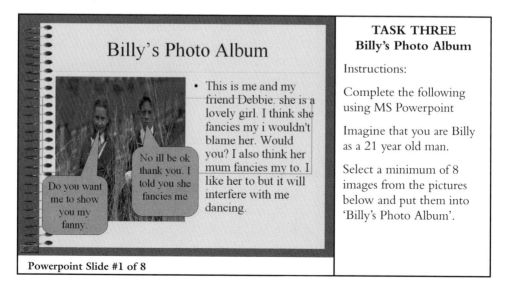

Powerpoint Slide #1 of 8

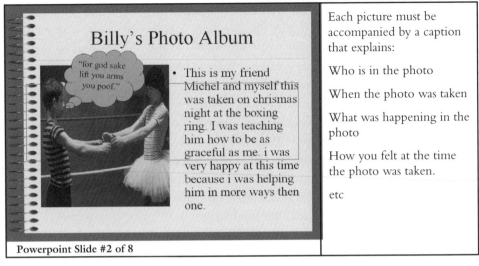

Figure 3. Copy of Paul's work

When I look at the way Paul brought the characters to life through his use of dialect and dialogue in his *Billy Elliot* 'Photo Album' written response, it is clear to me why he said that this class was 'fun' and 'easy'. Paul was not only working in a space where he had established positive social relationships with his teachers and some students, where 'you usually always get a teacher when you need one'. The classroom also provided a space where he was able to engage with interesting and challenging curriculum that allowed him to play with language, construct meaning and communicate in meaningful ways.

Conclusion

As I reflect on what it was that we as English teachers were trying to achieve when implementing the Year 9 literacy program, I am reminded that all of us, students, teachers and school administrators, are entangled in familiar school practices and traditional ways of thinking about learning that make it difficult to imagine alternative ways of conceptualising and experiencing teaching and learning, social relationships and what counts as knowledge (see Doecke & McClenaghan, this volume.) Deborah's shock and horror at our working conditions in the opening vignette made me aware that I had become so accustomed to my surroundings that I no longer saw the 'problems'. Although we tried to spend as little time in that room as possible, when we were in there I no longer noticed the dampness or saw the lack of space and light. In fact, at the beginning of the year we had spent a lot of time trying to find teaching spaces for these extra literacy classes, and the memory of walking around the school like gypsies looking for a room with my Year 7 literacy class was still fresh enough in my mind for me to be grateful to have a teaching space at all. These poor working conditions had become as 'normal' and 'natural' to me and to the students as they were 'unnatural' and confronting to Deborah, who was seeing and experiencing them for the first time.

Although it might at times seem that teachers have the autonomy and agency to bring about social change, we are in many ways locked into practices that are not always of our own making, and we often find ourselves producing and reproducing the same injustices that we seek to expose and eliminate. This contradiction is evident in the suggestion that these Year 9 students embark on a letter writing campaign. There was no more effective way to reinforce these students' powerlessness and their 'deficit' status in their own eyes than by assuming that they had not noticed their physical environment. Deborah and I were also unwittingly setting them up to fail by asking them to tackle a genre that was characterized by social and cultural conventions that were not a part of their daily textual practices. Although our intentions may have been to empower the students, the suggestion and subsequent attempts to enforce the exercise reflected our own cultural preferences and negated their experiences and literacy practices. It would be similarly disingenuous to ignore the fact that by withdrawing students from English and Languages Other Than English (LOTE) classes and establishing separate 'literacy' classes, we were responsible for creating the false dichotomy that came to exist between English and literacy and reinforced in the minds of students that those involved in the literacy intervention program were, indeed, 'not normal'. It seems that at the very time we were attempting to teach these literacy students in ways that interrupted culturally dominant ways of thinking, acting and seeing who and what was 'normal' in schooling, we ourselves were guilty of reproducing the very same practices that further oppressed the already oppressed and marginalised.

Rochelle and Paul were two of the fourteen Year 9 students who had been labeled 'at risk', removed from their mainstream English class and positioned as individuals with a 'problem' that needed to be 'fixed'. They were among a number of students whose difficulties with learning stemmed from a range of complex factors, such as family breakdown, poverty, and social isolation, not simply from any learning deficiency. The reality was that even against the state's measures of success – 'engagement', 'attendance', 'retention' – the initial testing regime and functional approach to literacy failed to make a positive impact on the learning of these students and only further alienated them from school life. Whereas what these students needed was to have access to rich and flexible curriculum and literacy practices with the power to crack open and demystify schooling and the learning process.

Paul's regular attendance, creativity and enthusiasm for the work we were doing in this Year 9 literacy class was much more than 'good fun'. The 'fun' and 'easy' time that Paul was having in class stemmed from being engaged in interesting and challenging literacy practices that acknowledged his situated history, experiences, beliefs, and the characteristic ways in which he used oral and written language to communicate with others in the classroom. In this class he knew that he did not have to struggle on alone because learning did not have to be an individual activity, but something that happened with and between people. He came to feel that he had something to offer to the learning in which everyone was participating and that he was capable of authoring his own experiences through his writing in a way that would have significance for others. These students perceived their learning as 'fun' and enjoyable because they were working out of spaces and within social relationships that did not define them according to what they could not do, but by their potential. Certainly, they still farted, chewed gum, made loud noises and gave each other nipple cramps, but through their writing they also demonstrated a wonderful capacity for being clever, funny, ironic, honest, inspiring and so many other things that cannot be captured in any single account of their achievements.

As I turn a critical lens on our own practices in implementing this literacy intervention program, I ask myself: What will happen to these Year 9 literacy students if they return to their mainstream Year 10 English class next year? What are the possibilities available to them within 'normal' schooling? What is 'normal'? Have we only set these students up for failure – again? Did we make a long-term difference in the lives of these students? Did they really need remediation? What 'progress' did they make? What did they get from this program and would they be able to transfer what they had learnt to other settings? By the end of the year they would arrive in class and walk straight up to a computer and continue with the writing they were doing, while continuing their conversations with each other and their teachers. At the start of the year it had been a matter of coming to class and waiting for instructions about what they were doing that day. I have come to feel that working with students is as much about negotiating social relationships as it is about negotiating curriculum. We had been able to provide a space where the students had the opportunity to talk and engage in reading and writing that was meaningful to them because it connected with their world. Neither the opening vignette nor the pen portraits that I have written present a complete and finished 'reality' – to suppose so would be to deny these students their histories and their futures. But standardised tests capture their potential as human beings even less! By the end of the year, Paul was finally writing with more confidence and enjoyment, but I was still left hoping that some day he would take it upon himself to revisit a text and go beyond the first draft. One thing I know for certain is that we didn't change their lives. All we did was temporarily validate them.

References

Bakhtin, M. (1984) *Problems of Dostoevsky's poetics*, C. Emerson (ed.), Minneapolis, MN: University of Minnesota Press.

Board of Studies, Victoria (BOS) (2000) *English: Curriculum and Standards Framework II*, Melbourne.

Daldry, S. (dir.) (1999) *Billy Elliot*, Tiger Aspects Picture Ltd.

Doecke, B. and McClenaghan, D. (2005) Engaging in Valued Activities: Popular Culture in the English Classroom, this volume.

Department of Education, Employment and Training (DE&T) (2002) *Education Times* Budget Special Issue, 9 May.

Freebody, P. and Luke, A. (1990) 'Literacies' Programs: Debates and Demands in Cultural Context, *Prospect* 5(3), May 1990, pp. 15

Illesca, B. (2004) Teachers' Work and Professional Identity: Living a Contradiction on the Margin, in *English Teaching: Practice and Critique* 3(3), December 2004, pp 79–87. Accessed in March 2005 at: http://www.tmc.waikato.ac.nz/english/ETPC/narrative/pdf/2004v3n3nar3.pdf

McClenaghan, D. (2004) Unpublished paper.

Nelson, J. (dir.) (2001) *I am Sam*, New Line Cinema.

Popkewitz, T.S. (1998) *Struggling for the Soul: The Politics of Schooling and the Construction of the Teacher,* New York and London: Teachers College Press.

Street, B. (1997) The Implications of the 'New Literacy Studies' for Literacy Education, in *English in Education* 31(3), Autumn 1997, p. 51

Chapter 12

'I want you to write me a poem . . . and I don't want it to rhyme.'

Val Kent

Val Kent taught at Huntingdale Technical School, now South Oakleigh Secondary College, before becoming the Education Officer for the Victorian Association for the Teaching of English. The following essay, written in 1995, provides a fascinating glimpse of how she was able to encourage her students to experiment with language and to make connections between poetry and their values and concerns. For this volume Val has written a coda to this piece, in which she reflects on how she might tackle the challenges of teaching poetry today.

'You can use any word you like as long as it doesn't rhyme with truck or shunt.'

Robert was fourteen and absolutely obsessed with footy. In science, catering and maths, every formulae, recipe or equation catapulted him into a description of a match, a score, a player, a referee. He drove us all crazy.

Everyone was writing in their journal. Robert was hanging over the stairwell shouting a kick by mark description of Saturday's footy and I lost it, frog-marched him into the adjacent staffroom, slammed his journal and pen in front of him and hissed 'write'.

'Write what?'

'Write anything.'

'Anything?'

'Anything at all.'

'ANYTHING?'

I knew what he meant, and was in no mood to get into the 'no bad language' versus 'it's what my dad says, so why shouldn't I put it in?' argument; or the more sophisticated version, 'If you want us to write about real life then we have to use real language don't we?'

'You can use any word you like as long as it doesn't rhyme with truck or shunt.'
He smirked at me, looked thoughtful. 'I'll write about the dream I had last night.'
Footy dreams, I thought, gritted my teeth, bit my tongue.
'Good idea.'

He looked self-conscious when he handed it over and very pleased with himself at the enthusiasm of my response. It was a long poem about street kids, not divided into stanzas, randomly capitalised and without punctuation. The following lines are part of the final version:

> They're fighting a battle a day.
> Their clothes are made
> from leather, spikes and fox-skin.
> They're the ones who fight for
> freedom,
> And the ones who fight
> for a living. (Robert 14)

It wasn't a 'good' poem. I could have sat down with him and talked about the repetitiveness of some of the language, how he could cut at least a third of it and the indeterminate nature of the final lines but it would have been a mistake. This was his first poem, he'd chosen the title himself – The Fighting Boys – and there was absolutely nothing in it about Australian Rules. I could have kissed him but he wouldn't have liked it, so we discussed the punctuation – where it should go, why a comma and not a full stop, where he wanted to leave in the capital letters and what difference this would make to the poem.

I talked to him about how effective his images were, why they were visual, how I could see the kids, the rats and the fires and I asked him about the lines

> Where are all the angels that
> Were falling through the night.

'What are the angels doing in the poem, Robert?'
'Dunno. I just liked the sound of it.'

Fair enough, so did I. I read the poem to the class, to his pastoral, maths and phys. ed. teachers, all victims of footy mania, and they were astonished. It was published in the sub-school's newspaper and if writing poetry never replaced footy in Robert's mind, it certain trailed a close second for a number of years.

With many students, you have to be particularly careful when responding to their poetry. A poem is not an argumentative essay, a report or a film review where there is little room to experiment with structure. Suggesting that a word, a rhyme or the structure itself could be changed can too easily be read as a criticism of the ideas or feelings that inform the poem. Just as I've heard students say that they can't write because someone has criticised their hand-writing, I've also seen them translate criticism, whether written or verbal, however kindly or thoughtfully stated, into believing that their poem is worthless because of what it is saying, rather than how it has been said. The time to move into a more serious critical mode is once they become confident, especially if the poetry begins to pour out, or to resemble birthday card lyrics or pop songs.

Several years later Robert fell in love with Zoe who was sixteen going on twenty-five. He wrote, but never gave her, a poem which signalled both a change in style and an awareness of his own sexuality. He called it, appropriately enough, 'The 11.30 Poem'. The conventional sentiments, rhythm and rhymes of the first two lines:

> *Just one more night and I'll say goodbye,*
> *I'll leave your body and walk on by*

are in sharp contrast to the rest of the poem:

> *I touch you, my sweat against your cool body,*
> *Your mouth is alive, my tongue inside.*
> *Your hands take a grip on the side of the bed,*
> *The sheets are pulled back on the heat of the night,*
> *Our bodies are close, the heat is divided,*
> *Our minds are hooked on love.*

His images not only suggest physical closeness, the warmth of both night and flesh, but 'Our minds are hooked on love' brings in an extra dimension. Here is a warmth which is more than physical, an emphasis that is all the stronger for being made in the final line and an indication of its importance to the writer. Robert's best friend reported to him that Zoe, on hearing of his feelings for her, had said, not unkindly, 'Oh – the footy man.' His next poem was a shout of rage entitled – in large, bold letters – 'I'm no footy man because these days I like dancing with my headache intact 2 Hookey's Low-Life Basslines while Barney sings and waves his arms,' and the poem ended with:

> *. . . you don't know me.*
> *I am no footy man.*
> *This is a poem I've enjoyed writing,*
> *And I hope you get the message.*

'Why would you want to teach in a tech school?'

Fifteen years ago I chose to do my teacher training at Hawthorn Teachers' College because it meant that I would be in a classroom two days a week for most of the year. It seemed to me then, and it still does, that this is a far more effective way of learning to teach than being tossed into several schools for a few weeks of teaching rounds. 'Why would you want to teach in a tech school?' several of my male friends asked. 'Don't do it,' said one of them darkly, 'you'll get beaten up.'

I wanted to teach in a tech school because having passed the 11+ exam (this was in England) and entrance to the local Grammar School, I was streamed into a C class, where I remained for the rest of my time at school. The emphasis was on uniforms and uniformity, passing exams, aiming – if you were in an A class – for Oxford and Cambridge, and being good. 'Be good sweet maid, and let who will be clever,' the Head Girl wrote in my autograph book. 'Bullshit' wasn't part of my vocabulary then but it would be my response today. I wanted to teach in a tech school because my own school taught me that I was, if not stupid, then not particularly bright and because I found this difficult to reconcile with the first class honours degree of twenty years later.

I wrote that last, rather immodest sentence because it is one of the reasons why I felt good about teaching in a school where the vertical structure of the classes was firmly based upon the belief that students are not homogeneous, and will not dutifully move from Years 7 to 12 at a similar pace, with the same responses and degree of enthusiasm. This meant that we could not teach from a class set of books, nor could we assume that our students were now ready for Shakespeare or even for Roger McGough. We planned our classes and taught with the recognition that the almost illiterate, the very bright, the integrated students and those who had been labelled failures and firmly believed it to be true, sat side by side, as they still do in many schools.

Because the classes were vertically structured, staff offered electives in their subject areas which students in Years 7–10 could choose to contract into. Although the Year 10 students had their own English, maths and science classes, they, together with the younger students, negotiated with the help of parents, carers and pastoral teachers, the rest of their curriculum. At this particular point in time students were at Huntingdale Tech either because its structure and philosophy appealed to them and to their parent(s) or those who cared for them, or because other schools, persuasively or forcefully, had indicated to the students that they really would be much happier elsewhere. Everyone would be much happier if they were elsewhere!

The students who booked into my poetry contracts fell into several categories: they loved poetry and enjoyed writing it; they couldn't get into any of the contracts they wanted and it was a choice between poetry or a subject/teacher they disliked; their pastoral teacher suggested that they needed to 'do more English'; or they just didn't give a damn since they weren't planning to attend anyway.

Although there were often times when I bolted into the bunker of my senior

English and literature classes, the pleasure of teaching poetry with a class where age and experience ranged from years eleven to sixteen far outweighed the attendant realities, and sometimes terrors, of mixed ability teaching. I came almost immediately to believe that not only could every student write poetry but that they should be encouraged to do so as often as possible.

'Have you got any more by him?'

The image of everyone making love on the bus in McGough's 'At Lunchtime A Story of Love' can convert a whole class who began by shouting 'WE'RE NOT DOING POETRY, ARE WE?' to instant attention.

'Why are people described as "white mothballbodies" doing naughty things?'
'Because their bums are in the air.' Triumphantly.
'I think this is a pretty rude poem.'
'Funny but. Have you got any more by him?'

Humour was particularly effective in breaking down initial barriers and when they next came to class and found tables covered with books and instructions to find a poem, say what they thought it was about and be willing to read at least one verse to the rest of the class, there was rarely resistance. The Rory Harris and Peter McFarlane collections (e.g., 1985, 1997), where student poetry lies alongside, and is not distinguished from, the poetry of established writers, were an invaluable source of encouragement, ideas and models. Reading poetry aloud, identifying themes and writing responses in their journals gave them ideas for their own poetry, which was the next step.

'You should join this class, we get to talk a lot about love and sex and stuff.'

This was shouted out to a passing student. Teaching in an open area which included a flight of stairs, doors to other classrooms and was next to the library, had mixed blessings. One of the advantages was that students passing through on urgent trips to the toilets, the smoko, or just in the process of making it a short day at school could see their peers reading and talking about poetry. Sometimes they sat down and joined in.

Because the boys rarely chose poems about love I encouraged them to write them. Rodney's first three pieces, love of one's family, of pets and the love of a mother for her child were childish in both form and content but his fourth poem was quite different.

> *Lust*
> *over each other*
> *visit each others bed*
> *enjoy*
> *Rolling in the grass —*
> *sexual fantasies come true. (Rodney 13)*

'There aren't any commas or full stops here, Rodney. What do you want to do about this?'

'Well, I reckon that, um, sex is pretty exciting, so I think there shouldn't be any punctuation because then it sort of moves faster. Like, er, sex.'

'Fine. What about the capital R in 'rolling'?'

'Shouldn't be there – I'll take it out.'

It wasn't until I saw the typed version that I realised it was an acrostic, a form we'd used in an earlier class. The structure had dictated not only the brevity, which was quite different to anything else he'd written before, but it had also affected the language and tone. I read the poem to the class and watched him move up several notches in the estimation of the boys and noticed thoughtful looks from a few of the girls.

Rick had written:

> *I look at her and she turns away,*
> *I think to myself – why?*
> *When all I want is her to look.*
> *Her eyes meet mine,*
> *We know we have to be together,*
> *But there are walls between us,*
> *I will break them down and*
> *Meet her once again eye to eye*

But after listening to Rodney he changed it to this:

> *I look at her and she turns away*
> *and I think to myself – why?*
> *when all I want is her to look,*
> *her eyes meet mine,*
> *to know we have to be together.*
>
> *But there are walls between us.*
>
> *I will break them down and*
> *Meet her once again, eye to eye (Rick 13)*

'What have you done here, Rick?'

'I've made it faster, changed the punctuation. See?'

'Yes. Good. What's happened here?' Pointing to 'But there are walls between us'.

'Well, that's why she looks away; I put a space each side so it looks like a real wall because that's what's gotta be broken down.'

Brad was extremely resistant to writing poetry, snorted with derision at the idea of writing a poem about love but finally handed one in.

> *We went to the beach*
> *Because we wanted an outing.*
> *We went for a swim,*
> *Because it was warm.*
> *We had a barbie*
> *Because we were starving.*
> *We had to go home*
> *Because it was dark. (Brad 16)*

I read it to the class.

'Not much in it about love,' observed his best friend, whose own poem, which he was noisily pleased with, verged on the erotic, making me wonder what his parents would say when he took it home. Brad respected Daniel's opinion far more than he did mine and he immediately added

> *And then we went outside*
> *And made love among*
> *The warm and wet leaves.*

'Brad, this is ...' He snatched it from me.

'Yep, it's finished, it's good, it's a love poem, just what you wanted and you gotta promise not to read it to the others or I'll set light to it.'

'PUT THAT LIGHTER AWAY.'

Martin and Lucy fell in love in front of everybody in their literature class. They gave me the poems they had written about each other but my response was deliberately tentative. What they were wanting to say to each other and the pleasure they took in doing so was far more important than 'getting it right' could be. Sometimes the best response is to leave well alone.

'I wish I could write like that.'

Sometimes I give them a poem simply because I like it myself. This is not always a good idea; Benjamin Britten's recording of 'The Lyke-Wake Dirge' produces looks of incredulity and mutters of 'turn it off, turn it off.' But students with or without religious beliefs sit up straight for Charles Causley and once I gave them his 'Keats at Teignmouth' because of the last lovely stanza.

> *Then I saw the crystal poet*
> *Leaning on the old sea-rail;*
> *In his breast lay death the lover,*
> *In his head, the nightingale.*

This Year 10 class was not ready for Keats's 'Ode to a Nightingale.' But they did read, and respond in their journals to his 'La Belle Dame Sans Merci', Tennyson's 'Lady of Shalot', Manifold's 'Griesly Wife' and Rossetti's 'Goblin Market'. By this somewhat circuitous route, women as enchantress or enchanted, we arrived at Angela Carter's richly metaphoric short story, 'The Company of Wolves', compared it to earlier versions of 'Little Red Riding Hood' and to Neil Jordan's film version. The journey was pleasurable; it produced considerable discussion and argument, but the creative responses were disappointing. I tried to find out why and came to the conclusion that perhaps on some occasions, literature can be intimidating.

'I can't write like that.'

'But I'm not asking you to.'

'Good, because I'm not going to try.'

'Why can't we just enjoy the poems?'

However, Christina Rossetti's 'Remember' did produce this:

> *Remember me.*
> *Remember me, the girl*
> *Who never talks*
> *Who hides her face*
> *And is too shy to make*
> *A noise*
> *Who is not able to say*
> *'Remember me, you know me*
> *I am here.*
> *Just because I don't*
> *Talk it doesn't mean*
> *I am not able to feel*
> *That you don't notice*
> *Or remember.'*
> *Remember me. (Suzanne 16)*

'I wish I could write like that,' she said, meaning Rossetti.

'You have,' I told her.

The girls responded to Rich's 'Aunt Jennifer's Tigers' and Hope's 'Advice to Young Ladies' with stories and poems of their mothers' lives; their own lives, they assured each other, would never be as circumscribed. I gave them e.e. cummings and Dorothy Parker and received, in return, poems reflecting a wry disenchantment with love.

> *Like dimming a room*
> *that's been lighted for years*
> *my love I once felt*
> *is now over my dear*
> *you can sit there and say*
> *that to me you can't lie*
> *but I know that you have*
> *a new slice of pie. (Melanie 15)*

Tracey refused to write a poem about love.

'Come on, Tracey, write about how you feel about Jamie.'

'Nah. It'ud be gross.'

'I need another piece of writing from you before I can write your report.' Blackmail.

She scowled and five minutes later offered to read it aloud. It went down very well.

> *It was 5.14*
> *My eyes were tight.*
> *I'd been drinking and smoking*
> *All last night.*
> *I smelt a bit*
> *And I looked like mud.*
> *I'd been mucking around*
> *With a Huntingdale thug (Tracey 13)*

'Don't try and make it rhyme.'

'Don't try and make it rhyme,' I tell my students. They look puzzled, belligerent or obstinate. 'Poetry should rhyme,' they argue, in spite of the free verse, found verse, concrete poetry, performance poetry, etc., that we have read and discussed, 'I want to make it rhyme.'

Rebecca, who has cerebral palsy, was writing a poem for the class newspaper. An aide whispered, 'I think it's a poem her mother has read to her.' I didn't believe it. The class, which met three times a week for a double session to write and publish a newspaper, had been discussing violent parents. 'When you've finished that,' I said to

Rebecca, 'I want you to write me a poem about what we've been talking about, but don't try and make it rhyme.' She tapped out on her typewriter, 'why?'

I explained, as I was to explain on dozens of other occasions, how concentrating on the search for a matching word or phrase could stultify a poem; that it was all too easy to lose your way in shallow rhymes that obliterated genuine feeling and original ideas. She typed out, 'I agree,' sat for several minutes gazing at the typewriter keys, then wrote a five stanza piece, every line of which rhymed, and concluded with:

> *'I bumped into a tree,' said the policeman's daughter,*
> *To the men she lies about the man who haunts her.*
> *They don't believe her anyway,*
> *So with her father she has to stay.*

'It rhymes, Rebecca, it rhymes.'

She smiled and tapped out, 'I prefer it that way.'

I didn't, but I did like the first two lines of the stanza very much and told her why. She had also demonstrated to others in the class that a poem could say as much, and sometimes more, about a topic than their essays could and this encouraged several of them to turn what they had written into poetry. It also proved, not only to the aide, but to her peers that she was capable of writing thoughtfully and sensitively, and that a damaged body was no reflection of the intelligent child within.

Karen's poetry was idiosyncratic, never written to any formulae and only attempted when she felt like it. I looked over her shoulder and read:

> *I was born in a lighthouse*
> *My mother was the sea,*
> *I never knew my father*

'Terrific. Tell me when you've finished.'

'Nah. I'm not going to finish, I can't go any further.'

'Of course you can. Who's the speaker? Why didn't she know her father?'

'Who said it was a she?'

When I came back ten minutes later, she'd added 'And he never knew me.'

I groaned. She grinned at me.

'It was the only way I could finish it.'

We had a number of skirmishes where I tried to persuade her to finish the poem and lost every one.

One fourteen year old student showed me the scars on her wrists and handed me a poem, saying, 'I don't care what you say, it's my poem and it's going to rhyme.'

> *As the blade cuts my skin*
> *I can feel it dig deeper in.*
> *I am sure the scars will fade someday,*
> *However they will never really go away.*
> *As the blood drips down my arm,*
> *It finally gathers in my palm.*
> *My blood is a rich red,*
> *I sometimes wish that I were dead.*
> *The anger builds inside of me,*
> *When I slash I set it free.*
> *School has now become a release,*
> *Here I can find some peace.*
> *When I'm at school I feel OK,*
> *Sometimes I wish that I could stay.*
> *Will this pain ever go?*
> *At times I really do not know.*

This was in class; not the time to talk about the source of the poem.

'Good, now I want you to re-write it, but this time don't make it rhyme.'

'Stuff that, I like it as it is.'

'I know you do, and there are some really great lines in it. Just do me a favour and give it a go; humour me, OK?' She wrote:

> *To cut myself is to release pain;*
> *Anger also goes when the blood drips out.*
> *The fear of dying was quite real;*
> *Anger and the fear of living overcome it now.*
> *The people that care will never understand.*
> *A move or a change,*
> *That's what I need,*
> *But I am stuck.*
> *I don't want to go forward but I can't stay,*
> *The scars I have inside of me will be there for life,*
> *And the visible scars will stay for a while.*
> *I want to give up and let go of life,*
> *But two people keep me here and will do so for a while.*

In the first version words and phrases had been chosen for the sake of the rhymes, and 'I sometimes wish that I were dead' is unnecessary given the content of the rest of the poem. In the second version there was an elaboration of experience and feeling that had not been there before. But there was also something missing. The evocative image of the 'rich red' blood gathering in her palm had gone. 'The anger builds inside of me/When I slash it sets me free' had also been lost; however, 'I want to give up and let go of life' in this version becomes the impetus for the whole poem whilst the last line reflects both the dilemma and the courage of this particular student.

'Can you see how in this poem, every line says something that was, or is important to you?'

'Yeah. But I like the other one better.'

'Why?'

'I just do. It rhymes.'

'Well, I have to say that these two lines in the first version are very powerful.'

'There you go; see, I was right; it has to rhyme.'

'How do you feel about combining the best of both poems, keeping the ideas and the feeling in the second poem and perhaps going for some internal rhymes?'

'Not bloody likely!'

Most of Jessica's poetry was free verse but in this one, rhyme, rhythm and meaning coalesce into a jauntiness which is deliberately vulgar and colloquial, demanding to be read aloud.

> Gee. I love my Target trousers; ya know that they're the best.
> I love the way they squeeze and crackle, when I laugh & jest.
> Gee, I love my Target trousers; I love the fluoro hues,
> Soon I'm gonna get myself a matching pair of shoes.
> When I wear my Target trousers all the blokes just think I'm cool,
> We all get together and we hang around at school.
> Gee I love my Target trousers when we huddle in the halls,
> We talk of footy, beer and chicks and the hugeness of our balls.
> Gee I love my Target trousers, I think they are just swell,
> I never take them off to wash, so they've begun to smell.
> Gee I love my Target trousers, I just think they're
> Mega, massive, corker, Brucey, spot ya bloody digger.
> Thursday afternoon and I'm pissing on a shed,
> Stretched a bit to read some writing and I piddled down my leg!
> Mum washed them ten times in a row but the smell just wouldn't go.
> Gee I loved my Target trousers, ya know they were my life.
> Now that I ain't got none, I feel that I'm in strife.
> I'm really glum, I feel real stink, I'm gonna slit my wrists I think. (Jessica 17)

'Guess who wrote this?' I asked.

Not one student suggested a female name and a great deal of discussion and argument over what constitutes a male or female 'voice' ensued, as well as a number of notably entertaining failures when others tried to emulate Jess. It was also an excellent performance poem to use with younger students and a choral rendition of it riveted a group of visiting Japanese Principals and, via video, made its way to Japan.

'I think I'd like to read this to the rest of the class.'

Whenever I get the chance I read their poems aloud, often dancing around the room reading as they try to wrench it from me. Of course you have to be able to recognise when a student really doesn't want their poems made public, and respect this, but most of the time their protestations stem from the belief that what they have written is worthless. Reading it aloud legitimises it for the writer and often encourages others in the class to attempt their own poems. I see them sitting there, thinking, 'I could do that,' and they do.

'I want you to listen to Natasha's poem and tell me what you like about it. It's called 'Sunday Summer Heat'.

> *Backyard sunbaking, 34,*
> *suntan lotion,*
> *no tan,*
> *gone pink,*
> *music blaring,*
> *mind spinning,*
> *getting angry,*
> *music full blast,*
> *neighbours complaining,*
> *Mind yelling,*
> *headache worse, 37.*
> *Having an orange,*
> *getting sticky,*
> *turning on hose,*
> *washing hands,*
> *squirting towel,*
> *getting angry,*
> *spitting on ground,*
> *getting toe, 42.*
>
> *No fun,*
> *gone red,*
> *going inside,*
> *having shower,*

a little tan,
get changed,
date comes,
tan gone,
headache bad,
date bad,
real jerk,
get back home,
cry myself to sleep,
go to school,
look terrible,
bad zits,
feel bad,
fall over,
feel embarrassed,
go home,
go to sleep to forget it all
AND IT WORKED. (Natasha 14)

'It's real; you know how she's feeling.'

'It's fast so it's not boring.'

'Yeah; and there's a whole day in it.'

'It's good, the way she keeps putting the temperature in, so you see everything getting worse as the weather gets hotter.'

'I like the way she only uses two or three words in each line.'

'It's a performance poem!'

'Do we know the jerk?'

Another advantage of working in an open area rather than in a classroom was that the circle of tables could be easily adjusted to form groups of any size. There was room to write group poems, to rehearse a performance poem, to get down on the floor and read, or to go into a huddle and discuss each other's work. Doug and Grant decided to put the best lines of their two poems together but there was some disagreement over exactly which were the best lines. As each agreed to give up a line only if it were matched by one from the other, a small group set themselves up as judges and handed over this:

Violet is a wicked fragrance
Silver is a seductive unicorn
White as the glowing moon

> *Grey is a gang of girls*
> *Brown as a batch of buns*
> *Gold as a ticking watch*
> *Silver is a silken sheet.*
> *(Doug 14 & Grant 15)*

I talked to them about which line was a metaphor and which a simile and asked them what they preferred and why, and they changed the poem so that it was all metaphor. Then I read them that old perennial, 'The Highwayman' and we played spot the metaphor and ignore the printed questions at the end of the sheet. We read it again, this time around the class, and they re-wrote it as narrative, either from the point of view of Bess, the Highwayman, the Ostler or some other person who may have been on the scene.

'I reckon he got that from the Top Ten.'

> *Could not sing an old*
> *Song now; it is not because*
> *I don't want to—*
> *I can't remember how the*
> *World goes. (Win 12)*

'Do you want to make it clearer who it is who can't sing? Is it you?'
'No.'
'Who is it then?'
'Anyone who doesn't understand how the world goes. If you don't understand this, how can you write about it?'
'I thought you were writing about singing.'
'So. You have to write the song first.' Reasonably.
'Do you have to understand the world to be able to write?'
'No, but you have to remember it.'
'Remember?'
'Know it.' Patiently.
'Ah. Right. This is a very good poem, Win, I think we'll leave it exactly as it is.'
'I think Win's a cheat, I reckon he got that from the Top Ten.'
'Did not!'
I didn't think he had either. Although I was left with the feeling that he was responding to my questions rather than to the poem itself, I liked its simplicity, the way it was open to interpretation and that he was willing to think and talk about what he had written.

'Not another poem! What am I supposed to do with this?'

I use any excuse to give them a poem. I like to think that perhaps some of them hang on to their photocopies even if they never buy a poetry book or write a poem again. If one of them is writing about their own animals I give all of them Monro's 'Milk for the Cat', Smart's 'My Cat Jeoffry', Spenser's 'Shepheard's Dogge', and Brooke's 'The Little Dog's Day'. If they want to write about the weather I shower them with Spring poems by Nashe, Shakespeare, and Hopkins and the opening of *The Canterbury Tales*. If they write about the sea everyone is given Masefield's 'Sea Fever', extracts from 'The Ancient Mariner' and the translation plus the original Anglo-Saxon version of 'The Seafarer', which I can read to them because they won't recognise where memory is replaced by invention.

If someone is writing an essay on animal liberation we read Ewart's 'A Black Rabbit Dies for its Country', Hughes' 'The Death of a Stag', and Davies' 'Sheep'. A rabble of Year 9 boys can be reduced to silence by Harwood's description of the mutilated owl, shot by a child and hobbling in its own blood and bowels. A racist remark produces poems by Langston Hughes, Oodgeroo Noonuccal, Jack Davis and the inscription found by the poet Adrian Mitchell in the Children's Graveyard at Dimbaza:

> Beauty Douglas was born 7.12.68
> ShE DIE 19. 1.69

When the boys enthusiastically launch themselves into homophobia we read Brass's 'I Think the New Teacher's a Queer', and sometimes in the discussion that follows, the combination of memory and fear in the poem elicits a response that surprises us all. Poetry can confront prejudice and speak more powerfully than any words of mine.

If we're discussing anorexia we may begin with the lines from Cornford's 'To a Fat Lady Seen From a Train.'

> *O WHY do you walk through the fields in gloves*
> *... O fat white woman whom nobody loves?*

If we're studying *Dr Strangelove* we read Paul Dehn's dark nursery rhymes, and listen to Sting's lyrics, and if the text is *Night* they learn about the holocaust, so many of them for the first time, from Lily Brett's *Auschwitz Poems*. When they read Tony Harrison's poem, 'A Cold Coming', the photograph of the charred Iraqi soldier on the jacket together with the poem, caused more thoughtful discussion of the Gulf War than any media piece. It also had the added bonus of introducing them to sexual punning, Eliot's 'Journey of the Magi' and the notion of the responsibility of the writer.

'Because I saw her do it.'

Amanda, an intelligent, Creative Arts student, who during the course of the year had converted my response to rats – one of which was usually concealed about her person – from 'aaagh' to tolerance, was one piece short of completing her CAT, due in on the following morning. Potentially an A student, her lifestyle, living in utter chaos with other students – and a rat – was frequently at war with her talents.

'You need another piece for your folio: I want you to write me a poem.'

'Haven't written any poetry since I was in primary school.'

'You've just been telling me about your mother's visit; write a poem about that, and for God's sake ...'

'I know, I know, don't try and make it rhyme.'

She sat down and after ten minutes handed me the poem. 'Out of the louvres & onto the backyard trolley' describes a frantic cleanup of her student household just before a visit from her mother. We talked about the structure of the poem, its paciness, humour and punchline.

'Now go over there,' the other side of the library, 'and write another.'

I gave her the first line, 'When I Was Young', and sent her off twice more with 'Now I'm Older', and 'Sometime in the Future'. She chewed her pencil and edited as she went along. We discussed the punctuation and she made half a dozen alterations. There wasn't enough time to do any more but it was fine as it was anyway. Her own authentic self, humorous, thoughtful, and occasionally quite desperate, shines through the four poems and when some months later, at a verification meeting, someone said, 'How do we know she really wrote this?' I was able to say, 'Because I saw her do it'.

'Why isn't it an A?'

I'd just bought Tammy's charcoal drawing, 'Bottles', and told her that when she was rich and famous she could have it back for the same price. Neither of us had any idea that she could write poetry.

> 'I want you to write me a poem about your painting.'
> The splendour of the curving shapes
> The sticky liquid poured from them
> The broken jagged edges
> The mirrored reflection of the light in the glass
> The distinct, cold, hard surfaces. (Tammy 16)

Tammy's poems were often very painterly; her images were vivid and hard edged and her imagination was stirred by the sea. As far as I know, she had never read T.S. Eliot when, in one of her poems, she wrote:

> *I am walking on the bed of the ocean*
> *Where the mermaids are singing harmoniously*

and I gave her Browning's 'Meeting At Night' after she had written:

> *The sun's rays scan the water as*
> *it disappears into the night,*
> *leaving the sea dark and grim.*
> *The beach is silent except for the*
> *roar of the waves crashing against*
> *the beach and then sidling back to*
> *the depths of the ocean.*
> *The moon comes out and*
> *brightens the night.*
> *The sea is alight again.*

We discussed the internal rhymes which had not been deliberate, and she brought in her painting of an angel at sea and wrote:

> *Here beneath the heavens the*
> *oceans become silvery surfaces*
> *inhabited by Angels and Gods.*
> *Rows of tiny wind waves flow*
> *up to the seas surface.*
> *A pleasing shade has fallen o'er*
> *the sea.*
> *An Angel rises to the surface.*
> *Waits.*
> *Then departs mysteriously into*
> *the dark water.*

She spent hours in the library writing and re-writing an essay, frustrated with her inability to transfer her spoken ideas and argument to paper.

'Why isn't it an A?' she said, when she finally handed it over.

'Why can't I write poetry?' I replied and read her latest one to students who could get an A but who couldn't write a poem with as many lovely images as this one:

> *The lights soften into gold*
> *as darkness starts to fall.*
> *They walk on.*

The stars rain into her hair like
snowflakes,
as silence stretches its arm over
the mountains.
The night air sends out a chill.
But a fire burns between them.

'Oh my God, this is disgusting.'

I gave my senior English and literature students a collection I've made of vulgar, bawdy and erotic love poetry from the fifteenth century to the present day which included Donne, Rilke and Jong. This was partly because I wanted them to think about and discuss the differences between each genre, but it was also as a way into a discussion of pornography. I wanted them to produce their own definitions, one that they might remember when they were watching their Dad's/boyfriend's/own blue movies or reading *American Psycho*. I didn't give them any pornography, although when I handed out the poems, some of them immediately said, 'Oh my God, this is disgusting.' My response to Mark's poem was one of pleasure because it evolved out of heated, illogical arguments and his own change of heart. I also, as did the rest of the class, appreciated his cunning use of footwear:

pornography injures the human heart
erica jong's flying you know what
(it rhymes with sock)
I thought was pornography
but now I see
the wheeling, graceful metaphor
for what it really is –
a part of me. (Mark 17)

I find, somewhat to my surprise, that what I've written appears to be as much about an approach to teaching poetry as it is to responding to students' writing. But perhaps we can't, or shouldn't, have one without thinking carefully about the other. What our students write must to a large extent depend on the models we offer, the expectations we hold and the chances we give them to be successful.

Sometimes this may involve seizing the moment, but more often it means providing it. Whenever possible I give them poetry which I hope will resonate for them in some way. I want them to make the links between what they read, discuss and write, and their own lives; even if I didn't want them to do this, they would anyway. I want them to read poetry which encourages them to consider or confront deeply held beliefs and prejudices, which are not necessarily their own, but which sometimes are.

Many of my students had never written poetry before. 'What me?' they said, 'me write a poem, you've got to be joking.' Much of what they wrote arose not just from a response to other poetry and prose, but also from an attempt to understand and articulate their own place in the world. Often it was a combination of both. Sometimes, their poems illuminated such disorder in their lives, or reflected their deepest fears and anxieties and at such moments they were entrusting me with more than a poem. And of course they also wrote with humour, verve and courage. Many years ago, David Holbrook wrote, 'I think there is no child who is not capable of fine feelings, of sorrow, of sympathy, love and delight.' I agree, and find such fine feeling in their poems as well as in their response to poetry and to each other.

Coda

What would I do differently now? Well, to begin with I would use far more visual texts including comix, cartoons and picture books and spend more time moving in and out of poetry and crossing over to other narratives and genres.

My students might welcome a close analysis of Hardy's poem, 'The Convergence of the Twain (Lines on the loss of the Titanic)' if we had first compared the scene where the ship hits the ice in three film versions: the 1953 *Titanic* directed by Negulesco; the 1958 British *A Night to Remember* and the recent James Cameron (1999) *Titanic*. The design of the Titanic and the disaster itself would become evident as a class construct, once we looked at the first class passenger list and menus, the map of the layout of the ship (Sauder & Brewster 1998) the lists of survivors and the transcript of the Senate Investigations (Kuntz, 1998) and survivor stories (Foster 1999, Maxtone-Graham 1998).

I would use extracts from Seamus Heaney's translation of *Beowulf* together with the animated *Beowulf* and John Gardner's fast-moving, meta-fictive, mythic and poetic *Grendel*. This novel is told from the monster's point of view, as are Charles Keeping's illustrations to Crossley-Holland's translation. Here, Keeping, deliberately chooses to resist the text and the usual opposition of good and evil, and depicts Grendel 'not so much as a monster, but more as a deformed outcast of society' (Martin 1989, p. 44).

I would introduce my students to other texts referenced by their own poetry. Robert's angels in his first successful poem would suggest Janeen Webb's short story 'Blake's Angel', set in a future where living angels are prized. A captured angel is sold to a poet with writers' block; angel song, it is said, will cure him, but the angel for a long time refuses to sing. Robert would enjoy this story and so would everyone else. We could examine why the author calls her poet Blake William; this could involve some research on William Blake's poetry, and his paintings and engravings of angels, which would almost certainly take us to Milton's fallen archangel in *Paradise Lost*. The Argument, which precedes each Book (Milton 1991) summarizes the poem and this could be read against biblical and other versions of the fall of the archangel; and of the fall of man, caused by a woman, which would lead to a number of very different arguments.

I would show them two large format editions of *Paradise Lost*. The one illustrated by Ian Pollock (Milton 1991) is of a techno world; his brightly coloured, highly symbolic watercolors are awash with detail. They place Milton's fallen angel, skull-for-a-head, carrying an umbrella, dressed in a striped suit in a modern landscape of tyres, guns, planes, globes, skyscrapers and blood. His illustrations give us a far more hellish Satan than Milton's heroic verse does, unlike Mary Groom's romantic wood engravings (Milton 1937). Blake said of Milton, that he 'was of the devil's party without knowing it' (quoted by John Wain in Milton 1991, p. vii), and Groom stands together with Milton; her delicate engravings offer us an elegant Satan with shapely limbs and hung with jewels; he is as gorgeous as the poet's East.

Homophobia, racism and sexism were always challenged but now I would be more overt about this. Dealing with homophobia in the classroom is difficult; but there are novels and short story collections (Macleod 1996, Pausacker 1996), which present alternative images of sexuality and texts of real life narratives by young people, their families and teachers, together with excellent classroom strategies (Pallotta-Chiarolli 2005). I would also send my students home to see *Angels in America*, *Boys Don't Cry* and *Shame*.

I would teach far more contemporary, Australian indigenous poetry especially the poetry and music of Romaine Morton and Archie Roach together with the report of the national enquiry into the stolen generation. The 'grief and loss,' the 'tenacity and survival' (Human Rights and Equal Opportunity Commission 1997, p. 3) recorded in the report are evident in much contemporary poetry, lyrics, picture books, documentaries and film. Richard Frankland's powerful, 28 minute film *Harry's War* (1999) not only has all the necessary filmic requirements to teach 'film as text', it is also a powerful story of friendship, love and reconciliation.

We might well look at various constructions of femininity and masculinity using the South African critical literacy comic *Heart to Heart* (Watson & Mashigo 1994), Angela Carter's short story and film script of *The Company of Wolves* and Anthony Browne's picture books. The two stories in *Heart to Heart* and the meta-narrative could lead into any number of poems and other texts about love, including those that offer alternative constructions of gender. These could include Carter's Little Red Riding Hood (in Carter 1979), Browne's small boy who goes into the forest to find his father (Browne 2004), and the not-so-innocent fairy tale world of Sondheim's *Into the Woods* (Lapine 1999).

The subtitles on the school textbooks published by the Rethinking Schools movement in the USA are upfront in their intention to address social justice and equity issues within the curriculum. I can't imagine an Australian primary/secondary textbook, where the introduction would state that the curriculum should be explicitly anti-racist, activist and visionary, and that their textbooks 'begin from the premise that schools and classrooms should be laboratories for a more just society than the one we now live in' (Bigelow, Harvey, Karp & Miller 2001, p. 3).

Perhaps we should, whenever we can, privilege texts that are concerned with how to respond to each other with empathy and humanity. We often teach to war films and poetry; perhaps we should devote more of the curriculum to the specific *causes* of war such as poverty, racism, xenophobia and gender politics. Simon Schama's description of the Irish Hunger Memorial shows us landscape as text. A ruined cottage from County Mayo, a field of clover, rocks and bog grass, overlook the Stature of Liberty, Ellis Island and commercial skyscrapers; it commemorates the victims of the nineteenth century, Irish potato famine.

Schama asks, 'How could the greatest famine in nineteenth century Europe have persisted in the backyard of the greatest empire in the world?' (Schama 2004, p. 276) Janet Frame's 'The Terrible Screaming' answers this. In her short story everyone can hear the screaming, but it's too uncomfortable to acknowledge, easier to pretend it doesn't exist. The story concludes with the observation that the terrible screaming was silence and 'Silence had found its voice' (Frame 1991, p. 107). We need to teach our students to understand that they too have voices, and can use them towards building a more just society.

References

Bigelow, B., Harvey, B., Karp, S. and Miller, L. (eds) (2001) *Rethinking Our Classrooms: Teaching for Equity and Justice, Volume 2*, Wisconsin: Rethinking Schools Press.

Browne, A. (2004) *Into the Forest*, London: Walker Books

Cameron, J. (dir.) (1999) *Titanic*, Lane Cove, N.S.W.: Twentieth Century Fox Home Entertainment.

Carter, A. (1979) *The Bloody Chamber*, Penguin: Melbourne.

Foster, J. W. (ed.) (1999) *Titanic*, Melbourne: Penguin Books.

Frame, J. (1991) The Terrible Screaming, in *You Are Now Entering The Human Heart*, London: The Women's Press, pp. 105–107.

Franklin, R. (dir.) (1999) *Harry's War*, South Melbourne: Australian Film Institute.

Gardner, J. (1972) *Grendel*, London: Andre Deutsch.

Harris, R. and McFarlane, P. (1985) *A Book to Perform Poems By*, Adelaide: AATE.

Human Rights and Equal Opportunity Commission (1997) *Bringing Them Home: Report of the National Enquiry into the Separation of Aboriginal and Torres Strait Islander Children from their Families*, Sydney: Sterling Press.

Macleod, M. (ed.) (1996) *Ready or Not*, Sydney: Random House.

Martin, D. (1989) *The Telling Line: Essays on Fifteen Contemporary Book Illustrators*. New York: Bantam, Doubleday, Dell Publishing Group.

Maxtone-Graham, J. (ed.) (1998) *Titanic Survivor: The Memoirs of Violet Jessup-Stewardess*, ACT: Boronia Press.

McFarlane, P. and Harris, R. (1997) *Doing Bombers Off the Jetty!: Models for Writing Poetry*, South Melbourne: Macmillan.

Milton, J. (1937) *Paradise Lost*, M. Groom (illust.), London: Golden Cockerel Press.

Milton, J. (1991) *Paradise Lost*, I. Pollock (illust.), London: Folio Society.

Pallotta-Chiarolli, M. (2005) *When Our Children Come Out: How to Support gay, Lesbian, Bisexual and Transgendered Young People*, Sydney: Finch Publishing.

Pausaker, J. (1996) *Hide and Seek: Stories About Being Young and Gay/Lesbian*, Melbourne: Mandarin.

Sauder, E. and Brewster, H. (1998) *The Titanic Collection*, San Francisco: Madison Press.

Schama, S. (2004) *Hang-Ups: Essays on Painting (Mostly)*, London: BBC Books.

Lapine, J. (dir.) (1999) *Into the Woods*, S. Sondheim (music and lyrics), Chatsworth, CA: Image Entertainment.

Watson, P. and Mashigo, I. (facilitators) (1994) *Heart to Heart*, Johannesburg: The Storyteller Group.

Some further suggested resources

Clark, M. (1982) *A History of Australia IV*, Melbourne: Melbourne University Press

Dann, J., Campbell, R. and Etchison, D. (eds) (2003) *Gathering the Bones*, Sydney: Harper Collins.

Dinenage, F. (ghostwriter) for Kray, R. and Kray R. (1989) *Reg and Ron Kray: Our Story*, London: Pan Macmillan

Ellin, S. (1979) *The Speciality of the House and Other Stories*, New York: Mysterious Press

Gee, J.P., Hull G. and Lankshear C, (1996) *The New Work Order: Behind the Language of the New Capitalism*, St. Leonards, N.S.W.: Allen & Unwin.

Gilbert, P. (ed.) (1995) *Challenging the Text: Critical Literacy Units for Secondary English*, Townsville: James Cook University.

Hancock, J. and Simpson. A. (1997) *Reflecting on Viewing: Final Report*, Canberra: Dept. of Employment, Education and Training.

Hirsch, E. (1999) *How to Read a Poem: and Fall in Love With Poetry*, New York: Harcourt Brace & Co.

Lankshear, C. with Gee J.P., Knobel, M. and Searle, C. (1997) *Changing Literacies*, Buckingham: Open University Press.

Ondaatje, M. (1992) *Running in the Family*, London: Bloomsbury.

Pearson, J. (1995) *The Profession of Violence: The Rise and Fall of the Kray Twins, 4th edn*, London: Harper Collins.

Rogers, T. and Soter, A.O. (eds) (1997) *Reading Across Cultures: Teaching Literature in a Diverse Society*, New York: Teachers College Press & NCTE.

Stephens, J. and Watson, K. (eds) (1994) *From Picture Book to Literary Theory*, Sydney: St. Clair Press

Stevens, W. (1971) *The Palm at the End of the Mind: Selected Poems and a Play*, New York: Random House.

Chapter 13

Hybridity, Creativity and Learning

Writing in the Science Classroom

Gaell Hildebrand

Hybrid
Imaginative/scientific writing
Involves creative thinking,
Synthesis and active researching.
Demonstrating that you can
Appropriate the language
Of power.
Pushing the boundaries of genres,
Combining, blending, bending;
Showing the teacher more than they knew
About you
And your constructions of science.

An early memory I have in my personal history as a writer occurred when a careers advisor told me that although I was equally interested in writing and science I would have to choose one or the other. 'You can't do both', she declared. I left the room puzzled: 'Why not? Scientists write. Writers write about science. Why can't I bring science and writing together?'

These days I am confident enough to say: 'Bleah!' (with tongue protruded). 'I am doing both. I promote both. I am convinced each is informed by the other.'

Sadly, there are still many careers advisers, science teachers and – dare I say it? – English teachers who think that the 'two cultures' of science and the arts (Charles Snow[1] 1963) should remain unconnected. This is despite many studies critiquing this position, including Nobel Laureates in science, such as Peter Medawar (1963), who argued that most science writing does not follow the linguistic rules of discrete scientific genres – and he argued this way back in 1963, the same year Snow's treatise was published.

I have deliberately broken the conventions of academic discourse in writing this chapter. You will find poetic interludes, as well as other types of writing that I have brought together to create a hybrid text. I do this deliberately in order to disrupt the established practice of separating the discourses typically associated with the arts from those used in the sciences. I am trying to be one of Arthur Koestler's (1959) 'creative trespassers' (*The Sleepwalkers*) moving freely between the two cultures of science and the arts. As Mike Watts observes: 'Science and poetry are so often caricatured as being at opposite ends of a cultural spectrum, the one so dour, impersonal, detached and stone-cold logic, the other emotional, irrational, imaginative and artfully eloquent (Watts 2001, p. 198). In my writing and my teaching I try to transcend these binaries, thereby opening up new possibilities for language and learning in my classrooms.

> *My purposes*
> *In using poetry*
> *Are to:*
> *Evoke feelings,*
> *Prod reflections,*
> *Act politically,*
> *Enjoy complexity,*
> *Use metaphors,*
> *Shift gear, and*
> *Create connections.*

I write poetry despite being warned: 'use the linguistic and stylistic resources of the poet or artist for scientific communication, and you will not have standing as being scientific' (Jay Lemke 1995, p. 178). I am prepared to take the risk – even though it feels extremely risky to expose my poetic efforts to an English teaching audience. I choose to play with the linguistic conventions in order to illustrate, by form as well as content, that our pedagogical practices in (science) teaching are informed by our belief systems, our frames of reference, our past experiences, our aesthetic appreciation – by our subjectivities.

Whose interests have been served by the divide between the arts and sciences? Certainly not those of the learner. Particularly not the commonly disenfranchised learner – those who are not white, not Anglo, not male. Mainstream science – the 'malestream' as Mary O'Brien (1981) described it – has benefited from the construction of a specialist zone where highly technical language has created the impression that science is neutral – even value-free – while at the same time building borders that are difficult to transgress for those outside this specific domain. This Western science, this knowledge/power generator of 'truth', has created itself through the collective voices of many men, as something that is absolute, beyond question, and supremely 'rational'. None of these men – to borrow Ruth Wallsgrove's words – want to confront the paradox that 'you can't be rational if you pretend that everything you do is rational; if you don't examine and come to terms with what you feel, your feelings will interfere anyway, but in a hidden and uncontrollable way' (Wallsgrove 1980, p. 235).

Feelings matter. Emotions influence learning. Knowledge is never neutral. These things I have learned in the process of critiquing science from a feminist perspective. Science is for all – not for a small group of white boys/men who ridiculously pretend they are always 'rational'. Through the act of writing – including rehearsing their writing, revising their writing, and presenting their writing to an engaged audience – students actively construct meaning that is personally significant to them.

This chapter draws on teachers' experiences of using hybrid imaginative/scientific writing with their students in order to facilitate their learning in science. These hybrid genres create learning spaces where students can (re)locate themselves into a new frame of reference, synthesising ideas, anthropomorphising them, transforming scientific ideas into their own language, and demonstrating their learning.

Writing in/forms science learning

I want to play with the notion of 'in/forms'. Firstly, writing 'in' science and in science learning becomes the artefact – the trace left behind through which we infer and interpret meaning. Science itself has always been informed by imaginative writing – writing using metaphorical devices, allegories and imagery. I will report some science teachers' voices here, each of whom is an experienced user of hybrid imaginative/ scientific writing in their science classrooms where they set hybrid writing as assessable learning tasks. Their focus was on poetry, anthropomorphic narratives and travel brochures as representative hybrid genres – all forms they used to scaffold students' learning.

Secondly, writing 'forms' science learning through the very act of writing itself, enabling us to construct particular perspectives on what it means to learn science. Traditionally certain types of writing tasks shape science discourse and these must be challenged because a) the available texts construct science as a rational field that 'discovers' through the mythical 'scientific method', and b) the allowable genres construct science learning as merely a project focussed on recalling facts, processes and theories. Stepping outside the genre constraints usually imposed on, and by, science teachers provides opportunities for a new view of science learning to become visible.

Thirdly, writing 'informs' science, and science learning, as the writing becomes a tool, or medium, for proposing possibilities, for playing with thinking frameworks, and for the clarification of ideas. Hybrid imaginative/scientific genres generate new ways of 'thinking' science and teachers who use such tasks come to understand their students' learning in ways that teachers who rely solely on so-called 'factual' writing rarely can. Hence, writing equals learning in science classrooms – if the boundaries of what is written are diversified beyond conventional, so-called 'scientific', genres.

> *Our discourse on pedagogy*
> *Is shaped by our frame of reference,*
> *Our ideological positioning.*
>
> *Through my feminist lens,*
> *I re/vision ways of learning science:*
> *By interrupting the hegemony*
> *Of science-as-usual,*
> *Of power-as-usual,*
> *Of pedagogy-as-usual,*
> *Of writing-as-usual.*
> *Changing power*
> *By*
> *Crossing borders.*

What is 'hybrid imaginative/scientific writing' in secondary school science?

I define hybrid imaginative/scientific writing as any hybrid, or blended, genres that use 'scientific' and/or 'factual' genres (i.e. recounts, procedures, reports, explanations, expositions, discussions, etc.) in conjunction with imaginative genres. The genres for writing to learn science are therefore immediately expanded. The following examples serve to open a window of possibilities on hybrid imaginative/scientific writing:

> Imagine you are a water molecule: describe five changes of state that you have recently experienced (anthropomorphic narrative).
> Prepare a travel brochure advertising a trip to another planet (advertisement).
> You are a parachutist – or dancer, or basketballer . . . – describe the forces acting on you throughout a jump – or dance, game . . . – (realistic recount).
> Write a poem describing a monotreme, in the shape of that animal (poetry).

Other forms of writing included under this rubric are:

- a range of narratives (horror, romance, adventure, science fiction, comic strips);
- diaries and journals (travel, autobiography);
- letters (home, To the Editor, Dear Dorothy Dix);
- poems (ballad, ode, limerick, cinquain);

- song lyrics (rap, rock, ballad);
- scripts (live production, screenplay, radio show);
- advertisements (brochures, jingles, posters); and
- journalistic writing (news and sports reports, editorials, obituaries).

Further examples are described by Leonie Gianello (1988), Hildebrand (1989), Liz James (1989), Sue Lewis and Anne Davies (1988), McClintock Collective (1989), and by Vaughan Prain and Brian Hand (1996). You can see from the publication dates that the value of using hybrid genres in science classes is nothing new. Yet this insight may still be new to many teachers, including English teachers and Literacy Coordinators who may not have considered the possibility of using imaginative writing to facilitate learning in science.

> *Science,*
> *Powerful, creative, evolving,*
> *Challenging, exploring, thinking, learning,*
> *Writers actively constructing meaning,*
> *Science.*

The most commonly used hybrid genre is anthropomorphic narrative. In science there are many concepts that have been given anthropomorphic names: electrophilic (electron–loving), hydrophobic (water–hating) and so on. Such scientific terms ascribe human feelings, forms or other attributes to things not human. Science is both enriched by anthropomorphic and metaphorical language and enriches our everyday language through lending terms such as the uncertainty principle, fermentation, bonding, memory bank, and so on. In some discourse communities, any use of hybrid imaginative/ scientific genres, such as anthropomorphic writing, is dismissed as an inappropriate tool for learning science merely because it steps outside the documented patterns of some conventional scientific writing in papers and textbooks. This is a position I contest by drawing on what teachers know, their 'wisdom of practice' (Shulman 1987), as they intuitively set tasks that have the goal of writing to learn science, rather than (merely) learning to write science, as currently written by some scientists in some contexts.

In Table 1, I have catalogued a spectrum of different writing to learn tasks used by the sample of four science teachers I am quoting in this chapter.

I have written at length elsewhere (Hildebrand 2002) about the controversial notion of anthropomorphism in science hybrid writing where I concluded that the evidence from both students and teachers is clear: writing anthropomorphically enables students to synthesise science concepts and see relationships within a new frame of reference, and it provides a positive affective element, as it engages students, a necessary precondition for learning to occur.

Sample Writing Tasks	Year level	Science area	Writing artefact (product)
Alex			
You are Roula, the red blood cell. Describe a day in your life.	9	biology	narrative (anthropomorphic)
Yesterday was a freaky day; I woke up to find myself in a world without friction.	9	physics	narrative (fantasy)
The circulatory system as a city transport map.	9	biology	annotated map with metaphors
Describe a trial to determine if something is living or not with arguments for the defence and prosecutor.	7	biology	legal report
Katie			
Prepare a travel brochure for a part of the solar system.	7	astronomy	advertisement
Write a letter home from space.			letter
Write a song about four elements.	7	chemistry	poetry/song
Write a book for primary students on safety with electricity.	8	physics	manual
Rosemary			
The rock cycle – from the rock's perspective.	7	geology	narrative (anthropomorphic)
The atoms' party – and who went home with whom.	9	chemistry	narrative (anthropomorphic)
Write a set of postcards home from your trip down the gut – one from each major organ you visit.	9	biology	narrative (anthropomorphic)
Sandy			
The fate of a ham sandwich.	9	biology	narrative (anthropomorphic)
You are a molecule in crude oil; describe your progress through a fractionating column.	10	chemistry	narrative (anthropomorphic)

Table 1: Writing Tasks Used by Collaborating Teachers

Whose story?

So far, this text has portrayed my perspective, my construction and my story. But shortly I will introduce some teachers' voices, disguised with pseudonyms. Each teacher was purposefully chosen as they had been using imaginative writing within science for a period of three or more years and were considered to be typical of expert users. I knew these teachers through our shared commitment to gender-inclusive pedagogy and they had all taken on hybrid writing as one facet of their work toward that goal. They were not novices to the practice, nor were they coerced into trying hybrid writing as a learning tool in science. There is no random sample here.

In the generation and analysis of the data that indicates these teachers' perspectives, my role involved empathetic understanding and partiality, rather than detachment and objective portrayal, and the process rested on a premise of respect for the daily complexity of their pedagogical realities. I recognise that I have interacted with the collaborating teachers in this research, not just measured their views from a distanced vantage point at a particular instant in time.

For practical purposes, this paper draws only on the interviews of four women teachers – 'Alex', 'Katie', 'Rosemary' and 'Sandy' – whose voices reflect the larger group of twenty teachers studied. Their schools provided a student population that embraced the ethnicities, first languages and class patterns of Australian students. While I also observed their classes, and surveyed and interviewed their students, I am not drawing on that evidence here.

'Discourses are about what can be said, and thought, but also about who can speak, when, where and with what authority' (Stephen J. Ball 1993, p. 14). Science, including its off-spring school science, is a discourse of 'power/knowledge' in Michel Foucault's (1977) terms – the discourse of science is given status and power in society as a source of 'truth'. I seek to interrupt the discourse of dominant science pedagogy, 'hegemonic pedagogy', because of my belief that it acts to reproduce science-as-is, science that is directly linked to hegemonic masculinity and power through language. By pedagogy I mean all those interactions between the teacher, the students, the formal and the hidden curriculum, and the resources that work together to produce the lived experience of school science. In particular, I seek to interrupt the hegemonic writing practices in science – those practices that have been established over time through patterning school science writing on particular artefacts, the selected writings of scientists. This is clearly my story, embroidered with science teachers' voices. The links between ideology and pedagogy are the broad fabric of this chapter.

> *Discourses on appropriate genres in science*
> *Avoid questions of whether the conventions*
> *Inculcate a positivist view: an over-reliance,*
> *And ought to be the subject of contravention.*
>
> *There is no 'scientific genre' – as a singularity,*
> *And to insist that school writing be in compliance*
> *With restrictive styles is to effectively guarantee*
> *Limitations on learning through writing in science.*

Writing IN Science Learning

Writing is one of the pedagogical tactics that teachers can use to enable the building of students' scientific capability. As students write they are developing expertise and confidence in thinking about and working with science concepts, models, arguments, and inquiry processes. Both writing to learn science and learning to write science are valuable activities for students to experience. The value of writing to learn is now widely accepted by science education researchers because 'the act of writing in science is seen as a process of constructing understanding and building knowledge – the minds-on complement to hands-on inquiries' (Larry Yore et al. 2003, p. 712). In concluding his comprehensive review of writing to learn science, Prain (2002) argued:

> for the continuation of the two broad orientations identified in this field. The genrist position is strong on the content of science to be learnt, where content refers broadly to both knowledge about, and participatory skills in, the practices of science, while the diversified writing perspective is strong on likely conditions for building student broader understanding and engagement with science, as well as the development of critical perspectives towards this subject. (Prain 2002, p. 15)

I am drawing from the 'diversified writing perspective', providing examples from the evidence generated from teachers when they used hybrid imaginative/scientific writing genres as a vehicle for learning science ideas (Hildebrand 1998, 2002). I am thus focussing on writing to learn science, rather than learning to write science.

The word 'writing' is both a verb and a noun and as such it signifies both a process and a product or artefact. The process of writing enables many of us to learn what we think as we write/type, cut, paste and deliberate over our writing – in that sense writing is a medium for learning. As writers we are active in constructing meaning for ourselves: interrogating our thoughts, re-arranging our ideas, clarifying our position. One way we learn is to write something new – something we have to struggle with, are challenged by, and develop ownership of, as we transform the words on the screen/page to build our meaning.

A thought bubble on my writing:
As I struggle to formulate my ideas and sharpen my thinking in this chapter I re-write, insert, delete, and rearrange in an effort to send a clear message to you, the reader. I am engaged in the act of sense-making for myself. However, what I decide is a clear position may be interpreted by you in quite different ways from my intentions. The text evokes diverse responses, has multiple meanings, initiates a critique that is dissent or concord depending on your frame of reference, your prior understandings, your subjectivities.

The writing sample, or product, is the artefact left behind: the record of thinking that others can read, review and synthesise into their own thinking. The writing artefact takes on multiple meanings as your understandings, as the reader, filter, critique and reconstruct concepts as you interact with my text. Your meanings are informed by your expertise and your experiences. Meaning–making also depends on your particular ideological orientation within your own discourse community.

A thought bubble on scientists' writing:
As scientists write they are engaged in meaning-making, in creating a case, in staking a claim, in arguing a point. As they re-write, insert, delete and rearrange their words to form a text, they are engaged in a struggle to formulate their ideas and clarify their thinking so that they may convince their peers that they have generated a new conceptualisation of our physical world, or some aspect of it. Their audience is the discourse community of other scientists producing knowledge in their field, and the broader public. In their struggle to write with clarity they also draw on rhetorical tools and metaphorical language to help persuade their readers.

The scientists in Yore et al.'s study (2004, p. 361) reported that 'writing served to generate insights, deepen understanding, help eliminate ambiguity, show gaps in data and argumentation, uncover errors, solve problems, and lead to new areas of inquiry'. Similarly for our students, as they struggle to write, they construct meaning for themselves. The artefact, or written product, that they complete becomes a record of where their thinking has moved to during the writing process.

As argued by Hand and Prain (1996, p. 26) 'the use of different writing types for different audiences requires students to conceptualise their own knowledge from a different perspective'. By using a broader spectrum of writing tasks teachers may also interest and engage some students in science who have been previously disengaged from this powerful field of knowledge. Providing a route into science for such students is in itself a worthwhile reason for diversifying writing practices in science. Patricia Rowell (1997, p. 47) in her wide-ranging review of writing to learn in science, concludes that 'writing in school science could be used to move in multiple directions among discourses' rather than constraining students to write within set genres all the time. This freeing up of writing constrictions will provide alternative ways of thinking about and through science. She argues that:

if multiple roles for writing in science are recognized, the taken-for-granted communication function, tied to transmission of information … could be dislodged from its predominant position. (Rowell 1997, p. 48)

Douglas Barnes (1992) reports on an earlier study he undertook (Barnes and Shemilt 1974) which showed that science teachers saw writing as predominantly a 'mechanism for rehearsing and recording information', compared with the view of English teachers that writing was 'an opportunity for the learner to make sense of his or her learning' (Barnes 1992, p. 21). The practising science teachers whose voices you will hear in this chapter had similar motivations to those English teachers reported by Barnes and Shemilt, i.e. they were interested in how writing might enable students to learn science, rather than simply teaching them how to write science. Clive Sutton thinks that science teachers have generally 'accorded too low a status' to writing tasks as they focused on practical investigations and yet learners clearly need 'thinking, talking and writing activities' in order to have space to 'reflect on ideas' and science teachers need to 'organise the means for them to do so' (Sutton 1992, p. 3).

Writing FORMS Images of Science Learning

I challenge the norms of writing in science classes because I think that writing forms (shapes, defines) science learning through the texts that are *available* for students to read and interpret which in turn dictate what is *allowable* for students to write and produce. Although science education constructivists (e.g. Roger Osborne and Peter Freyberg 1985) and feminist educators (e.g. Alison Lee 1996) hold a range of views on learning, both groups agree on the centrality and power of language in shaping our understandings and constructions of the world about us. Lemke's assertion that the use of scientific terminology is interpreted as a 'claim to power' and people come to accept that 'superior' people master it (Lemke 1987) is related to the concern of many feminist science educators, myself included, that science is directly linked to hegemonic masculinity (Evelyn Fox Keller and Helen Longino 1996) through, among other means, the discursive practices associated with its learning and teaching.

The writing genres traditionally available for students of science construct science as positivist, a discourse that can be traced back to simplistic – and unrealistic – Baconian notions of science. The texts set for students to read imply that there is a right way to write science, presenting science as a process of induction that proceeds smoothly without discontinuities until a self-evidently correct view is reached. In such a discourse, the third person passive voice permeates the writing in order to distance the knower from the known, to create a feeling of observations speaking for themselves, and to generate apparently unchallengeable conclusions based on rational arguments that are, seemingly, uninfluenced by the ideological framework of the scientist. The passive voice can also be used to abrogate responsibility as shown by comparing these two examples of text: 'the third sample was rendered unusable' rather than 'I dropped the third sample'.

These writing artefacts do not fairly represent the process of science, as was argued by the Nobel laureate, Peter Medawar (1963) in his classic exposé of the hypocrisy of the conventional genres of scientific papers. Some researchers in the history, philosophy and sociology of science (e.g. Bruno Latour 1987) agree that the image of science constructed by the formal artefacts of science, the written traces of scientists' work in journals and textbooks, do not correlate closely with the practice of science as it is actually conducted today. Yet the implicit ideological assumption within hegemonic pedagogy has been the belief that the 'natural' genres of writing used to learn science ought to be in one-to-one correspondence with the narrow genres employed to formally report science.

The available texts construct science as masculine. Feminist critics of science (e.g. Sandra Harding 1991, Fox Keller and Longino 1996) argue that presenting science as positivist aligns it with hegemonic masculinity. Both of these constructions – hegemonic masculinity and positivist science – are based on a common set of asymmetric dualisms where the concepts in the left column are valorised, taken as the norm, and used as the measure of worth. The concepts in the right column are associated with the 'other', are of lower status, and represent a supposed inherent inferiority. These dualisms create implicit assumptions about (hegemonic) masculinity and femininity, as well as science and non-science. Some sample dualisms are:

rational	emotional
logical	intuitive
objective	subjective
abstracted	holistic

As a feminist I argue that both sides of these dualistic concepts are present in science and should be portrayed within the available texts in schools. Science involves both the logical and the intuitive, both the objective and the subjective, as Linda Shepherd (1993) has shown.

The writing genres usually allowable for students to produce in school construct an image of what counts as science learning. This image is established through an emphasis on recalling facts, concepts, and theories; solving algorithmic problems; and adopting scientists' models and metaphors. I cannot condone this view of learning as simply receiving and reproducing information – authentic learning always involves constructing and reconstructing, internalising and personalising. I contend that the current emphasis in many science classrooms on using only so-called 'factual' or 'scientific' genres in the process of learning science may:

- inhibit learning processes;
- alienate many students, especially girls;
- construct an imaginary world of science; and
- promote a sexist, Western, neo-Colonial science-as-usual.

The discourse patterns within the texts that are available for students to read, and allowable for them to write, shape their thinking in, of, and about science. Whilst I agree with Jim Martin (1990) that students need to be explicitly taught how to deconstruct and use the hegemonic genres of power in science they can also be fruitfully asked to 'bend the genre' and not leave this task only to 'the most prestigious members' of science (Carol Berkenkotter and Thomas Huckin 1995, p. 159). The texts that students produce can therefore be vehicles for challenging what is understood as science and as science learning.

The Politics of Disruption

In looking at hegemonic pedagogy, as enacted within secondary science classrooms, Lorraine Code asks: 'out of whose subjectivity has this ideal grown?' (Code 1991, p. 70). When considering the *politics of disruption*, it becomes clear that those who are in some way marginalized by established practices – anyone constructed as 'the other' – have a greater personal investment in fractures or interruptions.

> *Marginalised as the other:*
> *Not white,*
> *Not male,*
> *Not heterosexual,*
> *Not speaking English as a first language,*
> *Not living in privileged neighbourhoods.*
> *The other*
> *Has become the majority.*

I speak here from the perspective of someone who is committed to interrogating the gender/education system as a source of disenfranchisement from science and from power, while recognising that voices from positions exploring ethnicity/race, post-Colonialism and sexuality also challenge current practices in science classrooms.

At times there appears to be an impenetrable barrier to change, as though current practice is the 'natural' order. Yet interrupting and contesting dominant discourses, as history shows us, is always possible – even in science. 'We must all, women and men, become aware of the power dynamics which are discouraging for women and, most importantly, work to change that atmosphere' (Sharon Haggerty 1995, p. 7). As Haggerty argues, it is the responsibility of each of us to change the inequities of the current situation; we can no longer leave it to the marginalized groups, the victims of othering, to right the wrongs of hegemony. All educators (science teachers, English teachers, teacher educators and science education researchers) must become informed and act for change if we are not to be complicit in maintaining power for a small elite and marginalising the majority of the population.

Using the Politics of Disruption lens

I present here some voices from Victorian schools framed through the politics of disruption lens. Up till now, this has been my voice, my perspective, my story. Now it is time to mute my voice and introduce the teachers' voices to you.

While I am mindful that teachers' perspectives and experiences can never be fully captured by my cutting of their words into selected 'sound-bites', I have none-the-less organised them in a way that seemed to me to usefully structure their reasons for disrupting hegemonic science writing practices. These can be categorised as:

a)   A dissatisfaction with teachers' own learning processes in science;

b)   A belief that science is creative;

c)   A belief that science is dynamic and not fixed;

d)   A belief that an imperative of teaching is facilitating learning;

e)   A belief that science is linked with power through its language; and

f)   A commitment to try to bring science to all students.

Space restricts the number of teacher quotes that I can reasonably present, but I trust there are sufficient for you to clearly hear what these teachers have to say about their reasons for disruption.

(a) A dissatisfaction with teachers' own learning processes in science:

Learning equals memory – that was the way science was taught when I was at school. I was good at that and therefore I was successful at science, because that was the way the learning was promoted . . . But it's significantly different from myself as a learner now, reflecting on what I'm doing and why I'm doing it and 'what is learning, anyway?' (Alex)

When I was in secondary school . . . I found learning very threatening: it was always very competitive, the teachers were fairly authoritarian, there was nothing friendly about learning. Probably my love of science came more from my parents than anything I did at school. So I try to make learning in my classes non-threatening and non-competitive and more welcoming. (Rosemary)

I didn't gain a good understanding of science until I had to teach it. I really didn't. When I think that I went through a whole degree but some of the really basic ideas in science I don't think I ever really understood them before I taught them . . . I learnt by rote learning. I could get through the tests. That shows you how pathetic those tests were in terms of whether we really understood anything. (Sandy)

(b) A belief that science is creative:

Scientists are creative people . . . The important discoveries that have been made have been made by very imaginative and creative people . . . Scientists are interesting people too, and I think it's getting them [students] around the idea that scientists are these straight people getting around in lab coats and so on . . . and lots of scientists who have made interesting discoveries haven't been your conventional sort of scientist — as students perceive them. (Katie)

I think if you don't have the creativity and imagination, you can have all the knowledge in the world, but you'll still just put one foot after the other. It's the hop, skip and jump — sideways, forwards or backwards, or up or down — that makes the discoveries, that leads to new ideas and new fields. (Rosemary)

(c) A belief that science is dynamic and not fixed:

I guess what we'd encourage kids to do would be to start thinking, and not stop thinking, about stuff that they come across in the lab. And not to think about science as a collection of 'facts' that haven't changed and won't change. And to think that it's more of a dynamic process — and I think by doing things that encourage kids to write and think and talk divergently, by using kids talking to each other about their work, by using creative writing, by using role play, we're encouraging them to move away from the stereotyped image of what science has been and to think about it in a more evolutionary way. (Alex)

(d) A belief that an imperative of teaching is facilitating learning:

I've been aware of difficulties in learning things in certain ways and I've tried to make things more accessible for students. That's the whole point of this: I'm trying to make things more accessible. (Katie)

I like the idea that you can get some divergent thinking going in a topic and explore it more thoroughly. Explore it in different ways than the kinds of exercises that you might be getting from a textbook or from question-answer things, where you're limited to one kind of response and that was in the mind of the person who devised it in the first place . . . There are strategies that you'd want to promote for good learning or understanding to happen . . . and this is one of them. (Alex)

(e) A belief that science is linked with power through its language:

The function of language is to help people communicate — to facilitate communication. It's not meant to be exclusive you see . . . I think there is a bit of academic snobbery too, in a lot of the so-called scientific language. There's more than just using the scientific language: there's politics and power at play there . . . it's the politics of language. (Katie)

(f) A commitment to try to bring science to all students:

I think having an understanding of the different types of kids [is important] and where they're going and what they're going to be doing . . . [and] understanding that different people need different tasks in order to show their abilities and their potential. (Rosemary)

My original premise when I started teaching science was that 'science is for all', it isn't just for people who were going to be studying at university or whatever . . . I guess one of our aims in science education is to produce a scientifically literate population, a scientifically aware population that can really take part in the decision-making process. (Katie)

Enabling Pedagogy

Hegemonic pedagogy, the dominant form implemented as a set of conventions, has worked well in the past for many 'malestream' students and is still the mainstay of most of the world's science teachers. However, hegemonic pedagogy has quite rightly been critiqued by writers within feminist and critical pedagogies, largely on the grounds of its complicity in producing students who are gendered, powerless and 'governable' (in Foucault's terms). It has certainly not worked well for the majority of the world's students, those constructed as 'the other'.

After engaging with the arguments from critical and feminist pedagogies, I must reject many conventions within hegemonic pedagogy because of the way they send messages to students about science, about learning, about gender and about power. I reject, for example: the presentation of science as fragmented scraps of knowledge that are divorced from the social lives of students; the presentation of science as the 'truth', a quest for the right answers to add to the catalogue of facts, algorithms and fixed models; the pressure to coerce students to conform to 'scientific' models; and the unexamined ways science is used as a powerful gatekeeper for future pathways for students.

However, I cannot adopt without modification feminist and critical pedagogies. They themselves might be subjected to critique as 'regimes of truth' (Jennifer Gore 1993). A major concern that I have is that they appear to embody a conception of power that can be given to others, stored and used later, in a banking model. A second inherently arrogant assumption of critical and feminist pedagogies exposed by Gore is that teachers claim to know what is best for the students who are to be empowered.

So where do these concerns leave me? I propose an alternative, enabling pedagogy (Hildebrand 1998), that engages students in significant, challenging, and meaningful learning, that is sensitive to their diverse learning interests, concerns and needs and that addresses their social contexts, values and life experiences in an enjoyable and intriguing manner.

Enabling pedagogy *both* pragmatically accepts that the authority of a teacher in a regular school classroom cannot be given over entirely to the students *and* expansively seeks to shift the power balance within the classroom, within science, and within the broader society. An enabling pedagogy recognises the systemic constraints that operate on teachers' daily work, such as an intended curriculum content and structures that are prescriptive, even in sites where school-based curriculum development prevails. An enabling pedagogy accepts that there are no universals that apply to all teaching contexts, all students and all teachers, nor does it presume deficits in students who have traditionally been positioned as 'other'.

Enabling pedagogy draws on and addresses at least five pedagogical facets:

a) the affective;
b) the creative;
c) the critical (as articulated in both feminist and critical theories);
d) the cognitive; and
e) sociocultural contexts.

Using the Enabling Pedagogy lens

I will now use the facets of enabling pedagogy to amplify teachers' voices, as they speak about hybrid imaginative/scientific writing.

(a) The Affective

Part of the pleasure of it for the kids, is that it allows them to have a bit of fun when they're doing it. So they can be imaginative and creative in what they're doing . . . I generally find that most kids love doing it. (Sandy)

I'm trying to actively engage them in the task by setting them a writing task where they've got an opportunity to use their imaginations, and to be creative, because I see science as a creative endeavour after all! And I want them to try things out. I think it's called risk-taking these days. I think to learn something effectively you have to be engaged in it, and they enjoy that sort of thing. (Katie)

If you're going to thrust the very scientific and very technical writing on kids who aren't ready for it you're going to turn them off and they're not going to like science. What I found is that by making science enjoyable and making them interested they're prepared to 'hack' something a bit harder next year because they can see some meaning to it now. If they don't get that con-nection, you lose them . . . It just brings science to being something that is enjoyable, that is relevant, [and] something that they can understand. (Rosemary)

(b) The Creative

We're fostering that side of science by telling kids 'it's OK' to use your imagination . . . If you can do the task and get some sort of positive feedback for it, well, it has a huge impact on their confidence . . . I think that's what the kids look forward to in a lot of the creative activities because they know it's something they can do and they will be successful . . . I think it's having the lateral thinking, the imagination, the creativity that helps them to enjoy science. (Rosemary)

If you really think about it, for example in chemistry, no one has ever seen atoms or electrons or particles, you're asking people to have an imagination, aren't you? You're asking them to think in an abstract way, to use their imagination . . . I'm not saying chuck the evidence out, or anything like that. I'm just saying that we're still asked to imagine – because we've not seen any of these things. We're assuming or we're inferring . . . It still requires a degree of imagination. You still have to have a picture in here [pointing to her head] that tells you that's the way such and such happens. (Katie)

We try and teach science creatively, as far as possible. (Katie)

(c) The Critical

I also get them to do a media analysis [of] an article from a magazine or a newspaper. We talk about the tools that the writer uses to engage an audience and how the message is being communicated . . . It makes them much more aware of how journalists operate [and they] start to question terms and so on and you look at an article much more closely and the kids will say 'Oh, now I see what they're trying to do there'. They can look at a piece of writing, scientific or otherwise, and the skills are going to transfer into other areas too. They can look at a piece of writing much more critically. That's one of the skills that I think they develop in this . . . by doing these sorts of tasks you're helping kids use the language of science and feeling comfortable with the language of science . . . just using language, and analysing language and being critical of the way language is used, say by journalists. And not being fooled by journalists. Science is empowering for some, it should be empowering for all. Those who can manipulate the language of science are in a very powerful position because you can exclude people, and 'bamboozle' them with facts, and whatever. But if people can become more critical of what's being said and how it's being said, perhaps they can then look beyond the obvious. (Katie)

The way we think about things now may not be the way we think about them in the future: and possibly that might happen because people are encouraged to think about them differently, in school. (Alex)

(d) The Cognitive

Using science to teach students to think:

> *It's one of those tools where you do have to put yourself in a [new] situation, and write about it. And you have to understand it be able to do it and that, I think, is where the strength comes from . . . anything that gets kids to perceive an idea in a different way, or play with it in a different way, has advantages, I think. It's freeing up their thinking processes. It's getting them to be a bit more flexible in the way that they're operating. (Sandy).*

Learning science is about broader skills than recalling knowledge:

> *They're learning scientific skills, they're clarifying scientific ideas, they're learning context, they're also learning skills in terms of communicating science. (Katie).*

Synthesising and seeing holistically:

> *I see it as a synthesis kind of activity and you need to develop some kind of understanding about what you're doing to be able to synthesise the ideas about it . . . I'm not saying that the creative writing piece is the be-all and end-all, but it was a point when we wanted to see it reflecting the synthesis of ideas and understandings that we had been working through. Because we didn't have a lot of time to spend on this unit our focus was, 'how was the thing a co-ordinated whole?' We felt that it had been too often studied in isolation before: this is the bit about the blood, and this is the bit about the heart – but the kids didn't understand how it was a whole system and why it was all necessary. So the tasks that we've done have tried to promote the idea of a system, and I think the [imaginative] writing lends itself reasonably well to a synthesis of the different functions and how it all works together. (Alex)*

Using imaginative writing to assess conceptual understandings:

> *It's one of the quickest ways to pick up misconceptions the kids have about anything. You find if they haven't got a clue about this, or they haven't made the connection between this and that . . . I think they like having other opportunities to show what they understand. Some students, in fact, find it an easier way to show what they understand than other methods. Often kids who hate tests really do well at a creative writing response . . . it really gets the kids to internalize [ideas] and understand what it's all about . . . They can't fool you in creative writing tasks . . . They have to re-organize it, they can't just take information and transcribe it. They have to be able to understand the information in their head to be able to write the story. (Sandy)*

(e) Sociocultural Contexts

Connecting with students' interests and worlds:

It's really interesting to see how kids think. I think if you have an idea in your head – this is the way I'm going to do this topic and I'm not going to allow for flexibility: this is the information I want them to know, it really cuts you off from any ideas that might be coming from them ... Kids themselves are a valuable resource – their questions are really resourceful and you can use those as a starting point for lots of things. I think if you don't allow that, if you don't set up the conditions for that, you're really cutting off a huge area that you haven't tapped into ... You have to have an open mind ... and you have to be able to accept kids' ideas, and be able to work with those, be prepared to develop ideas ... the idea of a disease booklet, came into my head purely from responses that students had to watching the video on body systems. (Katie)

Starting where students are:

The other reason that I think they quite like it [anthropomorphic writing], is because kids are self-centred and they like talking about 'I' and 'what I'm doing'. It's a stage of their development, especially for the younger kids ... It's an easier thing for them to do. To talk about 'I' rather than talk about something that's more abstract, or divorced from them. (Sandy)

Catering for differences:

There should be achievement even for the less able student. So even if they don't deal with the scientific concepts in great depth, at least they've learnt something about the concept. Whereas you can cater for the really bright students and you'd expect much more depth in their handling of the scientific concepts. That's another point I meant to make: that in the writing tasks you can allow for that varying range of abilities ... it allows for that, that's one of the advantages of it, I think. We're all trying to cater for individual differences. And if you've got any ESL students, for example ... you might simplify some of the language for them, or spend a little bit of time making a connection between the scientific terminology and the terms they might have used to explain something. So I think it's very helpful for ESL students ... But, having to put something in your words, and having to present it as well, certainly makes it part of you. (Katie)

And my starting point with these teachers, gender:

I find the girls like playing with the ideas more often than the boys do. They're more challenging of the ideas; the boys will accept the ideas. You could put it up on the board, and the boys will go 'yeah, that's OK', we'll go away and apply it. But if there's a little bit that one of the girls doesn't understand, that can be just an enormous barrier. That's one of the advantages of this [writing], it helps them put the big picture together, in the types of tasks that I use . . . [And] it's often the girls who hate tests, who have this phobia that 'I can't do tests', they love assignments . . . Part of this, too, is that they can do it in their own time and they can think about it. One of the concerns that a fair percentage of the girls that I teach hate about tests, is that they just don't have the opportunity to sit and think about what's going on. It's 'bang, bang, bang', working through all of these ideas, fast. (Sandy)

Playing with language = Writing to learn

Many of those who advocate the use of imaginative writing as a feminist practice promote a sense of playfulness in learning through writing (e.g. Gianello 1988, McClintock Collective 1989, James 1989). The concept that it is permissible to have fun in a science lesson is not new; neither is the idea of having fun through playing with writing. As Joan McLane writes:

it seems likely that play with written language can help children develop greater awareness and understanding of how it can be manipulated – of what can be done with it and of what they can do with it . . . Playing with the processes and forms of writing seems likely to give children a sense of 'ownership'. (McLane 1990, p. 312)

She describes play as allowing students to stretch their learning and feel as though they 'were already competent' or in Lev Vygotsky's words:

play creates a zone of proximal development of the child. In play a child always behaves beyond his [*sic*] age, above his daily behaviour; in play it is as though he were a head taller than himself. (Vygotsky 1978, p. 102)

Some students would be familiar with playfulness in popular books like those presented in Joanna Cole's (1989) *Magic School Bus* series – and its Microsoft® multimedia re-incarnations on CD-ROM. We ought to remember that not only young children like to play. So too do secondary students and their teachers. As Lemke exhorts: 'Make trouble. Play!' (Lemke 1995, p. 184). Powerful learning occurs when students are able to playfully engage in acts of hybrid writing in science.

Snippets from three year 9 students voice their view that through playing with hybrid genres these students do learn (the whole study included 144 students and these three are typical).

You get to learn more about it: things that you didn't know and after doing it you know a lot more. (Wesley, year 9 boy)

I liked doing the writing task because then you can go into more details of things. It really tests if you understand what you're talking about because you have to imagine it and visualise it. And sometimes you have a doubt so then you come up with a question and then you have to answer it and then you learn even more by doing it, without realising it. (Francesca, year 9 girl)

I think it helps you when you're actually learning the ideas. You just get virtually told about them [in class], and then you write a story, and while you're writing it then you learn about it. (Nigel, year 9 boy)

Writing INFORMS learning in science

Powerful learning occurs when students are engaged in acts of hybrid writing in science. Their teachers are thinking ideologically (disrupting hegemonic pedagogy) and acting practically (creating an enabling pedagogy). The teachers' goal is enabling scientific capability for all their students and this means thinking about how writing informs science learning. These teachers recognise that the sociocultural context of the classroom matters for their students and so they create an environment where play is supported, where ideas from students' social worlds connect with their learning; and where pleasure in the pursuit of learning is possible.

I conclude that the policing of genres that are allowable for students to produce while learning science, premised on the maintenance of hegemonic power relations and a chasmic separation of science and literature, is based on a fundamentally flawed positioning of boundaries. As Watts argues:

> any move which probes the human and imaginative aspects of science and which allows expression of feelings must act to make the learning of it less empty and less alien. (Watts 2001, p. 207)

The teachers whose voices we have heard here have resisted pressures to conform to a view of science and science teaching that they do not value. They have chosen to disrupt hegemonic pedagogy and by incorporating hybrid imaginative/scientific writing into their repertoire they have moved into the zone of enabling pedagogy. These are powerful teachers. They are re-shaping the discourse on quality pedagogy in science – and their voices are in sharp contrast to the advocates of a purist approach to scientific writing genres in science classrooms (e.g. Michael Halliday and Jim Martin 1993, Jerry Wellington and Jonathon Osborne 2001). Rowell argues that such purists allow for no critique of the underlying ideological position that scientific genres construct, an image of the nature of science that is in direct conflict with current philo-sophical perspectives. She says that 'the portrayal of science as an accumulation of undisputed 'factual' information is a setback for those who would characterise science as a human, interpretive activity' (Rowell 1996, p. 32). While I agree with Stephen Norris and Linda Phillips (2003) that scientific capability must incorporate literacy, in its fundamental sense (being able to read, write and use scientific language) it is not, on its own, sufficient. Learning science requires thinking creatively, synthesising ideas and using your imagination to relocate yourself in unusual frames of reference. Hybrid writing genres can be a purposeful medium to achieve these ends.

The allowable genres for writing to learn science do not need to be in one-to-one correspondence with the available genres in school science texts. There are at least two reasons to write in science classrooms: *learning to write* scientifically is one; the other is *writing to learn* science. The second reason should not be constrained by the same linguistic rules as the first because it has a different social purpose. There is more than one right way to write in science classrooms.

> *Fractures that interrupt the teaching of science,*
> *Thinking beyond the old pedagogies of compliance,*
> *Remembering those whose science lessons were for nought*
> *Creating contestations in how*
> *Science could,*
> *And should,*
> *Be taught.*

References

Ball, S. J. (1993) What is Policy? Texts, Trajectories and Toolboxes, *Discourse: The Australian Journal of Educational Studies* 13, pp. 10–17.

Barnes, D. (1992) The Significance of Teachers' Frames for Teaching, in T. Russell and H. Munby (eds) *Teachers and Teaching – From Classroom to Reflection*, London: Falmer Press.

Barnes, D. and Shemilt, D. (1974) Transmission and Interpretation, *Educational Review* 26, pp. 213–228.

Berkenkotter, C. and Huckin, T. (1995) *Genre Knowledge in Disciplinary Communication: Cognition/Culture/Power*, Hillsdale: Lawrence Erlbaum.

Code, L. (1991) *What Can She Know? Feminist Theory and the Construction of Knowledge*, Ithaca: Cornell University Press.

Cole, J. (1989) *The Magic School Bus Inside the Human Body*, New York: Scholastic Inc.

Foucault, M. (1977) Truth and Power, in C. Gordon (ed.) *Power/Knowledge: Selected Interviews and Other Writings*, Bury St. Edmunds: The Harvester Press.

Gianello, L. (ed.) (1988) *Getting Into Gear: Gender Inclusive Teaching Strategies in Science Developed by the McClintock Collective*, Canberra: Curriculum Development Centre.

Gore, J. (1993) *The Struggle for Pedagogies – Critical and Feminist Discourses as Regimes of Truth*, New York: Routledge.

Haggerty, S. M. (1995) Gender and Teacher Development, *International Journal of Science Education* 17, pp. 1–15.

Halliday, M.A.K. and Martin, J.R. (eds) (1993) *Writing Science – Literacy and Discursive Power*, London: Falmer Press.

Hand, B. and Prain, V. (1996) Writing for Learning in Science: A Model for Use Within Classrooms, *Australian Science Teachers' Journal* 42(3), pp. 23–27.

Harding, S. (1991) *Whose Science? Whose Knowledge?* London: Open University Press.

Hildebrand, G.M. (2002) *It's Electrophilic, It's Hydrophobic . . . That's Anthropomorphic Language!* Paper presented at the international conference, Ontological, Epistemological, Linguistic and Pedagogical Considerations of Language and Science Literacy: Empowering Research and Informing Instruction and Teacher Education, Victoria, BC, Canada, September.

Hildebrand, G.M. (1998) Disrupting Hegemonic Writing Practices in School Science: Contesting the Right Way to Write, *Journal of Research in Science Teaching* 35(4), pp. 345–362.

Hildebrand, G. M. (1989) Creating a Gender Inclusive Science Education, *Australian Science Teachers' Journal* 35, pp. 7–16.

James, L. (1989) The Atoms' Party, *Australian Science Teachers' Journal* 35, p. 72.

Keller, E. Fox and Longino, H. E. (eds) (1996) *Feminism and Science*, Oxford, UK: Oxford University Press.

Koestler, A. (1959) *The Sleepwalkers – A History of Man's Changing Vision of the Universe*, London: Hutchinson.

Latour, B. (1987) *Science in Action*, Cambridge, MA: Harvard University Press.

Lee, A. (1996) *Gender, Literacy, Curriculum – Re-writing School Geography*, London: Taylor and Francis.

Lemke, J. (1995) *Textual Politics – Discourse and Social Dynamics*, Chicago: Taylor and Francis.

Lemke, J. (1987) *Talking Science: Content, Conflict and Semantics* ED282402, Paper presented at the Annual Meeting of the American Educational Research Association, Washington, DC.

Lewis, S. and Davies, A. (1988) Gender and Mathematics and Science Teaching – GAMAST – Professional Development Manual – Gender Equity in Mathematics and Science, Canberra: Curriculum Development Centre.

Martin, J. R. (1990) Literacy in Science: Learning to Handle Text as Technology, in Frances Christie (ed.), *Literacy for a changing world*, Melbourne: Australian Council for Educational Research.

McLane, J. B. (1990) Writing as a Social Process, in Luis C. Moll (ed.) *Vygotsky and Education – Instructional Implications and Applications of Sociohistorical Psychology*, Cambridge, UK: Cambridge University Press.

McClintock Collective (1989) Creative Writing Ideas, *Australian Science Teachers' Journal* 35, pp. 72–73.

Medawar, P. (1963) September 12th. Is the scientific paper a fraud? *The Listener, BBC Publications*, pp. 377–378, reprinted in Bernard Dixon, (1989) *From Creation to Chaos*, Oxford, UK: Basil Blackwell, pp. 170–175.

Norris, S.P. and Phillips, L.M. (2003) How Literacy in its Fundamental Sense is Central to Scientific Literacy, *Science Education* 87, pp. 224–240.

O'Brien, M. (1981) *The Politics of Reproduction*, Boston: Routledge & Kegan Paul.

Osborne, R. and Freyberg, P. (1985) *Learning in Science*, Auckland: Heinemann.

Prain, V. and Hand, B. (1996) Writing for Learning in Secondary Science: Rethinking Practices, *Teaching and Teacher Education* 12, pp. 609–626.

Prain, V. (2002) *Learning from Writing in Secondary Science: Some Theoretical Implications*, Paper Presented at the International Conference Ontological, Epistemological, Linguistic and Pedagogical Considerations of Language and Science Literacy: Empowering Research and Informing Instruction and Teacher Education, Victoria, BC, Canada, September.

Rowell, P. (1996) The Images of Science in the Genre Debate, *Australian Science Teachers' Journal* 42(2), pp. 29–33.

Rowell, P. M. (1997) Learning in School Science: The Promises and Practices of Writing, *Studies in Science Education* 30, pp. 19–56.

Shepherd, L. J. (1993) *Lifting the Veil: The Feminine Face of Science*, Boston: Shambhala Publications.

Shulman, L. S. (1987) Knowledge and Teaching: Foundations of the New Reform, *Harvard Educational Review* 57, pp. 1–22.

Snow, C. P. (1963) *The Two Cultures and the Scientific Revolution – And a Second Look*, Cambridge, UK: Cambridge University Press.

Sutton, C. (1992) *Words, Science and Learning*, Buckingham, UK: Open University Press.

Vygotsky, L. S. (1978) *Mind in Society: The Development of Higher Psychological Processes*, Cambridge, MA: Harvard University Press.

Wallsgrove, R. (1980) The Masculine Face of Science, in Brighton Women and Science Group (eds) *Alice Through the Microscope*, London: Virago.

Watts, M. (2001) Science and Poetry: Passion V. Prescription in School Science? *International Journal of Science Education* 23(2), pp. 197–208.

Wellington, J. and Osborne, J. (2001) *Language and Literacy in Science Education*, Buckingham, UK: Open University Press.

Yore, L.D., Bisanz, G.L. and Hand, B.M. (2003) Examining the Literacy Component of Science Literacy: 25 years of Language Arts and Science Research, *International Journal of Science Education* 25, pp. 689–725.

Yore, L.D., Hand, B.M. and Florence, M.K. (2004) Scientists' Views of Science, Models of Writing, and Science Writing Practices, *Journal of Research in Science Teaching* 41(4), pp. 338–369.

Note

1 As a feminist political act I have included the first names of authors when I first cite their work, to signify that I believe that knowledge is always personalised through its construction by real people. By using people's first names I seek to create a more human connection with each author and remind us that we all look through particular frames of reference that re/present our complex mix of multiple subjectivities. Knowledge does not stand outside of people, over there, existing in a neutral space, even – or especially – in science.

Chapter 14

Writing, English and Digital Culture

Catherine Beavis and Claire Charles

It is no longer possible to think about literacy in isolation from a vast array of social, technological and economic factors. Two distinct yet related factors deserve to be particularly highlighted. These are, on the one hand, the broad move from the now centuries-long domination of writing to the new dominance of the image, and, on the other hand, the move from the dominance of the medium of the book to the dominance of the medium of the screen.

(Kress 2003a, p. 1)

[What we are seeing is] a broad-based shift from print to digital electronics as the organising context for literate-textual practice and for learning and teaching.

(Durrant and Green 2000, p. 89)

The tensions and future/present gazing embodied in statements such as these have been objects of concern for English teachers for some time. It's not as though English has not already wrestled mightily with the implications for the subject of the changing configurations of our students' textual worlds, as with changes in conceptions of the nature of texts and reading, and the nature of the world more generally. Indeed, English is remarkable for the resilience and flexibility with which it has confronted and responded to such changes over time. As historians of the subject note, for its whole history English appears to have been engaged in identifying, defending and redefining its core concerns, cast largely in terms of Literature and Literacy, or Literature, Grammar and Writing (Green & Beavis 1996). In recent times, much of this struggle and reflection has revolved around the question of text, and the place of (print) literacy and literature. As Green describes it, 'a marked shift in emphasis has been argued for *and* enacted, in syllabi and in classrooms: from 'literature' to 'text' (Green

2003a, p. 11); it is a move, he wryly notes, received as both liberating and a cause for lament by those both within and outside the profession.

The now widespread incorporation of visual texts such as film, television and picture books into the curriculum is a reflection of English teachers' awareness of the multimodal nature of the textual world out there, with texts such as these becoming the focus of the sorts of analysis, reflection, celebration and critique that have traditionally been part of the curriculum. When Alloway, Freebody, Gilbert & Muspratt (2002) call for attention to a repertoire of resources when addressing issues around boys' literacy they stress the need for the incorporation of popular texts. When Kress, in pondering on the place and nature of English in an unstable world puts aesthetics, ethics and texts at the heart of the purposes of English (Kress 2003b), he is similarly asking a question about not only what texts 'count', but how meanings are made, and what we might do with them—what 'reading' might mean in English in a multimodal, digital age.

And that's the rub. While at a theoretical level 'reading/viewing'—i.e. 'reception'—is balanced by 'writing/making'—i.e. 'production'—in the classroom, it's much harder to imagine how writing might be reconceived in manageable ways that reflect the range of modes and affordances of digital technologies, and the richness of the textual worlds young people are familiar with in their out of school lives. A key tension here, apart from simple questions of practicality, arises from the centrality of writing, still, to most forms of curriculum and assessment in educational settings, and its status, still, out there in the broader community. As Kress puts it, although 'language-as-writing will increasingly be displaced by image in many domains of public communication ... writing will remain the preferred mode of the political and cultural elites' (Kress 2003a, p. 1). Further, over centuries—millennia—ways of using writing have evolved that have become highly valued and valuable as a means to craft an argument, present a point of view, tell a story, evoke what paradoxically seems unable to be spoken and so on. The work of Vygotsky (1962) and others hypothesising complex connections between language and thought and the ways in which meaning comes into being through language underlies much of the ways in which we have become accustomed to think about writing. However, the transition we are envisaging is not an easy one. The situation is complicated by the fact that such (Vygotskian) understandings of writing are at times in sympathy but more often in conflict with other agendas for school uses of writing, and the ways these are superimposed as we ask students to use writing, the tasks we set, and the judgements and assumptions we make as we assess. Other purposes are served by school writing than learning and the construction of meaning, and in arguing for the need to recognise the importance of multimodal forms of communication we find ourselves up against more than simply a traditional view of the role of writing in learning and meaning-making.

While work in multiliteracies (New London Group 2000) and Media education (Burn 2003, Sefton-Green 2004) points ways forward that shift the emphasis away from print-based writing and on to more multimodal forms of creativity and design, there are still unresolved issues about how to conceive of, teach, and respond to writing in the 'changed communicational landscape' (Kress 2000) of the present day. We need to find ways to work with writing that acknowledge societal expectations about levels of formality and accomplishment in traditional terms, but that also respond both to the more complex semiotic forms of engagement and meaning-making going on in many out of school forums in which our students participate, where writing is but one of many modes, and to the ways in which writing itself is changing in the digital age.

As Lankshear and Knobel (2004) note, 'it does not follow that because some practice is widely engaged in outside school that it should be addressed, or even taken account of, in school ... Pedagogy and curriculum cannot be "hostaged" to every change in cultural tools and uses that appears on the horizon' (2004, pp. 78, 80). This is true. By the same token, however, if young people's experiences of narrative, engagement, communication and sociality are shaping their expectations of how texts work and what 'reading' and 'writing' might be, it is useful to consider what might be gained from understanding more about how 'writing' operates in the digital world, and to explore whether there are aspects of its functions and organisation that might be usefully brought into the ways we teach and use writing in schools. Some of the greatest advances in current understandings of how literacy is learned and used, particularly by children from less privileged or mainstream areas, have come from studies of out of school literacy practices (Hull & Schultz 2002). Gee's 2003 study of learning, literacy and computer games has particular relevance to the unit this chapter describes. The challenge is to see how and whether understandings drawn from studies of out of school usage of new and old 'cultural tools' have the capacity to facilitate learning for all students, and to extend and strengthen school curriculum through subject renewal that holds on to what is core, but reenergizes both the purpose and the form the subject takes, bridging between past and present, old and new.

As Kerin and Nixon argue, 'the integration of ICTs and critical literacy are no longer academic or innovative pursuits but are now framed as the responsibilities of all educators within curriculum frameworks and syllabuses from the early years through to post-compulsory education across Australia' (2005, p. 20). In this context, games provide a glimpse of the 'multimodal' literacies that challenge and extend print literacies, and are exemplars of the kinds of digital texts that teachers in Australia and elsewhere are increasingly being asked to help students analyse, master and critique. Consistent with such imperatives, this chapter reports on a small research project with a Year 8 English class, built around the study of computer games, where writing was used both as a tool for textual analysis and as 'creative response'. It focuses on the strategies and dilemmas that arose as we – teachers, students and researchers – used the 'old' modalities of talk and writing to imagine, analyse and explore interactive and multimodal textual forms. In particular, the chapter considers the opportunities and constraints imposed by using the affordances (Kress 1997) of one mode, writing, to describe those of digital, multimedia texts, and the questions this raised for us about the ways in which interactive and multimodal texts might be studied within English at school.

The unit and the writing it produced presented confronting questions about the tools available for undertaking multimedia analysis and response when multimodal texts such as computer games are brought into English, and for the ways in which writing is influenced in the immediate context of the genre of the computer game. At a broader level, it also served to refocus issues around the nature of English. These included tensions around the incorporation of popular culture within mainstream curriculum, issues of framing and analysis when there is a disjunction between the modes under study and the modes available as tools, and the preservation of core features in a way that is more than just 'business as usual' (Green 2003a), but still recognisably English and reflective of core qualities such as those identified by Kress and Green.

Introduction to the study

The English unit in which the writing we are exploring took place was part of the initial phase of a study investigating the literacy practices of successful female and male computer game players. We intended to harness existing research suggesting that computer games are one of the fastest and most efficient means through which young people become familiar with digital technologies and the new literacies involved in these practices. The phase took place within a co-educational independent school in the relatively affluent southern suburbs of Melbourne, and involved developing and delivering a small unit of English curriculum for a Year 8 class around three age appropriate computer games. The main two aims for this phase of the project were, firstly, to investigate the literacy practices of successful male and female gamers whilst delivering the unit, and secondly, to trial ways of successfully integrating new media technologies into existing English curriculum practices used when studying films and novels. Throughout the development and delivery of this unit we experienced some interesting tensions, which have implications outside the immediate concerns of the project. The tensions this chapter will explore centre on the implications of literacy practices associated with digital technologies for the way we understand and approach writing in the English curriculum.

The three games upon which we developed a unit were: *The Age of Wonders*, *The Age of Mythology* and *The Sims*. We chose them on the grounds that each game differed in terms of the practices required for 'successful' playing, and also in terms of the textual worlds created in the games. *The Age of Wonders* is a role-playing game or RPG, requiring the player to undertake quests. *The Age of Mythology* is a more strategic game, which requires the player to create and maintain armies, villages, and food supplies whilst simultaneously battling invaders. *The Sims*, as suggested by its name, is a game that supposedly simulates American suburban life. The player is required to create characters, develop families and build houses, careers and lifestyles. The strong consumer values in the game, as well as its popularity with young people of both genders made it an excellent candidate for critical evaluation. The literacy practices required of players in all games involved attention to multi-modal cues, and having to concentrate on multiple tasks at once.

Given that this was the first phase of the project, we had not yet investigated in detail the nature of the literacy practices used by young people in engaging with new media technologies, specifically those around writing. At this point we knew that we wanted to capitalize on the students' experience with the multi-modal nature of these technologies in order to investigate how the various modes such as graphics, sound and print work together to create a textual world.

The writing elements of the unit

We developed writing tasks for the unit that might provide students with the opportunity to critically evaluate the values and worlds constructed in the texts, paying specific attention to the multi-modal ways of creating meaning in computer games. We modelled our tasks on the kinds of curricular aims one might have in studying films or novels, encouraging students to explore how texts work to create meaning.

The two writing tasks we included in the unit were a short creative response to the game and a work sheet inviting students to undertake an analysis of how the various elements within their game worked together to create meaning.

English and Computer Games
... The aim of these classes is to look at computer games the way you might look at a novel or film. We will be asking you to get to know your game, play it a bit, and do some talking and writing about the world of the game, your ideas about its values, and to look at some sections very closely to see how the different aspects of the game (like images, sound and colour) are working together to make the game work ...

Session 1: Wednesday 9 June
In pairs, you will spend the first 50 minutes or so playing one of these games and getting to know the characters, story line and worlds. We will be asking you to think about two things as you do so:
1. What you have to do to make sense of the game, and how it works.
2. Start thinking about a new episode or character you might create around the game.

In the second half of the lesson you will be asked to write a story about your game, inventing a new character, episode or location.

Figure 1: Overview Handout, Lesson 1

The dilemma we faced was how to talk about multimedia texts and analysis in terms that would be familiar within English curriculum. We needed to find ways to use language that worked not just for students, but for ourselves, while nonetheless pointing outside and beyond the constraints of familiar forms to investigate and imagine texts that were interactive and digital. In our introductory handout, we relied explicitly on frames of reference we assumed students would know, using language that we hoped would be sufficiently familiar for students to see what we were hoping to explore. By the time we came to describing the 'creative response' task in detail, however, we tried to move beyond these terms.

The students were provided with two writing options for this short task. Option one asked them to design an 'Expansion pack' for their chosen game. In setting this task, we sought to create a closer match between the kinds of texts students were studying and the kinds of texts they produced, and to foreground the multimodal and interactive elements, while still setting something that resembled other 'creative response/dependent authorship' forms of writing familiar from more print-based literary contexts.

English and Computer Games
Create your own . . .

You have been commissioned to design an expansion pack for *The Sims*, *Age of Mythology*, or *Age of Wonders*. For your brief you need to:

Outline the scenario for your expansion pack
Describe the characters who will take part in it
Write the introductory movie clip or tutorial

Remember you will need to include those signpost features that have made this game so popular. This will include things like:
The landscape or setting
The atmosphere
The ways characters look
The ways characters speak
The kinds of episodes, adventures or challenges that happen in your game
The kinds of challenges people usually face
The ways they usually overcome them
The way the screen usually looks
Extra features to appeal to players, e.g. extra traps, weapons, spells, animals etc.

You may write your expansion pack as an outline for the company marketing division (in which case you will be describing it to them) or as a tutorial (in which case you will be explaining to a new player what they need to do, and why).

Take a few minutes to plan your expansion pack, then start writing!

Figure 2: Creative response task

(Expansion packs build on the original game, modifying and extending it without introducing the level of change in scope and concept that would require a 'sequel' to the game, as happened for example at the end of 2004 with the release of *The Sims 2*). The 'story' mentioned in the overview handout shifted genre to become a description or explanation – 'you may write your Expansion pack as an outline for the company marketing division (in which case you will be describing it to them) or as a tutorial (in which case you will be explaining to a new player what they need to do and why)'. Option two invited them to imagine an opening clip or tutorial – that is, a short piece of multimodal narrative or instruction that would mimic the operation of the game.

Expansion Packs: Andrew, Natalie and Nick

Within the limits imposed by the written form, Andrew, Natalie and Nick all took up the invitation in their writing to cross boundaries between the features and modalities of computer games and those afforded by conventional print representation and narrative. A characteristic of 'creative response' or dependent authorship, as utilised in the study of literary texts, is the need to catch and reproduce aspects of the original. All three pieces do so, but in very different ways. They also foreground and critique aspects of both context and ideology, and reflect each player's different experiences and preferences in relation to game play. They make an interesting comparison.

The Sims – New York   *Andrew*

The Sims New York will be about one male or female person aged 18–30. You can design this person and will be given $20,000 to use. They have to eat, learn and live. Eventually you would need to get a job, but to do so you would need to read or do weights to apply for a job. You could also steal money, but you might go to jail. Any job is open to you, as long as you work and before you apply for it. Be careful who you are friends with, they could turn on you. If you talk to someone you can select from a variety of things to say to them, depending on who they are. The main characters in this are you, your boss or employees, your 'friends', your neighbours, and anyone you might bump into in the street.

The main objectives of this game would be to be the head of a business, have a wife and friends, and own one million dollars.

Figure 3: Andrew, *The Sims – New York*

Andrew's Expansion pack is notable for the ways it replicates and critiques the structure and ideology of *The Sims*, but also starts to shift genre through introducing parameters that focus his game more narrowly than the original, providing scope for narrative drive. Whereas in *The Sims* players can create any number of characters, Andrew has built in the requirement that play revolves around just one (a 'male or female person aged 18–30'), with other characters populating the game in a secondary role. This, and his shift from 'they' to 'you' to refer to this character, shows him reshaping the typical structure of the game away from the creation and manipulation of multiple characters as is typical of this genre to constructing a focalising figure who effectively becomes the player's avatar, bringing the game closer both to print narratives and to other genres of game, such as role playing games.

While it is not uncommon for players of *The Sims* to recreate themselves and their friends and families in the game, and set them in motion, for Andrew, the creation of a specific fantasy character around whom a drama can be built goes one step further. Mirroring this pronoun shift to refer to character is the shift in the ways the reader of Andrew' s piece is imagined – initially as someone engaged in game design (in the God role), but rapidly moving to become the player engaging through the avatar. Other measures that turn *The Sims New York* into a more narrative genre include potential threats (false friends) challenges (how to 'get a job') and objectives ('to be the head of a business, have a wife and friends, and own one million dollars'). In alluding to start-up money, what the avatar must learn, the need for a job, the choice of who to speak to and what to say, and the pursuit of happiness (in the form of status, money, a wife and friends), *The Sims New York* recognisably takes up structural features of the original. However, the darker side of life in this version of the game, in particular untrustworthy friends, arguably shows Andrew critiquing aspects of the somewhat toxic ideology of the game in its emphasis on success, materiality and external display.

Sims Expansion Pack
Reality   *Natalie*
- more modern furniture
- more clothes
- your characters can go next door
- more hair and faces
- kids can grow 2 adults (optional)
- more facilities
- U can travel to space
- Drive to a city
- Go shopping
- Go to school, be able to invite friends
- Ask friends to go out, e.g. cinema, mall etc.
- Be able to do job
- Give people your number
- Type in what you wanna say or choose an option
- Buses, trains etc.
- Hot air balloons
- Lottery

Why I chose this –
I chose this because it makes *The Sims* more real. At the moment it's still really limited so I want it to be more real.

Figure 4: Natalie, *Sims Expansion Pack – Reality*

Where Andrew's expansion pack pushes *The Sims* towards a role play genre or adventure, taking a familiar, discursive literary form, Natalie focuses on the functionality and characteristics of the elements required to build and play. That is, where Andrew effectively creates a scenario and story line, and relies on writing to convey the nuances and subtleties of his game, Natalie concentrates on the elements provided and what characters can do. Her attention is more squarely on the interactive, operational and multimodal aspects of the game. As she comments in her explanation – an innovation of her own design – her changes are designed to make *The Sims* 'more real'. Her innovations explicitly refer to the visual, verbal and spatial options provided. Her changes are about creating a greater diversity of alternatives that rely on the multimodal affordances of the game – more faces, more hair, more clothes, more facilities, complemented by more sites for play, more places to socialise with friends, more means of transport, a closer approximation of social life as it is experienced, presumably, in her world. In this respect, her expansion pack is closer to the original than is Andrew's, in that it reflects the 'making' imperative of the game. Where Andrew wants to shift the game to become more like other narratives, Natalie wants to shift the game so that it more closely approximates claims made about it replicating reality. If she has a criticism of the game, implicitly it is that is does not live up to its promise to be 'real'.

The contrast between Andrew's and Natalie's texts highlights one of the paradoxes entailed in using writing in relation to multimodality. In Andrew's writing there is a strong connecting thread, linking together the problematic nature of getting/earning a job, knowing who to trust and so on, that both relies on and benefits from the kinds of distinctions and connections writing affords. He pays less attention to (multimodal) individual features constituting what characters look like and can do. Natalie's piece, by contrast, initially looks disappointing, just a list. However, the items within the list, seen in the context of the game she is referring to, collectively present an extremely rich and detailed picture to 'the company marketing division' of the way the game will look and play, but a picture that in writing is rendered two dimensional, thin and flat.

Nick's piece combines many of the features of both Andrew's and Natalie's accounts. As with Andrew's piece, writing allows him to explain in subtle and complex detail the kinds of changes he wants and why. He establishes an easy relationship with his reader as he moves from one point to another drawing on his knowledge of this and other games. Like Natalie, he identifies specific multimodal features of the game (e.g. talking gibberish, more costumes and bodies) that he wants to develop and change. The level of detail he attends to includes not only the need for greater variety in the options for characters' appearance, sites and scenarios and new and improved functionality, but builds in instructions about features of the technical articulation of this version with the older game. In this, and in the ways he incorporates features drawn from other games and other genres of computer games (casinos, driving, plane piloting,

---

The Sims – Deluxo Schmuxo　　　　　　　　　　　　　　　　　　　　　　　　*Nick*

Additional features

- instead of talking gibberish they actually speak English. So you can know a bit more about what the characters want.
- there are a bit more character costumes and bodies for when you are creating families
- instead of The Sims leaving the house to go to work and not showing them working, you can help them at work and go to their office and stuff
- you can now live on other planets and work under the rule of aliens and you have to learn alien customs, but it is very expensive to get a rocket trip so you have to get a good job.
- there are highways between the Planets and if you get fired you have to become a drifter and build yourself up again
- there are also little interactive games to keep the Players interested e.g. casino' s, driving, Plane Piloting

other info

- it doesn't need a tutorial because it has little Popups about new bits in the game and the rest is in the same format of the old game.
- you need a previous version of the game so you can load this version onto it

I think that we needed to spend a lot more time on the computer games. We could not fully explore the world of the game and so we were a bit confused.

I think that there should be natural disasters in the game and you can get taken to different city's by tornadoes.

you should also be able to go the amusement Parks around the world. You should also be able to build them.

Figure 5: Nick, *The Sims – Deluxo Schmuxo*

building amusement parks and so on), his extended familiarity with the world of games provides the piece with a strong and convincing sense of authority and complexity.

Opening Clip: Lincoln and Tim. From Narrative to Spectacle

Lincoln and Tim, working on *Age of Mythology*, took the second option: to create a tutorial showing players how to play. They interpreted this as a request to present the opening clip, an animated sequence indicating the context and main players in the game.

While Lincoln and Tim are working within the constraints or parameters of written language, they are nonetheless able to identify and evoke multimedia scenarios vividly and effectively. This brief piece provides a glimpse in writing of the different, visual logic of computer games, and what Darley (2000) describes as a shift from narrative to spectacle as characteristic of entertainment in the late twentieth (and now early twenty-first) century – a shift is epitomised in theme park rides (e.g. *Pirates of the Caribbean*), Special Effects films (e.g. *The Mummy*), and computer games Lincoln and Tim' s piece is notable for the ways in which its structure and features replicate those

---

Age of Mythology   *Lincoln and Tim*
Opening Clip
- 2 armys are stationed on a plain (somewhere), 1 hero from each side are on the front line. At the back of the armies there is a range of Mythological creatures
- 1 side charges, while their infantry runs towards them, the opposing army shoots some of them down with arrows
- The 2 armies clash – (flash forward to the end when there is only 2 units, a metator (minotaur) and a normal human)
- The two have a fight and after a while of fearsome fighting the human jumps up and with a quick flick of his wrist chops off the monsters head

[Then it starts to load the game]

Scenario
The scenario for my expansion pack is relatively the same except you are more close to the action (by Zooming the screen in).

Figure 6: Lincoln and Tim, Opening clip

of the animated sequences starting the game. It progresses through a highly visual succession of tableaux, flashing forward in time but essentially set in a timeless present. It establishes the scene and the combatants, juxtaposing massed forces in ways familiar not just from other games but also from films like *Lord of the Rings*. Such films draw on the very set of images/possibilities that epitomise one aspect of what computer games do so successfully – the kind of remaking of one media form into another that Bolter and Grusin (1999) call remediation. In doing so, it carries traces not just of other computer games within this and related genres, but also textual references from elsewhere, for example in the high-flown language ('stationed on a plain', 'the two armies clash', 'fearsome fighting', 'a quick flick of his wrist'). The poetic evocations of such terms seem to build on textual experiences elsewhere in more literary print and mythological worlds.

Analysing interactive texts

In the second half of the unit, after asking students to discuss their games in small groups, we wanted to develop approaches to textual analysis that would highlight the contribution of different elements in the games to the creation of meaning and ideology. Here even more than in setting the imaginative task, however, we found ourselves constrained by language – in this case, how to find the words to alert the students to what we (and we hoped they) were looking for. Our worksheet for this section of the unit read in part:

We developed a grid picking up these points in an effort to focus more closely on the relationship between elements such as those we highlighted, and the construction of meaning and ideology. For many of the students, this proved quite difficult, and their

Your Task!

After playing for about 20–30 minutes, save and analyse a small section of your game, and talk with your partner about your understanding of the following points:

1) What is happening in your saved section?
2) The characters' personalities (what sort of person they are)?
3) The lifestyle of the characters (rich, poor, job, no job, interests, pastimes)?
4) What things are valued in the game (e.g. hard work, money, career, resting, having fun, sleeping etc.)?
5) Which jobs are the most important?
6) Does the character live now or in the future?

For each dot point, you need to consider three things:

1) How GRAPHICS, ICONS, MUSIC and SOUND EFFECTS help you understand,
2) How you would change the GRAPHICS, ICONS, MUSIC and SOUND EFFECTS to make this part of the game better,
3) How similar or different this is from your knowledge of our world as it is now.

Figure 7: Introduction to Analytic Grid handout

grids consisted largely of descriptions of aspects of the action, but in some cases they were also able to identify and nominate specific features and their effects.

Despite or perhaps because of *The Sims* being more of a game scenario than a game, some students chose not so much to show how to succeed at the game, but how to make it more game-like, by creating a dramatic end. Thus, where Natalie and her friends saved a clip where a genie was produced from a bottle in a house packed with luxury goods (although it did then overrun the house with cockroaches instead of providing yet more luxuries), Andrew's group subverted both these values and the openendedness of the game by manipulating options to the point where they set their Sims, and their house, on fire. The analytic grid filled out by his group in relation to this clip begins dramatically. At a number of points (for example, the first square: 'the fire illuminates the room and crackles as you run frantically'; possibilities for different voices, the symbolic value and placement of the car etc.), Andrew and his group are able to pinpoint at least some of the elements that contribute to the game's effect and meaning as a whole.

This seemed to us to be one of the central challenges of the unit: how to help students become critically reflective and aware of the ways in which design elements interacted in the production of meaning. As the most familiar and readily available technology, writing seemed the natural choice for undertaking this analysis, but we were conscious that this was likely to impose limitations when applied to moving inter-active texts, though we were limited in the degree to which we could anticipate and in what ways. As with other forms of textual analysis and close reading, the aim was for students to be able both to identify the ways in which small separate details work together, but also to make links between perceptions of this kind and the effect of

	How do the GRAPHICS, ICONS, MUSIC, SOUND EFFECTS help you understand?	How you would change the graphics, icons, music and sound effects to make this section of the game better?	How is this similar/different from the world of today?
What is happening in your saved section?	The fire illuminates the room, and crackles as you run frantically	I would have the guy running away from the fire instead of screaming at it	You freeze in a crisis so the man doesn' t automatically call the fire depot
Characters' personalities (what sort of person they are)	They all sound the same but the graphics are good	I would give them different voices	*similar* they are all different
The life style of the characters (rich, poor, job, no job, interests, pastimes)	Wherever your guy has a job, a car comes, the horn beeps, and it shows the car out the front	It is already good enough	they get frustrated and they have needs just like us.
What things are valued in the game (e.g.: hard work, money, career, resting, having fun, sleeping etc.)?	You get money when you have a job so you can hire a maid. Sleep gives you energy	It is generally pretty good, but maybe the guy could get logic points if he works hard	People are always happy when they get paid, and if they work hard they get smarter
Which jobs are most important?	When you get a better job the car you drive to work in gets better	It is already good enough	The more money you get the more expensive stuff you get
Does the character live now or in the past or future?	The graphics and stuff seem relative of today	I think its good to show present times, they could make everything old school for 'Sims 80s'	It' s fairly stupid, the way we live and wat not

Figure 8: Andrew's group, Analytic Grid

these interactions on the way the text is experienced as a whole. By confining students to written language both to make their analysis and in the construction of their imaginative Expansions, we were conscious of the limitations created by the imposition of one form over the other. On the other hand, at least in relation to the analytic grid, writing enabled them to be explicit about what they found, but only in a static mode. When it came to presenting their clip with the analysis, using a data projector and standing out the front talking as their clip proceeded (that is, when both print and non-print modes combined) it was much more difficult for them to slow down enough to present their commentary. Rather, they got caught up in the excitement and drama of the action, their displays of competence and authority, and the immediate and ongoing interactions with their friends.

Contradictions and Complexities: Writing In and Out of School – Where to From Here?

In hindsight, a deep irony is evident when comparing the writing tasks we designed with the textual nature of the games. We were asking the students to engage in sophisticated multi-modal textual analysis through the purely linguistic means of a writing task in highly structured print form. We had designed a task that resembled a fairly traditional pedagogical technique, the worksheet. The creative writing task was a little less constrained, but still attempted to blend the practices involved with new media technologies with more traditional genre kind of work found in English curriculum. This posed some complexities with regard to how we include new media technologies in the English classroom. One initial concern was that the students were not adequately interested or responsive to the writing tasks they had been given. The tasks did not appear to allow the students to adequately explore possibilities through the writing, or express identities they were forming through these games. They seemed to do this more rigorously when they were talking, during some interviews we conducted.

As we expected them to complete the writing tasks whilst they were playing the games in class time they generally appeared far more interested in the games themselves. Many appeared to approach the work sheet on multi-modality and the creative writing task as a 'chore' that needed to be done and was clearly being 'imposed' upon them by us as the 'teachers'. Indeed, in one lesson the class teacher literally had to stand over a group of boys in order to ensure that they completed the creative writing task.

This, however, was not the only way students responded to the writing tasks. One student who was not so familiar with computer games drew instantly on the literacy practices to which she was already accustomed from English curriculum in responding to the demands of the creative writing task. Where students were extremely familiar with the games, they responded to this task quite differently, so that the boundaries between literacy practices associated with computer games and literacy practices found in the classroom were blurry as for example in Natalie's case.

The question of how to build on out of school experiences of writing and digital culture in the school context continues to be challenging. Studies comparing in and out of school writing such as Chandler-Olcott and Mahar's (2003) present a stark contrast not just in writing practices but also in what they achieve for the young people involved. In their study of the textual experiences of two young women, Eileen and Rhianon, Chandler-Olcott and Mahar suggest that the literacy practices occurring in and outside schooling were like different worlds. Outside school, Eileen and Rhiannon engaged in practices that were 'not privileged in classes yet were highly valued beyond school' (p. 379). There, their writing practices were motivated by relationships with mentors and friends that they developed in on-line communities, so that 'both girls used their membership in on-line communities to create richer and more satisfying social lives than they had in real time' (2003, p. 375). Chandler-Olcott and Mahar compare these group identity practices directly with the girls' social identities in schooling. For example, out of school, Rhiannon's 'technology expertise gave her status within the community' rather than 'marginalizing her as a "geek"'(p. 375), while Eileen's use of technology

> helped connect her with others who supported her continuing artistic development and appreciated the quirky set of popular culture sources on which she drew. In stark contrast to her experiences in school where her interests often set her apart from mainstream peer cultures, pursuit of these common interests created bonds between her and other members of the mailing list. (p. 375)

The authors argue that the on-line (out of school) and off-line (at school) literacy practices were separate worlds in their study, observing that '[t]echnological integration at the school placed more emphasis on linguistic Design than visual, spatial or audio modes' (p. 372). Writing practices occurring in the on-line communities such as these appear to be collaborative, as though people are working together for a common goal. The writing practices also involve more multi-modality than those often found in formal schooling.

Just as the girls in the Chandler-Olcott and Mahar paper were writing their way into a community of practice, teachers of English belong to a community of practice. The writing tasks we set our students in this project had pre-existing 'benchmarks' or ideals, which we would routinely apply when responding to their writing. We had a pre-conceived idea of how the analysis table would look if it were to demonstrate understanding and depth of critical analysis. The fact that the responses were different from what we expected was not necessarily indicative that the students had not understood the task or that they hadn't undertaken critical analysis of the game.

In our case, in different ways, the purpose of both writing tasks was to encourage the students to critically evaluate the textual construction of their game and analyse the elements that make up a text. However, the parameters of this writing task were very clearly defined, and perhaps operated to constrain the students' responses. Most students completed the creative task, but did so through a brief paragraph or two, or a summary. Most students completed the tables 'successfully' but others forgot they were there or did not fill them out adequately. The nature of 'writing' in this task needed to be conceived, both by us and by the students, in a more open ended exploratory fashion if it was going to generate more rigorous critical analysis of the games.

Through studying young people's outside school engagements with new media technologies we see the communal goals of the writing they undertake and the way this writing is embedded within identity building practices (Chandler-Olcott & Mahar 2003). One challenge for English is to find means by which to extend this way of conceptualising writing to the tasks we set in subject English curriculum. Thought about in this way, writing does more than simply demonstrate a particular knowledge or competency. It becomes a tool for belonging to a community or forming an identity. If we want to explore in a rigorous fashion how students engage with new media technologies, we might usefully consider combining written tasks with conversation, or demonstration, in order to obtain a richer picture of these engagements.

As Reinking notes,

Figuratively speaking, it is as difficult for those who have become fully literate within a world dominated by print to see how their own literacy has been shaped – indeed limited – by the technologies used to produce and disseminate printed materials as it is for a fish to think about the water in which it swims. (Reinking 1998, p. xviii)

Our work with this Year 8 class on digital culture texts suggests that writing and reflection on the process of writing have a powerful part to play in the charting and analysis of waters such as these. This is as much the case for students as it is for teachers and researchers. We would argue that the writing and reflection should be addressing the 'difficulties' of mismatches between multimodal and more conventional forms of texts and at least a partial awareness of what slips away when the 'apples' of writing are mixed with the 'pears' of digital texts. And yet it could be a matter of what slips away being as important as what emerges unexpectedly.

'Subject English' should not be perceived as a pre-existing entity that somehow must 'adapt' in order to accommodate new media technologies and the practices surrounding them. Rather, subject English could be conceptualised as ever changing and constituted through the very practices young people bring to it, a dialogue between students' practices and knowledges, and other stakeholders such as teachers, parents, government and the wider community. At the same time, however, English remains positioned within specific and ongoing histories, discourses and concerns, and questions of its identity continue to revolve around relationships between language, identity and text (Green & Beavis 1996, Kress 2003a, Green 2003a, 2003b, Sawyer 2005). While we have come some distance in finding ways for English to address and accommodate digital culture through the incorporation of a range of visual and multi-modal texts for 'reading' and analysis, relationships between 'writing' and these texts remain, as yet, somewhat problematic and requiring further exploration. The paradoxes and promises encountered in our unit on computer games foreground the need for English teachers to keep wrestling with questions and issues such as these.

Acknowledgments

This research was funded by a grant from the Deakin University Quality Learning Research Priority Area. Thanks to the English teacher, Year 8 English students and the school for their energy, good humour and support in making the project possible.

References

Alloway, N., Freebody, P., Gilbert, P. and Muspratt, S. (2002) *Boys, Literacy and Schooling: Expanding the Repertoires of Practice*, Melbourne: Curriculum Corporation.

Bolter, J. and Grusin, R. (1999) *Remediation: Understanding New Media*, Cambridge, MA and London: MIT Press.

Burn, A. (2003) Poets, Skaters and Avatars – Performance, Identity and New Media, *English Teaching: Practice and Critique* 2(2), pp. 6–21.

Chandler-Olcott, K. and Mahar, D. (2003) 'Tech-savviness' Meets Multiliteracies: Exploring Adolescent Girls' Technology-related Literacy Practices, *Reading Research Quarterly* 38(3), pp. 356–385.

Darley, A. (2000) *Visual Digital Culture: Surface Play and Spectacle in New Media Genres*, London and New York: Routledge.

Durrant, C. and Green, B. (2000) Literacy and the New Technologies in School Education: Meeting the L(IT)eracy Challenge? *Australian Journal of Language and Literacy* 23(2), pp. 89–108.

Electronic Arts (2000–2002) *The Sims Deluxe*, Singapore: Electronic Arts.

Electronic Arts (2005) *The Sims2*, www.thesims2.ea.com

Gee, J. (2003) *What Video Games Have to Teach Us About Learning and Literacy*, New York: Palgrave Macmillan.

Green, B. and Beavis, C. (1996) *Teaching the English Subjects: Essays on English Curriculum History and Australian Schooling*, Geelong: Deakin University Press.

Green, B. (2003a) No Difference? *Literacy Learning in the Middle Years: Secondary Thoughts* 11(2), pp. 11–14.

Green, B. (2003b) A Literacy Project of Our Own? *English in Australia* 134, pp. 25–32.

Hull, G. and Schultz, K. (2002) *School's Out! Bridging Out-of-School Literacies with Classroom Practice*, New York: Teachers College Press.

Jackson, P. (dir) (2001) *Lord of the Rings*, New Line Cinema.

Kerin, R. and Nixon, H. (2005) Middle Years English/Literacy Curriculum: The Interface of Critical Literacy and Digital Texts, *Literacy Learning in the Middle Years* 13(1), pp. 20–35.

Kinzer, C. K. and Leander, K. (2003) Technology and the Language Arts: Implications of an Expanded Definition of Literacy, in J. Flood, D. Lapp, J. R. Squire and J. M. Jensen (eds) *Handbook of Research on Teaching the English Language Arts*, New Jersey, Lawrence Erlbaum.

Kress, G. (2003a) *Literacy in the New Media Age*, London and New York: Routledge/Taylor and Francis

Kress, G. (2003b) English for an Era of Instability: Aesthetics, Ethics, Creativity and 'Design', *English in Australia* 134, pp. 15–24.

Kress, G. (2000) A Curriculum for the Future, *Cambridge Journal of Education* 30(1), pp. 133–145.

Kress, G. (1997) Visual and Verbal Modes of Representation in Electronically Mediated Communication: the Potentials of New Forms of Text, in I. Snyder (ed.), *Page to Screen: Taking Literacy into the Electronic Era*, Sydney: Allan and Unwin.

Lankshear, C. and M. Knobel (2004) Planning Pedagogy for i-mode: from Flogging to Blogging via wi-fi, *English in Australia* 139 and *Literacy Learning: the Middle Years* 12(1), pp. 78–102.

Microsoft and Ensemble Studios (2002) *Age of Mythology*, Microsoft Corporation, www.microsoft.com/games/ageofmythology/

New London Group (2000) A Pedagogy of Multiliteracies: Designing Social Futures, in B. Cope and M. Kalantzis (eds), *Multiliteracies: Literacy Learning and the Design of Social Futures*, Melbourne: Macmillan.

Reinking, D. (1998) Introduction: Synthesizing Technological Transformations of Literacy in a Post-Typographical World, in D. Reinking, M. McKenna, L. Labbo and R. Keiffer (eds) *Handbook of Technology and Literacy: Transformations in a Post-Typographical World*, MahWah, NJ: Lawrence Erlbaum Associates, pp. xl–xxx.

Sawyer, W. (2005) English and Literacy: A More Open Marriage or Time for Divorce? *Literacy Learning in the Middle Years* 13(1), pp. 11–19.

Sefton-Green, J. (2004) *Literature Review in Informal Learning with Technology Outside School*, Report for NESTA Futurelab About the Role of New Technologies in Learning, Report 7.

Sommers, S. (dir.) (1999) *The Mummy*, Alphaville films/Universal Pictures.

Triumph Studios (2003) *Age of Wonders: Shadow Magic*, Take Two Interactive Software, www.ageofwonders.com.

Vygotsky, L. (1962) *Thought and Language*, Eugenia Hanfmann and Gertrude Vakar (eds and transls), Cambridge: MIT Press.

Chapter 15

Engaging in Valued Activities

Popular Culture in the English Classroom

Brenton Doecke and Douglas McClenaghan

We become who we are ... through engaging in culturally valued activities with the
aid of other participants and of the mediating artifacts which the culture makes available.
(Wells 2001, pp. 171–194)

Culture Wars

Many English teachers create opportunities for young people to explore popular
culture in their classrooms. This does not mean aping their tastes and enthusiasms, but
attending to the way popular culture mediates their social relationships and the formation of their identities. You need only wander around shopping centres on weekends
to find young people immersed in a range of activities, from lining up with huge boxes
of popcorn at the latest Hollywood blockbuster to single-mindedly pounding the
machines in games parlours. Not content to occupy one place and live through one
moment, they simultaneously chat into their mobile phones or text-message people
located elsewhere. They talk and laugh excitedly, parading their allegiances and identities in a veritable Shakespearean display.

Young people inhabit a rich semiotic environment, full of songs, dialects, slang,
corporate logos, cross-gartered vanities, moustachioed Violas and other personalities:
'A great while ago the world begun, With hey, ho, the wind and the rain ...'. It is vital
that English teachers cultivate a sensitivity to the cultural practices in which adolescents
engage in their everyday lives and that they open up a space for young people to
explore the meaning-making potential of those practices in their classrooms. The
challenge for English teachers is to break down the divide between school literacy
practices and youth culture, providing a curriculum that matches the richness of the
semiotic practices in which young people participate outside schools.

But developing this kind of appreciation of youth cultural practices is far from being an innocent pursuit. Champions of 'Cultural Literacy' like Kevin Donnelly lament the advent of a curriculum that supposedly sees 'classic texts such as Shakespeare disappear to be replaced by popular culture represented by the TV show *Neighbours*, *Dolly Magazine* or the pop novel *Puberty Blues*' (Donnelly 2004, p. 24). 'Allowing students to read only contemporary and popular texts,' writes Donnelly, 'ignores the argument that, to be culturally literate, students must be introduced to those classic novels, poems and plays that are a significant part of our cultural heritage' (p. 79).

Donnelly's use of the first person plural shows how much is at stake in these debates. In his view, teachers should feel 'obliged to challenge, extend and enrich students' knowledge and understanding' (p. 94), enabling them to learn about 'Australia's Anglo-Celtic culture and the growth of Western civilisation' (p. 58). Those of us who might identify with the Celtic but not the Anglo (Douglas) or whose grand-parents were threatened by anti-Hun sentiment during World War 1 (Brenton) could surely be forgiven for feeling left out of Donnelly's sectarian vision of 'Anglo-Celtic culture'. His is a politically correct vision of schooling that befits a society which has been prepared to lock up refugees behind razor wire in order to defend 'our' way of life against the threat of anything 'foreign' or 'un-Australian'.

The issue is not whether Shakespeare should be replaced by *Neighbours*, *Dolly Magazine*, *Puberty Blues* or (to embrace a wider and more current spectrum of cultural activities) video games, animé or text messaging. Advocating the inclusion of popular cultural artifacts in English classrooms is not at the expense of focusing on Shakespeare or other so-called 'classic' texts, although teachers might legitimately encourage their students to ask why certain texts have been accorded 'classic' status, and consider how such judgments compare with the judgments they make when they discriminate between the latest songs or videos or TV shows. Young people can make a Shakespearean text a vehicle for exploring questions of value and identity that are significant to them, as Terry Hayes shows in his account of staging *A Midsummer Night's Dream* at Hawthorn Secondary College, a play that is 'unusually attuned to adolescent energies and passions', which 'expands and adapts to kids' cultures in ways that make them feel as though, in discovering Shakespeare, they have made him their own' (Hayes 1999, p. 58). Significantly, he refers to 'cultures' in the plural, because 'in any state secondary school, kids' culture is not a single homogenous entity; rather it is a set of heterogeneous sub-cultures – homeys and heavy metallers, Goths and geeks' (Hayes 1999, p. 58). The staging of *A Midsummer Night's Dream* provided a space for the convergence of these cultures, an occasion for the young people who formed the 'community' of actors, stage hands and others who produced the play to joyfully affirm both their current pleasures and their hopes (Hayes 1999, p. 61).

English classrooms should be places for students to take pleasure in their conversations with one another and the pursuit of their mutual interests. Joy is jackbooted out of classrooms by the custodians of 'Cultural Literacy'. Malvolio-like, they unsmilingly parade their virtues, denying students any opportunity to take pleasure in the current moment. Indeed, Donnelly dismisses the significance of students exploring their 'immediate' and 'local' worlds, describing such a focus as 'narrow' and 'superficial' (Donnelly 2004, p. 94). Our argument is that it is precisely with the 'immediate' and 'local' that any worthwhile conversation in an English classroom begins, in a spirit of 'acceptance' (Britton 1972, p. 134) of what students bring with them into class, and a preparedness to build on their existing worlds in order to open up new dimensions of language and meaning. And, with some students, the challenge is not to accept what they bring into class, but to get them to come to class in the first place. A traditional academic curriculum of the kind that Donnelly envisages not only prevents academically able students from engaging in authentic inquiry into their culture, but reinforces the alienation of those students who can see no purpose in schooling. A genuinely inclusive curriculum begins by enabling students to focus on their 'immediate' and 'local' worlds.

'And gladly wolde he lerne and gladly teche . . .'

This chapter draws on practitioner research which Douglas has conducted over several years with his own English classes. During this time, Brenton has played the role of a 'critical friend', engaging with him in discussion about his pedagogy and the artefacts his students have created. Recently, Douglas also invited Bella Illesca, another experienced secondary English teacher, to observe some of his lessons, paying attention to the matches and mismatches between what he intended and what he actually accomplished in the process of enacting a curriculum with his students (cf. Barnes 1976, p. 14). Some of the insights developed in the following discussion arise out of Douglas's conversations with Bella.

Our aim is not to tell a good news story about one teacher's professional accomplishments in importing popular cultural practices into his classroom. Nor do we wish to simply illustrate a set of resources and strategies that other English teachers might use. Rather, the chapter describes the professional learning of a secondary English teacher, arising out of his interactions with students and his conversations with 'critical friends', as he set about exploring the semiotic potential of popular culture with his students. This has involved reviewing his habitual practices as an English teacher, and reconceptualising the role that English might play within the curriculum and the lives of his students. To capture this professional learning, we have selected a number of moments in Douglas's teaching practice that raise interesting questions about the ways students might appropriate popular culture in order to extend their language and literacy. All the vignettes show writing emerging out of the speaking, listening, reading and viewing in which students engage, both inside the classroom and beyond, thus challenging traditional understandings of English curriculum which treat these dimensions as discrete language modes. One of the vignettes problematises the very notion of 'writing', presenting an example of a multimodal text that resists being categorized in any conventional way. We shall try to render these moments in their rich concreteness, using them to illustrate some of the things that we – teacher and 'critical friend' alike – have learnt. To conclude the chapter we shall then engage in more general reflections about school curriculum and critical inquiry.[1]

Mama mia, Norman is a psycho!

Our first example of using popular culture is taken from a Year 11 English class, when a group of four girls presented their text response to Alfred Hitchcock's *Psycho* to their peers. You need to imagine them out the front of the class singing about Norman Bates to the tune of Abba's 'Mamma Mia'. They have written the song (see figure 1) as part of their response to *Psycho*, and they have decided to perform it, accompanied by a karaoke tape. They have tapped into Hitchcock's black humour and word-play and are attempting the same with their own words.

By choosing to perform their song rather than just hand in the lyrics, they have accomplished something far more pleasurable, for performers and audience alike. When the karaoke version of 'Mamma Mia' finally tinkles towards its end, the audience bursts into applause. Throughout their performance the girls have been half-embarrassed, and it was evident that as a foursome they were supporting each other as they sang the verses, but now they are obviously gratified by the way their work has been received. Like all good oral work, their presentation has grown out of and reinforces the class's sense of community and shared experience, and their presentation has been a social occasion as well as a moment for learning.

What did we learn from their presentation?

Alfred Hitchcock's *Psycho* has an interesting place in the popular cultural landscape of these young people. The film has an iconic status, having been released over forty years ago, and it was not necessarily something that the students found enjoyable (cf. Burns 2000, pp. 24–34). When Douglas showed it to his students, they respectfully noted aspects of the film that make it a famous example of horror movies, most notably the multiple shots of the murder in the shower (which many knew because it had typically been appropriated by *The Simpsons*). But you could not say that they experienced the same kind of pleasure in watching this film that they derived from *Scream* 1 and 2 or *I know what you did last summer*. The way the students read this film was in itself an interesting example of how they exercise discriminations and made judgments as participants in popular culture. It is surely questionable to draw a hard and fast line between popular culture and high culture, as though one is a realm of fantasy in which you suspend your critical faculties, while the other is characterized by sophisticated discriminations and deep and meaningful reflection. Just as it is wrong to suppose that popular culture can be equated with a fleeting immediacy while the other embodies the slow march of tradition. As John Frow observes, both are 'regimes of value' which are characterized by equally complex processes of discrimination (Frow 1993, see also Frow, 1995). In the case of *Psycho*, the students were able to acknowledge its status as part of a cultural tradition in which they were actively engaged, and to identify and name their continuing pleasures in horror movies.

Norman's mother's been dead since we don't know when
Norman poisoned them both as they were lying in bed
Look at him now
He has lost his mind
Dresses in skirts
Now he thinks that he is his mum
Wielding knife-point at everyone

Just one look and mother's back from the dead
Just one look and mother's inside his head
Woa woa

Mama mia, here she goes again
My my, Norman is a psycho
Mama mia, someone's dead again
My, my, mother's gone and killed them
Yes he's been broken hearted
Blue since his mum departed
Why, why, did he ever let her go?
Mama, mia, now we really know
Why, why, Norman never let her go

Marion wanted Sam, didn't know what to do
So she stole forty thou from her boss and shot through
Look at her now
At the Bates Motel
She's on the run
But she won't be around too long
Norman's lust for her is too strong

Just one look and mother's back from the dead
Just one look and mother's inside his head
Woa woa

Mama mia, here she goes again
My my, Norman is a psycho
Mama mia, someone's dead again
My, my, mother's gone and killed them
Yes he's been broken hearted
Blue since his mum departed
Why, why, did he ever let her go?
Mama, mia, now we really know
Why, why, Norman never let her go

Figure 1. Students' karaoke version of 'Mama Mia'

The choices the girls made in constructing their text response are just as interesting as an example of how students can appropriate popular cultural forms to make meaning. There was a good humoured kitchness about their decision to do a karaoke sing-along to 'Mama Mia', an activity they could locate as part of a cultural landscape embracing both them and their parents. The text as they presented it exceeded Douglas's expectations as their English teacher. In this respect, it is worth noting that this text was only possible because Douglas gave his students leeway to decide how they would develop a response to *Psycho*. It is not as though he prescribed a specific form of text response: Write a response to *Psycho* by emulating the verse of Abba's 'Mamma Mia', and present it to class in the form of a karaoke! The students themselves exploited the popular cultural resources available to them, constructing a richly multi-leveled text.

Still playing havoc in my head

The previous example shows how students can use popular cultural resources to achieve conventional learning outcomes such as a 'text response'. It is not as though by bringing popular culture into the classroom English teachers are ignoring their respon-sibilities to teach English literacy as defined by literacy continua like *English – A Curriculum Profile* (AEC 1994), although texts like the one we have just examined also exceed those expectations in significant ways. Julian Sefton-Green has argued that a hard and fast divide need not exist between school literacy practices and the cultural practices in which students engage outside school, that there can be significant areas of overlap, whereby one domain can productively reflect on the other (Sefton-Green 2000, p. 15). Although schooling still involves a strong tendency to regulate children and to contain their potential by requiring them to produce accepted 'school' genres (e.g. the ubiquitous 'essay' or 'book report' or 'assignment'), it can also provide a space where students can focus on aspects of a popular culture in a sustained and critical way, and reach greater clarity about the nature of the cultural practices in which they engage as part of their everyday lives.

James, a Year 9 student, decided to write a film review for his final assessment task. To wrap up the semester, Douglas invited his Year 9 class to reflect on the reading and writing they had done together, taking up an aspect of this work and developing it in some way. This meant that they could write poetry or a short story, create a video, or possibly produce a review of a novel or film. James's decision to review *The Ring* was made only after he had seen the film – he did not initially watch the film with the intention of writing about it. When James suggested to Douglas that he would like to write a film review, he was not entirely sure what the task involved. What is a film review? Who reads film reviews? In what kinds of publications do you usually find film reviews? Douglas advised him to read a range of reviews in order to identify their char-acteristic features without providing too much scaffolding. Film reviews come, after all, in all shapes and sizes, and it would be limiting to say that they all display the same generic characteristics.

This movie, though I hate to admit to it, got to me. I don't like the idea of a piece actually affecting my thoughts or actions, for that's all it is, acting, but somehow *The Ring* got past my barrier of rational thought and reasoning, and the more I thought about the movie, the more scary, well done and mysterious it seemed to become. I actually ventured back another day with a different friend, and ended up seeing the same film. Even though I'd seen it all before, and knew exactly what would happen where, it didn't stop my heart from racing a little faster and my hands from gripping the arm rests a little tighter. The first time around when I viewed the film the significance of what the story was about didn't quite sink in. I was with a group of friends and was talking to them partially throughout the movie. The complexity of the plot and spooky scenes didn't make an impression on me until I went back the second time. It so happened that when I met up with a friend a week later ... I found myself once again sitting in the darkness watching the same movie I had viewed only a week ago. This time however there was a distinct difference. The normal increased thudding of my heart and sweaty palms began, yet with a frightfully cold edge. The second time the meaning and absolute psychotic evil behind the storyline came to life, and seemed to tear at me through the cinema screen, grabbing at me. I was whisked away into a land where for a moment I was petrified beyond belief, and for a split second I was there. Tingles of confusion and horror rushed up my spine making me shiver, stunning me, turning me to stone. The deeper the story delved into the realms of evil now awakened, the scarier the implications became. A girl of such wickedness, with thoughts so unimaginably disturbing, with desires so gruesome and horrific they were almost impossible to comprehend ... As the movie drew to a bewilderingly disturbing close, I sat numb, with the fears of what had been unleashed in front of my eyes, still playing havoc in my head.

Figure 2. James's film review

James's review shows a number of levels of response to the text (Thomson 1987, Wilhelm 1997). He foregrounds the fact that the film is only an artifact – 'for that's all it is, acting' – but then explores how he was nonetheless drawn into the narrative, in much the same way that the story itself turns on the ways in which people become transfixed by mysterious images and forces over which they have no control. James appreciates that there are multiple dimensions to the story, and that those dimensions only become available to readers in the process of viewing and then re-viewing the text. He understands that reading involves an interaction between readers and texts, and – what is more – that each reading is a product of the social context in which it occurs. It is noteworthy that when he 'actually ventured back another day' it was with 'a different friend', and so although his deeply felt emotions are intensely personal ('the meaning and absolute psychotic evil behind the story line came to life, and seemed to tear at me through the cinema screen'), they are also implicitly experiences that he has shared with his companion. Indeed, his written review might be read as the outcome of a shared experience, involving not simply viewing the film with a companion, but the conversation they had together after the event. Writing the review is yet another attempt to construct a meaning out of his interaction with the text, whereby he is able both to relive the way he became totally immersed in the film and to reflect on the way the text worked. His review is itself a kind of performance, in which he relives the film's visceral effects.

Of the samples of classroom work presented in this chapter, James's review perhaps comes closest to being a recognizable example of 'school writing' (cf. Sheerin and Barnes 1991). It is easy to imagine how such writing might be produced in response to familiar school prompts: 'Write an essay on a film which you enjoyed recently ...'. Yet it still provides a small window on the cultural practices in which James participates outside school – the ritual of going to the movies with friends, the 'distress' and 'delight' of watching horror movies (cf. Buckingham 1995), and the pleasure of watching the same film again (and again). It also shows how English classrooms can provide space for students to develop a perspective on those practices. James would not have produced this writing if he had not been required to do so by his teacher, and it is doubtful whether he would have spontaneously articulated these insights into his changing response to the text to his friends. It is also difficult to imagine that he would have taken the trouble to explore his response to the film by writing about it.

I've got you where I want you

One of our aims in this chapter is to show how much we can learn from our students as we negotiate the curriculum with them from day to day. Douglas Barnes has remarked that a 'school curriculum' should be richer than 'what teachers plan in advance for their pupils to learn', that a school curriculum 'made only of teachers' intentions would be an insubstantial thing from which nobody would learn much':

> To become meaningful a curriculum has to be enacted by pupils as well as teachers, all of whom have their private lives outside school. By 'enact' I mean come together in a meaningful communication – talk, write, read books, collaborate, become angry with one another, learn what to say and do, and how to interpret what others say and do. A curriculum as soon as it becomes more than intentions is embodied in the communicative life of an institution, the talk, gestures by which pupils and teachers exchange meanings even when they quarrel or cannot agree. In this sense curriculum is a form of communication. (Barnes 1976, p. 14.)

Although Barnes's vision of curriculum emerged in response to a markedly different professional world to that in which we operate today, it remains a powerful model for working with students, and for accepting what they each bring to class (what Barnes calls their 'private lives outside school') as a basis for 'meaningful communication' with them. English classrooms should be characterized by mutual respect in which teachers and pupils alike are engaged in a joint inquiry into the complexities of language and meaning.

We know we are teaching well when we are surprised by our students' insights, when what they accomplish exceeds our expectations or even challenges our preconceptions about how an exercise should be done or a text might be read. Sue decided to write about alcoholism, producing a text which is instantly recognisable as a poem (see figure 3). She is a Year 9 student, and it is impossible not to be impressed by the way she has constructed a persona through her carefully chosen words, conveying a sense of the menace which alcohol poses to its victim who is implied in the poem by her use of the second person. Because the 'you' of the poem conflates the anonymous addict with the reader it becomes all the more confronting and disturbing. The poem creates a contrast between the all mockingly triumphant force of alcohol and the implied – silenced and powerless – victim.

It's too late now, you can't run, you can't hide.
I've got you where I want you, you need me to survive.
You live for just one sip, it's out of your control.
Don't deny it, don't fight it, you know I own your soul.
Alone you are weak, but I make you strong.
If it feels so right, how could it be wrong?
I permeate your thoughts, let you be all you can be.
You can't eat, you can't sleep, you can't breathe without me.
Sip away your problems till you're passed out on the floor.
Sip away your life till you can sip NO MORE

Figure 3. Sue's poem

So far so good. You can probably recognize in our response to Sue's writing the language which English teachers use to evaluate students' work. There is no doubt that her work stands up well against conventional criteria for assessing literacy development. To borrow the language of outcomes based assessment, she has been able to produce a piece of writing which 'reflect(s) on values and issues in ways that are interesting and thought provoking for a specified audience' (VCAA 2000, p. 82). This is a conventional and legitimate response to a sample of students' writing.

Yet this reading of Sue's work is disrupted if we examine the form in which she actually submitted her 'poem'. Figure 4 shows her text, which is a bottle made of papier maché, glued to a piece of 27 by 31 cm cardboard. The text of the poem forms the background of this image, which also incorporates other visual detail.

As a text this is far more striking and complex than the words alone. Sue has created a hybrid text in which visual elements do more than simply illustrate the printed text. The images combine with the print in a multi-modal fashion, offering the

Figure 4. Photo of Sue's full 'text'.

reader an opportunity to interact with the text and construct meaning at a number of levels. Indeed, the reader is simultaneously positioned as a viewer.

The text is dominated by the bottle, which symbolizes alcohol in a more confronting way than is done by the poem. The maniacal face conveys madness and cruelty with its crazed eyes, fearsome blood-spattered mouth and shark-like teeth – an impression which is enhanced by the fact that the papier-mâché model is thrust into the foreground, thus creating a 3D effect. The monster is raising its arms in triumph, and in its left hand it holds a hapless victim – a teenage girl – both as a trophy and a warning (see Figure 5). When Sue presented her model to the class, students took in all these details, spending as much time pondering its visual features as reading the written text in the background.

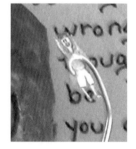

Figure 5. Detail

Lower down, Sue has drawn other characters representing a world in miniature (see Figure 6). People are lying around insensate amongst spilt and broken bottles, and what looks like their own vomit. There is an upturned car. The text constructs an image of social activities that centre on binge drinking, and in the background the characters lose their individuality, embodying an anonymous mass. The text is 'in your face', but it steps back from preaching or crude moralizing. Sue has managed to convey a powerful impression of the social world of teenagers and the risks that young people take.

Figure 6. Detail

To call Sue's work a 'poem' hardly does justice to this hybrid text. You might more properly describe it as a multimedia text, although significantly not in the way that this term is usually applied, i.e. to digital texts or texts mediated by a screen. Sue's text shows that it is not necessary to use ICT to create a multi-modal text and that the semiotic practices associated with multimedia are not necessarily a result of the growth of ICT. Indeed, her text has tactile qualities not replicable by digital multimedia. As a physical object that you can look at and hold, it has a different 'presence' to a text on a screen. Helen Nixon refers to the importance of 'the *material* aspects' (her emphasis) of such texts (Nixon 2003, p. 26), a term that might equally well be applied to the words Sue has printed as to the cardboard, papier-maché, paint and other media she has used. Similarly, Andrew Burn challenges teachers to 'move away from the idea of signification as an abstract practice, free from the taint of the material' (Burn 2003, p. 7). Signification is not simply a matter of the meeting of individual human 'minds', but is a function of the social relationships in which people participate, whereby they use shared material resources – including the 'material' of language – to construct meaning. Unfortunately, schools fail to recognize the complexity of such semiotic practices when they cling to traditional notions of language and meaning.

Reality Check

Culture, as Raymond Williams famously observed, concerns 'relations between elements in a whole way of life' (Williams 1971, pp. 11–12). Culture is not something we possess, but designates a complex range of activities in which we participate, as we go about the business of living. To reify culture as though it denoted simply a privileged body of texts and artifacts, and to imagine that schools should be responsible for inculcating such a narrow version of 'Cultural Literacy', is to deny students the opportunity to explore culture as 'a whole way of life' in which individuals and communities participate in various ways.

But the issue is not really one of choosing between 'high' culture and 'popular' culture. The conservative reform agenda heralded by champions of 'Cultural Literacy' like Donnelly is less likely to usher students into the 'sweetness' and 'light' of 'the best that has been thought and said in the world' than to see the perpetuation of dreary routines of whole class instruction and the endless recycling of assignments on *The Lord of the Flies*, *Macbeth* and *To Kill A Mockingbird*. Disputes about literary canons and canonicity do not necessarily influence the choices which teachers make when writing a school syllabus (cf. Guillory 1993), which often reflect pragmatic judgments about what 'works' at certain year levels. Whether the book embodies 'the best that has been thought and said in the world' is hardly a factor in their decisions. Syllabus construction has its own logic, often involving habitual practices that deny students the opportunity of making connections between the school curriculum and the issues that concern them. The threat posed by Donnelly's preferred model of school curriculum is that it legitimizes such practices precisely at a time when educators should be imagining alternative forms of teaching and learning.

To challenge these traditional practices is not simply a matter of introducing popular cultural texts or other 'relevant' content, but means reconceptualizing school and the social relationships enacted there. A glimpse of the classroom that Donnelly envisages can be gained from his approving remarks that in England 'there is a movement back to the teacher standing at the front of the room and actually directing and controlling the class' (Donnelly 2004, p. 35), and his defence of essay text literacy and the 'repetition' and 'memorisation' that examinations require (p. 34). This is less a vision of learning than a model of social control. By contrast, the samples of work that we have considered in this chapter reflect a lively classroom environment in which talk is a medium for learning and the exchange of views, where students take an active role in their own learning rather than compliantly doing what they are told to do.

Yet although we have presented these samples of students' work as a celebration of what they have achieved, we do not wish to idealise Douglas's classroom as a site where students can unproblematically engage in inquiry, or to ignore the complex and contradictory pressures that simultaneously shape his relationships with his students and their sense of community identity. One of the reasons he invited Bella Illesca to observe his classrooms was to trace possible disjunctions between what he was trying to accomplish and how the students understood the activities they were doing. Bella found, in fact, that not all of Douglas's students were comfortable with his approach to English curriculum and pedagogy. Sally, for example, was a 'successful' student who felt more comfortable with being told what to do and then doing it. This is not necessarily a criticism of her—she has simply been socialized into a particular way of being a school student. In conversation with Bella, she criticized Douglas's preference for negotiating the curriculum, reflecting attitudes and practices that have become naturalized through schooling and which some of her peers no doubt shared. Douglas's classes also contained a number of students who were radically disaffected from schooling, and he was unable to persuade them to change that stance.

To accept what students bring with them into class also means negotiating with conventional attitudes and expectations about what it means to 'do' English. Gordon Wells, who draws on Vygotsky to construct an alternative model of teaching and learning, calls this 'disputed territory', where a practitioner struggles with the demands of policy makers, administrators and mandated practices, and the situatedness of working with particular students in a particular place (Wells 2001, p. 172). Teachers do not only experience curriculum and conventional literacy practices as something imposed from above (in the form of mandated curriculum and the organizational practices of schooling) but as embodied in the individuals with whom they interact, all of whom bring their personal histories as students with them into class.

This is not to deny the promise of opening up the curriculum in order to engage the diverse range of individuals who make up our English classrooms, merely to recognise that such initiatives require complex mediations that are perhaps of a different order to those usually associated with 'negotiating the curriculum' (cf. Boomer et al. 1992). Teachers and students alike are caught up in habitual practices that make it difficult for them to imagine alternative ways of organizing schools and experiencing teaching and learning.

But the challenge remains of enabling students to make connections between social and cultural phenomena that otherwise appear discrete or isolated, drawing links between 'high' culture and 'popular' culture, between their local neighbourhood and global movements, as aspects of a 'whole way of life'. Not to recognise how things 'connect' is to fail to accept responsibility for others, to refuse a moral obligation to understand how our individual lives are bound up with the lives of others.

References

Australian Education Council (AEC) (1994) *English—A Curriculum Profile for Australian Schools*, a joint project of the States, Territories and the Commonwealth of Australia initiated by the Australian Education Coucil, Carlton: Curriculum Corporation.

Bakhtin, M. M. (1981) *The Dialogic Imagination: Four Essays*, in M. Holquist (ed.), C. Emerson and M. Holquist (transls), Austin: University of Texas.

Barnes, D. (1976) *From Communication to Curriculum*, Harmondsworth: Penguin.

Board of Studies (2000) *English: Curriculum and Standards Framework II*, Carlton, Victoria: Board of Studies.

Boomer, G., Lester, N., Onore, C. and Cook, J. (eds) (1992) *Negotiating the Curriculum: Educating for the 21st Century*, London: Falmer Press.

Buckingham, D. (1995) Distress and Delight: Children's Horror Talk, *The English and Media Magazine* 32, pp. 18–32.

Britton, J. (1972) *Language and Learning*, Harmondsworth: Penguin.

Burn, A. (2000) Repackaging the Slasher Movie: Digital Unwriting of Film in the Classroom, *English in Australia* 127–128, May, pp. 24–34.

Burn, A. (2003) Poets, skaters and avatars – performance, identity and new media, *English Teaching: Practice and Critique* 2(2), 6–21.

Burn, A. (2003) 'Two Tongues Occupy My Mouth' – Poetry, Performance and the Moving Image, *English in Education* 37(3), 42–51.

Burn, A., and Parker, D. (2003) *Analysing Media Texts*, London: Continuum.

Doecke, B. and McClenaghan, D. (1997) Reconceptualising Experience: Growth Pedagogy and Youth Culture, in W. Sawyer, K. Watson and E. Gold (eds), *Reviewing English*, Sydney: St Clair Press, pp. 204–211.

Donnelly, K. (2004) *Why Schools are Failing: What Parents Need to Know about Australian Education*, Menzies Research Centre, Sydney: Duffy & Snellgrove.

Frow, J. (1993) Regimes of Value, in P. Mead and M. Campbell (eds) *Shakespeare's Books: Contemporary Cultural Politics and the Persistence of Empire*, Melbourne: Department of English University of Melbourne, pp. 207–218.

Frow, J. (1995) *Cultural Studies and Cultural Value*, Oxford: Clarendon Press.

Guillory, J. (1993) *Cultural Capital: The Problem of Literary Canon Formation*, Chicago: University of Chicago Press.

Hayes, T. (1999) Puck in the Schoolyard: Crassing the Bard at Hawthorn Secondary College, *English in Australia* 125, August, pp. 56–61.

Kress, G. (1995) *Writing the Future: English and the Making of a Culture of Innovation*, Sheffield: NATE.

McClenaghan, D. (2000) Norman Bates, Abba, and Annoying Neighbours: The Importance of Oral Language in the English Curriculum, in *STELLA: English in Australia 129–130 and Literacy Learning: The Middle Years* 9(1) December 2000–February 2001, pp. 87–88.

McClenaghan, D. (2003) Writing Poetry – and Beyond, *English Teaching: Practice and Critique*, http://www.tmc.waikato.ac.nz/english/ETPC 2(2), pp. 97–103.

McClenaghan, D. and Doecke, B. (2005) Popular Culture: A Resource for writing in Secondary English Classrooms, in G. Rijlaarsdam, H. van den Bergh and M. Couzins (eds) *Effective Teaching and Learning of Writing*, Amsterdam: Kluwer.

Mercer, N. (1996) *The Guided Construction of Knowledge*, Adelaide: Multilingual Matters.

Nixon, H. (2003) Textual diversity: Who needs it? *English Teaching: Practice and Critique*, 2(2), pp. 22–33.

Sheerin, Y. and Barnes, D. (1991) *School Writing*, Buckingham: Open University Press.

Sefton-Green, J. (2000) Beyond School: Futures for English and Media Education, *English in Australia* 127–128, May, pp. 14–23.

Teese, R. (2000) *Academic Success and Social Power*, Oakleigh: Cambridge University Press.

Thomson, J. (1987) *Understanding Teenagers' Reading: Reading Processes and the Teaching of Literature*, North Ryde: Methuen Australia.

Wells, G. (2001) The Case for Dialogic Inquiry, in G. Wells (ed.) *Action, Talk and Text: Learning and Teaching through Inquiry*, New York and London: Teachers College Press, pp. 171–194.

Wilhelm, J. (1997) *'You Gotta BE the Book': Teaching Engaged and Reflective Reading with Adolescents*, New York and London: Teachers College Press.

Williams, R. (1971) *Culture and Society 1780–1950*, Harmondsworth: Penguin.

Note

1 We have discussed some of the following examples of integrating popular culture into the curriculum in other publications (see Doecke and McClenaghan 1997; McClenaghan 2000; McClenaghan 2003; McClenaghan and Doecke, 2005).

STELLA

Language Modes

The STELLA (Standards for the Teaching of Language and Literacy in Australia) Language Modes, as described in the following pages, emerged from an extensive project to articulate, and inquire into, standards for English literacy teaching in Australia (see www.stella.org.au). They were developed in workshops by English literacy teachers around Australia, and are meant to be accounts of how accomplished English literacy teachers conceptualise and teach speaking, listening, writing, reading and viewing. On the one hand, these accounts may seem to divide the teaching and learning of English literacy into five separate parts, of which writing is only one part. And yet, taken as a while, the STELLA Language Modes are clearly challenging the notion that English literacy teaching can be glibly compartmentalised into discrete modes. Rather, as in the preceding chapters in this volume, they argue for a dialogic conceptualisation of language and pedagogy, one that sees rich interconnectedness between these language modes, one that engages with the diverse professional voices (from diverse settings) that are reflected in them, and one that appreciates the range of socio-cultural factors that mediate the work of professional English literacy teachers in Australia.

Chapter 16

The Accomplished Teacher in the English/Literacy Classroom

Listening and Speaking

For accomplished teachers, talk is at the centre of English curriculum and pedagogy.

Their classrooms are rich linguistic communities in which all students participate. They give focused attention to various aspects of listening and speaking, teaching their students to listen actively and to share their ideas and experiences. Crucial in this respect is the establishment of a classroom environment that supports productive interaction between students in both small group situations and whole class activities. Accomplished teachers know how to structure such activities so that their students are able to jointly construct knowledge through talk.

Accomplished teachers understand that their students may belong to communities that speak a diverse range of dialects and languages other than English. They are adept at devising strategies that encourage all students to participate in the language of the classroom, including students who may otherwise be disengaged from schooling. They are sensitive to the needs of individual students, to the range of skills and abilities that students evince as listeners and speakers, and to the way oral language is bound up with self esteem. They understand the complexities of code switching, enabling their students to learn about the variety of discourses in which they participate from day to day, and the protocols associated with each. They celebrate this rich linguistic diversity, while teaching their students to handle the linguistic conventions of discourse communities or situations with which they may not be familiar, including discourses of power and influence.

They enable students to make their knowledge of oral communication explicit, building on and extending their knowledge of the diverse linguistic communities that constitute Australian society. Accomplished teachers teach their students to monitor their listening and speaking, encouraging them to internalise criteria with which to gauge the effectiveness of their exchanges with others.

Accomplished teachers value oral communication as a means for all students to participate in the English curriculum, and they are skilled at using oral work as a basis for writing and reading and critical thinking. Through listening and speaking, their students engage in imaginative play, negotiating issues of value and identity in a way that is unique to the English classroom. For such teachers, classroom talk is a vital medium for exploring the interface between school and community, for mediating between the formal demands of schooling and the linguistic communities to which their students belong.

Writing

Accomplished teachers value writing as a means of grappling with language and meaning. They have a finely tuned sense of the complexities of the writing process, and they use this knowledge to support their students to write texts for a diverse range of purposes and audiences. They encourage all their students to experiment with and to learn about new genres and forms of communication, including digital and multimedia texts. They know that learning to write is a process of learning how to mean, that each type of writing involves a specific set of conventions, a specific way of representing the world.

They encourage their students to see writing as a means of actively participating in their local community and the larger society. Their students might be writing letters to the editor of a local newspaper, designing picture story books for children at the local kindergarten, or developing multimedia texts to be published on their school's website – accomplished teachers seize every opportunity to promote writing for real purposes and audiences.

Accomplished teachers teach in the expectation that they will learn from their students. They recognise that their students bring a wealth of experience and knowledge into their classrooms which constitutes an invaluable resource for writing. They devise strategies that enable their students to draw on cultural practices outside school, including the rich semiotic resources of popular culture.

As teachers of writing, they are also conscious of the critical expertise and knowledge that they have to offer their students. They are committed to extending their students' repertoires as text producers, heightening their awareness of the enormous range of texts available to them. As well as the stories, poems and plays that are typically used in English classes, they are always seeking out new genres, including texts associated with the work place, politics, advertising and other public domains. Magazines, sit-coms, comic books, computer games, posters, prose poems, information brochures – all such texts provide potential models for students in their attempts to learn how to mean. Accomplished teachers know that learning to write is more than simply learning to emulate pre-existing conventions or knowledge, but a matter of experimenting with forms, testing boundaries and gaining critical insight into the ways texts work.

Accomplished teachers endeavour to motivate their students, even when they encounter resistance. They are adept at devising prewriting activities, giving students time to talk about possible ideas for writing and to consider what they would like to achieve. They establish classroom structures and routines that enable students to learn through revising their work. Their classrooms are writing workshops in which students are able to discuss their work with each other, benefiting from feedback from their peers. They encourage their students to internalize criteria that allow them to assess their own and each other's writing in supportive ways. Accomplished teachers also sense when they need to intervene and make explicit key skills and aspects of language, whether it be note taking or the use of nominalisations in argumentative writing or other linguistic conventions.

Accomplished teachers are acutely aware of the diverse range of abilities and needs of students in their class. They devise strategies that enable all students to engage in writing that is personally meaningful to them. When they assess their students' writing, they give them specific feedback that allows them to revise their writing in appropriate ways and to develop as writers. They are alert to opportunities to extend their students' range of written skills, building on their accomplishments to open up new dimensions of language. They are especially sensitive to the needs of students who are experiencing literacy difficulties, for whom writing may be a strange and alienating task.

Reading

For accomplished teachers, reading is always a purposeful activity. They might be giving support to beginning readers in their initial encounters with print texts, or working with adolescent readers as they investigate popular culture, or facilitating senior students' engagement with poetry – all reading should engage students in personally meaningful activities, allowing them to make connections between texts and their own knowledge, values, and experiences.

Accomplished teachers know that all forms of reading involve prediction and interaction, framing and interpretation, an active process of constructing meaning. It is never simply a matter of receiving or absorbing the meaning of a text. Meaning is always the product of an interaction or exchange between readers and texts.

Accomplished teachers understand how readers draw on a complex repertoire of cognitive skills when they engage with texts. With beginning readers, this means teaching them to employ a systematic range of strategies in order to make sense of print. Accomplished teachers make finely tuned professional judgements about the knowledge and skills of their students, and they know when it is appropriate to intervene in order to teach their students new skills when reading new texts.

Accomplished teachers know that learning to read is a life long process, and that different kinds of texts require a diverse range of interpretive strategies. They know that reading serves a variety of purposes, including information gathering, pleasure in the play of words and imaginative world of the text, as well as critical discussion and insight. Their aim is to enable students to develop an awareness of the different strategies required when interacting with texts, whether fiction or non-fiction, imaginative or practical.

Accomplished teachers recognise that adolescents engage in a complex range of literacy practices, and that their dialogue with students should embrace more than simply novels, plays or poems – the traditional fare of English classes. Their aim is to teach students to become discerning participants in the diverse cultural activities that constitute their daily lives. They understand the complex ways in which texts position readers, and they are committed to alerting their students to how they are positioned by texts. All texts have designs on the reader, and accomplished teachers have developed strategies that allow their students to identify and explore the range of viewpoints presented, as well as those which are silenced by the text. Accomplished teachers provide a classroom environment that allows their students to explore the multiple readings that might be generated by texts. Their classrooms are places in which students can investigate a variety of interpretations, where all texts are open to critical scrutiny.

Accomplished teachers are widely read in children's and adolescent literature, and exercise acute discriminations when matching the right book with a particular student according to their abilities and interests. They know how to use writing to facilitate generative responses to texts, and they are equally adept at devising speaking and listening activities that provide a base for engagement with and evaluation of texts.

When assessing reading, accomplished teachers devise strategies that will allow them to gain information and insight into the needs and abilities of their students and apply this knowledge to advance their reading skills. They are able to exercise discerning professional judgements with respect to professional development packages, intervention programs, diagnostic tests, and other reading materials.

Viewing

Accomplished teachers know that their students have acquired a rich repertoire of interpretive strategies through engaging with visual and multimedia texts and other popular cultural forms. They enable their students to make these interpretive practices explicit and to apply this knowledge to other texts. They understand that students' skills as readers of visual texts are often more sophisticated than their skills with print literacy, and that focused attention on interpretive strategies associated with visual literacy can provide a basis for students to reflect on their strategies when dealing with print texts.

Accomplished teachers draw on the analytical skills their students have developed through reading visual texts, encouraging them to articulate the critical insights and pleasures they gain from viewing, including the power of visual imagery and the range of emotions that images can evoke. They understand that students sometimes require encouragement and explicit teaching to gain a critical perspective on the films, television programs and advertisements they find entertaining. They devise strategies that enable their students to explore the complexities of framing and interpretation of visual texts, to recognise links between texts, and to acknowledge how their own experiences and values cause them to read these texts in certain ways. They also seek opportunities to introduce specific genres and conventions that might be peculiar to certain types of visual texts. Their aim is to teach their students how to engage in a sustained analysis of these texts without diminishing their pleasure.

Accomplished teachers understand that they must provide their students with the specialised language of viewing and visual texts in order to describe, deconstruct and critique these texts. This process commences in the early years by focusing on the use and effect of camera angles, the role of composition and framing, and other aspects of visual literacy. When teaching adolescents, accomplished teachers enable students to build on their existing knowledge of the technical, symbolic and written codes of visual texts, and to engage in an increasingly sophisticated analysis of the ways such texts imply a certain set of values and beliefs. They also focus on the impact that structural elements, such as linear narrative or non-linear hypertext, have on the way readers engage with visual texts.

Accomplished teachers understand that visual texts constitute a vital element of popular culture that shapes their students' understandings of self, society and an increasingly globalised environment. By focusing on visual texts in the classroom, students can begin to raise questions about inclusion and exclusion, stereotypes and archetypes, popular culture, mass media and marketing. They can critique the values promoted by popular cultural texts, exploring their own values and the values of the larger society. Rather than seeking to protect students from popular culture texts, accomplished teachers encourage them to critically evaluate such texts and to make an informed decision before accepting or rejecting them.

Accomplished teachers recognise the multimodal nature of many visual texts. They draw their students' attention to the ways that written texts are transformed when juxtaposed with visual images in picture books and display advertising. They also enable their students to explore how music, sound and voice can be used to support visual images in film and television.

When assessing viewing, accomplished teachers ensure that students have acquired the specialised language of viewing and that they are able to explain how visual texts are constructed and how this construction works on the viewer. In addition to these fundamental understandings of visual texts, accomplished teachers seek opportunities to assess the capacity of students to reflect critically on the way such texts are constructed and their own viewing practices. They focus their assessment on *how* rather than *what* meanings are constructed by engaging with visual texts, and provide opportunities, including the production of visual texts, to help students express and test their understandings.

Contributors

Catherine Beavis is an Associate Professor in the Faculty of Education at Deakin University. She researches in the area of young people and new media, with a particular focus on computer games, the changing nature of text, and the implications of young people's experience of digital culture for English and literacy education in schools. Her most recent book is *Doing Literacy Online: Teaching, Learning and Playing in an Electronic World*, edited with Ilana Snyder, Hampton Press.

Natalie Bellis is in her second year of teaching English at St. Paul's Anglican Grammar School, Warragul, Victoria. She is completing a Masters degree in Creative Writing at Monash University.

Scott Bulfin began his career teaching English at Highvale Secondary College, a government school in Eastern Melbourne, while also completing an honours degree about professional learning for early career teachers. He is an active member of the council of the Victorian Association for the Teaching of English (VATE) and works part-time as a research assistant at Monash University where he has also just begun a PhD looking at teacher and student uses of digital technologies in schools.

Claire Charles is a PhD candidate in the Faculty of Education at Monash University. She has taught at both secondary and tertiary levels in the areas of English, language and literacy. Whilst working toward her PhD she has been involved in two research projects, one from which this contribution arises. Her research interests include discourses of female empowerment, and constructions of femininity, in elite girls' schooling and the application of feminist media studies to this area.

Michael Clyne is honorary Professorial Fellow at the University of Melbourne and Emeritus Professor at Monash University, having held professorial appointments in

Linguistics at both universities. His reasearch and publications are mainly in the fields of bi-/multilingualism/language contact, sociolinguistics, inter-cultural communication, and second language acquisition.

Brenton Doecke is an Associate Professor in the Faculty of Education at Monash University. He is a former editor of *English in Australia*, the journal of the Australian Association for the Teaching of English, and has published widely on issues in English Education. He was involved in developing STELLA (Standard for English Language and Literacy Education in Australia), and has since pursued further research on the professional knowledge and practice of teachers of English.

Prue Gill is a long time classroom teacher, currently teaching English,Literature and Theory of Knowledge. She has taught in a variety of settings (government and private secondary schools, TAFE, and the Tertiary sector) and in many different types of class-room (disciplinary, inter-disciplinary, vertical age groupings, team teaching settings). She is a past president of the Victorian Association for the Teaching of English, and a current member of VATE Council.

Gaell Hildebrand is currently an academic who works in the field of teacher professional learning—both with pre-service and practising teachers undertaking Monash University courses and also with teachers in schools. She previously taught in schools both here and in Hong Kong in the areas of science, physics, chemistry and mathematics, and held several leadership positions such as curriculum, faculty and year level coordinator roles. Her research interests include writing in school science, the intersections between learning, assessment, curriculum and padagogy and she brings a feminist perspective to all her work.

Bella Illesca is an English teacher who has worked in government and non-government schools in Australia and overseas. She is currently teaching and working as a Research Assistant in the Faculty of Education at Monash University. Her areas of interest are English curriculum and pedagogy and professional learning. She is currently completing her Masters in Education at Monash University.

Val Kent has taught at Huntingdale Technical School, Monash University and the CAE in Melbourne. She was the Education Officer for the Victorian Association for the Teaching of English (VATE), and was extensively involved in organising conferences and professional development for teachers across Victoria. She has written *Exploring Narrative: A Guide to Teaching 'The Girl Who Married a Fly and other stories'* and has co-edited (with Michael Hyde) *Hunger and Other Stories*, both for the AATE.

Alex Kostogriz is a lecturer in TESOL and literacy education at Monash University, where he is involved in teacher education at both undergraduate and postgraduate levels. His research and teaching have been centered on exploring connections between students' cultural and social identities and learning. He is addressing this complex issue by bringing together perspectives from cultural studies, new literacy studies and socio-cultural psychology.

Terry Locke is Associate Professor of English Language Education at the School of Education, University of Waikato. His research interests include curriculum and assessment reform and their impact on teacher professionalism, constructions of English, the place of language in English classrooms and elearning. His most recent book is *Critical Discourse Analysis* (Continuum: 2004). He is coordinating editor of the journal *English Teaching: Practice and Critique*.

Judie Mitchell has taught English in secondary schools for over 30 years. She is currently Head of Teaching and Learning at Brentwood Secondary College in Melbourne. She has published widely on English teaching and professional learning, and for many years has been active in PEEL (Project for Enhancing Effective Learning). She has recently completed a PhD in the Faculty of Education at Monash University, entitled 'Constructing Professional Knowledge: Voices from a Teacher learning Community', from which her chapter in this volume is drawn.

Kevin Murray taught at Melbourne's Hawthorn Institute of Education. His essay 'Responding to Students' Writing' was originally published as a 'do-it-yourself-inservice kit' in *Idiom*, the journal of the Victorian Association for the Teaching of English, in Spring 1984.

Graham Parr is a teacher educator in the Faculty of Education, Monash University, where he lectures in English education, and curriculum and pedagogy. Previously he taught secondary English and Literature for 15 years, in Victoria and America. His research interests include teacher professional learning and professional identity, teacher knowledge, literary theory, and pre-service teacher education. He has published in national and international journals, and his PhD on teacher professional learning and critical inquiry is due for completion in 2006.

Wayne Sawyer is an Associate Professor and head of Secondary Teacher Education programs at the University of Western Sydney. He is Vice President, Curriculum, of the NSW English Teachers Association. Wayne is co-editor of *Reviewing English in the 21st century* and has edited or authored over 20 books on secondary English teaching. His recent major research has been in the areas of effective teaching across the curriculum, English curriculum history and boys' education.